INSANITY:
A MEMOIR

INSANITY

Fake it 'til you Make it

☼ ☼ ☼ ☼ ☼

A memoir told as a story – a story so twisted
that it took seven books to tell it all.

Book 5 in the *Powerless* Series

LELA FOX

☼ ☼ ☼ ☼ ☼

Cover designed by Queen Graphics; Fiverr, Photo via Deposit Photos
Contributing Editors: Ben Boyd, Teri Eicher, Noah Lloyd
"The Fifth Book" pun by a funny Lela Fox fan, Jennifer D.

Visit the author's website at LelaFox.com
First Printing September 2019 by A-FEX Books
ISBN 9781691278220

DEDICATION

I dedicate this book to my sister Karen who looks nothing like the picture above. She taught me all I know: everything essential in becoming a badass Fox woman. To this day, I ache for her big-sister approval.

We're best friends because we're so alike; she understands why I think it's funny to fart in public, why I laugh when I should cry, cry when I should laugh, and why I crack jokes when I'm nervous.

Karen, you make me laugh harder than anyone else in the world. And yes, I do think you're a radio or something. (Inside joke) LOL.

☼ ☼ ☼ ☼ ☼ ☼ ☼ ☼ ☼

TABLE OF CONTENTS

FAKE IT 'TIL YOU MAKE IT

"Perseverance is not a long race. It is many short races, one after the other."

–WALTER ELIOT

LIFETIME NUMBER SIX
THE SHATTERED LIGHT AT THE END OF THE TUNNEL

My childhood, Lifetime Number One, ended the moment I raised a cup of spiked punch to my lips. I didn't write about that Lifetime... sappy shit isn't my style. Picture-perfect families are boring, anyway.

Lifetime Number Two began with my first drink, and the story of my instant addiction, self-hate, and teen angst became the book *Powerless*.

In Lifetime Number Three, I rushed marriage and motherhood in a desperate attempt to run from the disease that threatened to consume me. The trek through this Lifetime became the book *Denial*.

Lifetime Number Four began when heavy binge drinking became heavy daily drinking. With shared custody of my son, I was the party-all-night girl one week and the inadequate-but-well-meaning mom the next week. It ended when the sham of my second marriage ended. That period of my life became the book *Chaos*.

Lifetime Number Five drove the book *Unmanageable*. That's when 24/7 drinking caused a frantic search for Mr. Right. I found him, right or wrong, and with his help, slowly became a selfish, unaware drunk, unable to take care of myself.

This book, *Insanity* (the fifth, which all alkies like), is the dramatic end of Lifetime Number Five and the beginning of an insane-but-sober Lifetime Number Six.

The series covers three Lifetimes beyond this one, each markedly different from the one before it. And each more catastrophic, cathartic, and curious.

Throughout my life, I've had some sort of faith to see something better for me. Somewhere out there, I believed, I'd find the elusive "something better" and escape what had been squashing my soul. I fought for the "something" for 27 years... yearned for it like an alcoholic yearns for his next drink. And I know a lot about that.

Through all my Lifetimes, I survived what would have killed a weaker woman. Each time, I would say, "This Lifetime is surely not the final one! This isn't the way it's supposed to end!"

I was right. It wasn't the end.

It was the beginning. Nine different times.

HOW I GOT HERE
nOT-SO-SUDDEn DYSFUNCTION

I've been through some bizarre shit. Some of it was caused by others, some by simple bad luck, but the worst of it was of my own making... brought by the desperate choices of a hopeless alcoholic.

As we arrive here at the end of Lifetime Number Five, I was scrambling to save my job and my third marriage, knowing my drinking was out of control.

But it wasn't the first time I'd come to that conclusion.

The same realization hit in my first marriage to Andy Winston, shortly after the sonofabitch told me he'd been having an affair and enjoying it immensely.

In my second marriage, Asswipe Miller McKeown called me an "idiot alcoholic" when demanding a divorce. After our nine-year marriage, he also said my "Bi-Polar crazy shit" drove him away. But I think he meant my "*On-Purpose* crazy shit."

After the second divorce, Shame, my old friend, become a constant companion. Then when my son told me he was ashamed of me and my alcoholic behavior, I dove to a new low. He went to live with his dad and Goody-Two-Shoes stepmother in a brick house with a white picket fence. I couldn't compete... so why not continue to be the fuck-up I'd always been? I was too far gone to have any sense of self-worth, anyway.

That's when I met Stuart. My savior, the man I thought could take care of me physically, emotionally, financially, and manage my day-to-day life with ease. He fit the bill and seemed more than willing.

What happened next became a free-for-all, my life in a swirl of dysfunction and foolishness.

My decision at the end of the book could have saved my life.

But it didn't.

THE END BEGINS

CHAPTER I

I remember stealing the ashtray from the bar; an oversized, white ceramic one with random splashes of bright-orange glaze. We'd been to a classic-rock bar on Highway A-1-A in West Palm Beach, Florida and we were both drunk, hardly able to stand or communicate. I'm guessing it was around two AM when we got home, thankful for the air conditioner's cooling of the early June heat.

Happily obliterated, I sat on the sofa looking at the birthday card from my husband of five months. "Happy Number Forty," it said. He signed it: "Have a good one, old bitty." What an asshole. He seemed to always find a way to mess up a good thing.

As I smoked a cigarette, I sang the classic-rock song *Fly Like an Eagle* by the Steve Miller Band in my typical key of flat and awful. Yona, our live-in Jamaican nanny, came out of her small bedroom to shush me. I supposed she thought I'd wake my stepson Jeremy, six years old and a light sleeper.

Just to piss her off, I quit singing but hummed the same song as loud as I could, louder than the singing had been. Yona stood with her hand on her right hip and bounced.

I thought it was hilarious and threw my head back for a long Tennessee laugh. The two of us had become friends, more than nanny-to-supervisor, but she disapproved of my "excessive drinking," she had said many times. I ignored her shit and her Goody-Two-Shoes judgement.

I stood to dance on the tile floor of the rental house, still humming.

Barefoot, I wore a flower-print mini skirt and no underwear. Golden-brown curls bounced to the beat in my head.

Stuart Weinstein, my husband number three, was in the bathroom and walked out zipping his fly. His beer belly was more prominent than usual in the profile view, I noticed, and his hair grayer in the shadowy light. In his brash New York accent, he said something smart-ass about how my "fat thighs" jiggled as I danced, and I yelled at him to shut the hell up. He yelled something back as he passed the French door to the back patio.

The next thing I knew, the stolen ashtray was in the air, sailing toward Stuart's head. He ducked, and the ashtray crashed through the patio door.

The rest is a blackout.

☼ ☼ ☼ ☼ ☼

Suddenly, though it must've been at least an hour later, I was in the driveway, overwrought and jittery. A pudgy hand held a Polaroid showing Stuart's scratched and bleeding face, pushing it toward me accusingly. With a smartass chuckle, the cop said, "I hear what you're saying, Ms. Fox, but *he* said you did it, and it sure *looks* like you did it, so the call is... you did it."

Then he snapped handcuffs on my wrists. Tight.

On the way east, I wondered how the Palm Beach County jail would differ from the others I'd seen. Maybe the floor would be sandy? The inmates would be more ethnically diverse, with less East Tennessee rednecks, I reasoned. Those thoughts came before the big questions: *What have I done? And how am I going to get out of this?*

The charge was domestic assault. After the fingerprints and mugshot downstairs, they threw me in the drunk tank. The cage was full of Haitian women, speaking their melodic language, laughing at nothing funny I could see. Miserable, I sat on the cold concrete bench, speaking to no one.

So who can I call? Who can post my bail? I tried to ignore utter defeat, but I knew there was nobody to call; I had no friends except Yona. My work friends were just that: nine-to-five friends, and I didn't like them worth a shit, anyway. Though I was groggy and still drunk, I was sober enough to know I was in big trouble. *How can I get out of here?*

An overweight female officer with a shock of frizzy black hair called my name. On our way to a cell downstairs, passing through four clanging cages of bars, I could smell her body odor. It added to the ugly reality of what I faced. I shivered in the heat.

When I asked for my phone call, I learned the bad news: there would be no easy-out tonight. That was for DUI arrests and minor things, not for domestic abusers like me, she said. I'd see the judge the next day, and he'd set my bail. Not only that, I'd need a proper home address before they would release me. Stuart had filed for a restraining order. I couldn't go home.

I continued to think of somebody to post my bail, but there was no one to call. For the past six months, I had isolated myself with the high-tech electric juicer and backyard grapefruit tree as my only friends. Oh, and of course the vodka, which was my main friend. The thought came: "my main squeeze" and I chuckled. *Who says a washed-up writer can't still make a good pun?*

The echo as we walked down the hall of cells deafened me, the smell of shit and vomit grew as we walked further into the cell block. Then the officer grunted and pushed me to the left, into the smallest cell I'd seen outside of a Hollywood movie. Like any cell, it had an eerie sense of coldness and the austerity of sharp angles, but this one proudly emitted the distinctive smell of solid human waste.

The flip-flops they provided caught on the wide crack in the concrete floor, a diagonal crack that divided the tiny space into two triangles all the way across.

As the guard removed the cuffs, I saw the bare and dark-stained mattresses on the bunk beds. No blankets, no pillows. In the corner, the toilet leaned questionably to the left.

No cellmate. I sat on the bottom bunk and put my head in my hands. *That sonofabitch has thrown me under the bus – on purpose! How could he treat me like this? His very own wife! Wouldn't LOVE stop him from this kind of cruelty.*

I peed on top of the existing poop, and knowing it wouldn't help to flush, I didn't. A squeaky voice in the next cell shouted, "Flush your stinky pee!" I mumbled an apology and flushed, but the toilet gurgled a few seconds and stopped.

Great. A stopped-up toilet in a jail cell. With a half-chuckle, half-belch, I blew a laugh at the irony of it all. *What the hell, Lela, you crazy drunk! You've really screwed yourself this time.* After a few sobs, which only hurt my head, I decided to sleep it off. Trying to avoid the biggest, grossest stains on the mattress, I closed my eyes. *Maybe you'll think of something in the morning.*

I woke with my contacts stuck to my eyeballs, as expected, and my head pounding, which surprised me. I wasn't usually one to have hangovers; Lela Fox was too adept at drinking for such kindergarten things.

I closed my eyes after the lights came on and willed the headache away. It returned with the faceless delivery of a cold-egg, raw-bacon breakfast. With a sigh, I ate the toast and the bruised apple. The germ of an idea formed in my mind.

Mid-morning, they led a chain of us to the courtroom, shackled together at the ankles and waist. *A damn chain-gang, as if I'm a common criminal!* The bailiff called my name first, and I stood, rattling the chains. The charges were now official: misdemeanor domestic assault. Bail was $5,000. In 1999, that was a lot of money.

Though I was antsy to set my new plan in motion, I had to wait for the other inmates' hearings before I could leave the courtroom. About an hour passed, and I needed to pee. After the last gavel fell, the deputies led us out in the same chain-gang. Complete humiliation, I thought, being treated like a criminal when I was innocent.

As I passed the District Attorney, I caught his eye and tried to garner a smile, but he looked straight through me. I wanted him to know I was somebody special within this chain-gang, somebody with sense, but his look of disdain burst my bubble of hope.

With a hard swallow, I accepted the truth. I was just a number in the system and my number was low, near the bottom. Yep, I was in big trouble, bigger than ever before.

My toilet was still clogged, and I complained to the deputy who deposited us back in our cells. She said she'd "get right on it." *Yeah, right.*

An hour later, she took me upstairs to make my phone call. The fat deputy slid the phone book across the counter and my shaking hands found the number for the liquor store in Wellington, Florida – the liquor superstore around the corner from our house in the upscale suburb of West Palm. Friendly Wine and Liquors, where they sold lottery tickets, too.

"Frank! It's Lela, your favorite customer."

"Hey, Lela! What can I do for you, hon?"

An upbeat voice will relax him, Lela. Don't let him think it's a big deal. "Frank, I'm in a little trouble. Can I use your address as my address so I can get out of jail?" A silent reply, so I continued. "And I'll pay you back two-fold if you bail me out."

"What? Wait! I'm not getting this... you're in *jail?*"

"No big deal, Frankie. But Stuart said I beat him up and he filed a restraining order against me. I can't go home and I can't leave jail until I give them an address where I'll supposedly live."

There was a gasp from the other end of the phone. "Wait, no! I'm not asking to stay with you. I can stay at a hotel until I find a place. It's just... I need you to bail me out and give your address. Can you? Will you? Please?"

"Let me get this straight. You got arrested for beating Stuart up?"

"Right."

"But he was in here this morning and he didn't *look* beaten up! Bought his regular bottle of Crown and about a hundred scratch-off tickets. Honestly, I think he has a problem with the scratch-offs."

Not giving a damn what the fidgety Stuart bought, I made sure I heard Frank right about the other. "No scratches on his face? No blood in his beard?"

"Nope."

"Just the same ol' donkey face?"

Frank spoke through his chuckle. "That's right."

"Dammit! I *knew* he set me up! The cops showed me pictures and stuff, but I don't remember a thing except those accusing steel-gray eyes. He probably scratched himself!"

"Whoa Lela, I don't want to get in the middle of something like th–"

"No! It's not like that! There's no 'something' to get in the middle of!"

"But–"

"Just a favor. And we can go straight to the ATM, Frank. I'll pay you back, twice the amount. No shit."

"How much is your bail?"

"Five hundred. Any bondsman will work. Have you done this before?"

"No, and I'm not really interested in doing it now."

"Frank! Hey! It's *me!* Your favorite customer! Do you think I'm the kind of person who would jump bail?"

"Uh, Lela..." It was a scolding voice, and I panicked. I interrupted the objection I assumed was coming. "Frank, paying bail is easy. Just look in the phone book, the yellow pages, under bail bondsmen. They'll be dozens listed there. A simple phone call, a dude will meet you at the jail, you sign some bullshit papers, and it's done. Then I'll need a ride to my van. Piece of cake. Surely I've given you enough business to pay for doing me this favor!"

"Lela, damn..."

"Please, Frank. I'm desperate. This is my one phone call. I have nobody else."

"That's why Lela... I mean, your only friend is the liquor store owner?"

With a chuckle, I said, "Pretty funny, huh?" My eyebrows pushed together as it hit me. No, this was not funny at all. With more humility, I begged, "Frank, please. I'm in a tough spot. And I'll pay you back immediately! You can *count* on that! We'll go straight to the ATM!"

The officer glared at me and cleared his throat. His double chin creased as he nodded. "That's enough time, ma'am," he spat.

"Look, Frank, I've got to go but I'm depending on you, begging you. I'll write a good review for the Better Business Bureau about the store, write a good article for the *Wellington Shopper*, maybe produce a professional radio spot. Anything!"

Still twitching, I stopped, knowing there was nothing more to say. The pause was unnervingly long. Frank sighed. "Okay, Lela, dammit. I shouldn't, but I will. But I don't want to hear another word about it. Nothing! I don't want to be in the middle."

"Frankie-baby, you are a good friend."

"Well, I try. But this is really cra–"

"Thank you, man. I'll make it up to you somehow. Oh! Wait! One more thing..."

"What?" He sounded irritated now.

I squinted one eye and gritted my teeth, knowing I was pushing my luck. "Can you call Stuart and ask him to put my purse in the van?" I said it fast, hoping to diminish it.

"Jeezus, Lela! This is beyond the scope of my–"

"But you won't have to talk to him, just leave a message." A *hmmph* exploded from Frank's end. "Please! I only get one phone call!"

"Okay, dammit! What's the number?" Thankfully, I had committed Stuart's work number to memory, even the foggy memory of the day after.

The officer took me back to the cell to wait for bail. *Would he come? Is my only shot at freedom going to come through?* Then I said aloud, "Frank, my dear Frank, please help me. And hurry!"

An hour later, a lunch tray slid through the bars. A bologna sandwich, or at least I *thought* it was bologna. A warm chunk of fat-speckled meat of an unknown variety on plain white bread, a side of equally warm applesauce, and another bruised apple.

As I gnawed on the apple core, a skinny black girl arrived to be my cellmate. In cuffs, nervous as a whore in church, or hopped up on something, maybe.

"Don't mess with me," she said as the deputy removed the cuffs. She held her menacing glare and, once free from the cuffs, put her hands and braced her feet as if ready to throw a boxing punch. She repeated, "Don't mess with me, Curly Bitch."

I rolled over to face the wall, seeing a roadmap in the rubberized paint, a roadmap I hoped Frank would soon follow.

I NEED A NOTEPAD

CHAPTER 2

My debit card didn't work. The account was "not found," according to the ATM. Head down and my lips quivering, I got back in Frank's car and slammed the door. Too numb to speak, I tasted bile.

Frank had been a real champ throughout the drama of leaving the jail; now he looked at me with serious concern and whispered, "What is it, Lela?"

"The account is closed, Frank. Stuart must have gone to the bank early. So... but... damn man, I'm sorry. There's no way I can pay you back." A rack of sobs hiccupped against my ribs.

Silence.

Five seconds later, Frank banged his hand on the steering wheel. "Dammit!" His continued mumbles included versions of "I *knew* better! I shouldn't have *done* this! What a *dumbass* I am!" Blah, blah, blah. I felt like a real ass, ashamed, sad that I'd hurt somebody I liked. *Some friend I am, huh?*

A thought struck. "Actually, Frank, Stuart will pay you back if you ask. He's only trying to screw *me*, not you. He wouldn't want you to be out the money. Underneath, he's a nice guy."

Frank's answer was a sarcastic laugh, but I believed what I said. Despite all the red flags I had ignored over the past two years, I thought Stuart was a nice guy. I was blindly in love with him and yearned for his approval.

"That's a bunch of bullshit, Lela. He tried to rip me off just this morning at the store. Like a sleight-of-hand thing, asking for change and scratch-offs at the same time. I still don't know if I got it right. He's a snake."

Why is everybody always against Stuart? I fought the urge to defend him, taking an all-business stance. "Take a left out of the lot. To Ashley Acres, our subdivision." The ride was silent, and when my house came into view, I blew a sigh of relief, "Yes! My van is there! Now I just hope my purse is inside. Did you call him, Frank?"

"Shouldn't have done *that*, either," he mumbled.

Stuart's car was nowhere in sight. And when I opened the van door, there it was: my purse on the driver's seat. *Thank you, Stuart! See, you're not a total asshole!*

I bid Frank a goodbye and used my key to open the front door. Yona stood in the living room holding a broom, eyes wide. "Mizz Lela! No! You're not supposed to be here!" Her normal sing-song voice had no song in it at all. "I'm supposed to call the police if–"

"No! Don't call! Yona, I just need some things. I have no clothes, no underwear!"

Though I knew I wouldn't be able to pay her back, I asked for money anyway. "My dear-dear-friend Yona, do you have any money I could borrow?" *This is bad, Lela, but you're too desperate to let morals interfere. And maybe Stuart will give her some money or something to make up for it.*

"Borrow money?"

Shooting for casual, I cocked my hip and through a friendly-as-hell smile, said, "Yeah, girlfriend! We can meet up for a payback, easy. I wanted to call you from jail, but I don't know your number without my cell ph... Yona?" When I realized she wasn't listening, I stopped talking. Her eyes were far away, her hands gripping the broom handle as if it might fly away. "Never mind. I'll be out of here in a flash. No worries."

Stuart's hiding place was stupid. I found five hundred-dollar-bills in his underwear drawer. Obviously, he had forgotten or he would've hidden them from me. I spent a max of three minutes collecting random clothes and underwear and stuffing them into a tote bag from the closet. *Hurry, hurry! You'll be in deep shit if Yona calls the cops.*

On the way out of the Master suite, I met Yona walking out of the kitchen. *The kitchen... where the wall phone is.* With a gasp, I asked, "Yona, did you call somebody?" She froze in place, her mouth open with no words coming out, just two feeble squeaks.

She snapped into motion, exaggerating her movements. "No, Mizz Lela.

I'm just sweeping. See?" Still holding the broom, she brushed the tips of the straw against the floor, back and forth quickly while standing in one place, not at all like a normal person would sweep.

"Damn you, Yona!" I screamed over my shoulder, heading for the door. *Get out of Wellington and FAST, Lela!*

Two blocks away, I pulled into the small lot at Friendly Wine and Liquors and gave two of the bills to Frank. "Some payback is better than none at all, right?" Again, Frank mumbled. He didn't look at me while stuffing the bills in his pocket.

Deep in my purse, I found another treasure, a stack of winning scratch-off lottery tickets. Small potatoes, but the winnings totaled $32.00 and three free tickets. I grabbed a bottle of Grey Goose and a bottle of tonic, cashed in the tickets, and took my change.

In the heat of the afternoon, I dashed toward the coast, toward last night's bar location. If I remembered right, there was an old-fashioned motel just north of it. The name was Blue-something, something odd. I held up traffic as I looked on both sides of A-1-A. Finally, I saw the motel on the left and pulled into the lot. The Blue Flamingo. "Well, that's stupid!" I said out loud. "I think they're mixed up with pelicans."

My room was on the far end of the last building, the size of a postage stamp, filled with a musty smell and an undertone of something worse, like soured milk. I went in search of an ice machine and found none. *Oh, well. God knows I've had hot vodka before.* It was my first drink of the day and my hands shook as I filled the provided plastic-wrapped cup. The breeze blew through the open door and dried my sweaty brow.

Fear brought the need to get shit-faced, but I fought it. *Nope, don't go there, Lela. Be strong and think hard. You need a plan and you can't devise a plan if can't think.* I stood outside the door on a crumbling sidewalk, then walked barefoot to the pool area. Oily globs and a green cast in the shallow end meant no swimming for me. After a defeated sigh, I plopped onto a lounge chair and stared into, listening to the traffic noise.

Thinking of all the things I'd left behind; I knew the most important was my medicine. Diagnosed "Bi-Polar As Hell" by multiple psychiatrists over the years, it was critical that I stay on the medicine, the five different prescriptions I took daily. Without my meds, I may drop into the depths of depression... or launch into a flying, manic voyage through the stratosphere. "Just hold it in the road, Lela," I said out loud. "Stay calm and don't drink too much."

A few minutes before five, I called Dale, my boss at Smyth Software.

"Lela! Where have you been? Are you okay?"

"Dale, uh... I have a few personal things going on. Trust me, you don't want to know. I was in a place where I couldn't call." Then I pulled out my silly persona and said, "So... my sweet, understanding, and fine-looking boss... I'll be there bright-eyed in the morning."

He mumbled a few unintelligible words, and then said clearly, "You know this gets reported to HR, right? No show, no call. And strike one of three."

"Yes, I'm aware of that rule. I'm calling HR next."

"Remember she's a friend of mine so don't be jerking her around."

"I'm not jerking anybody around, Dale. Mostly, I'm just sorry, truly sorry. But it couldn't be helped." Dale remained silent, so I kept babbling nervously. "And it won't happen again, okay? You can trust me on that."

"*Trust* you?" Dale blew a sarcastic laugh. "Lela, don't be ridiculous." I felt the tension through the line.

All I could do was ignore his scolding and assure him again in a cheerful tone. "Bright and early tomorrow morning, Dale. I'll be there!"

"Here's the problem, Lela... and it's a *big* problem. There was a program update today. You have a stack of projects, some little, some big. Yep... much to do, much to write. And since this is an unexcused absence..." His voice trailed off, but I understood his point.

"No problem. I'll catch up. As you know, you can always count on me."

When I heard his laugh, I could envision his head back, wide-open mouth, and that slender hand slapping his knee. The motherfucker. Still laughing, Dale said, "Lela, dear, I've learned that to count on you is bad management.

I faked a laugh. "Good joke, Dale! See you tomorrow."

With no intention of calling HR, I poured another vodka-tonic, this time disgusted by the lack of ice. In a hurry, I left the drink on the pitted dresser and maneuvered through rush-hour traffic to get a bag of ice, a Styrofoam cooler, another bottle of tonic, a pack of cigs, and a "Big Gulp" insulated cup. As I paid the man, I realized the remaining $300 wouldn't last long.

Payday was the following Friday. Ten days. I made good money as a technical writer for Smyth Software and their order-entry program called SIMMY, but my role was better explained as "translating technical stuff for the end user." But quite a bit of that "good money" had been in the checking account Stuart stole.

I opened my flip phone, thinking I should call Stuart... tell him I need money. *But that's breaking the restraining order. If I had my computer, I'd send an email... but I bet that isn't allowed either.* I snapped the phone closed and looked around at the pitiful room. As tears flowed, I lay back on the prickly bedspread and screamed out loud. "This isn't real! This is not happening!

After a few minutes of tears, I jumped from the bed. Determined to keep active and not fall into the dreariness of feeling sorry for myself, I washed the chemical smell off my new cup and fixed my drink properly.

To the beach! Where your soul can find peace. I hopped into the van and drove to a public beach access spot just down from the motel. A long walk should've cleared my mind, but I felt wound tight. Tight as a banjo string, my Daddy would say.

I waded in the ankle-deep surf, thinking about my plight and trying to find the kernel of a plan. *So much to think about! I need a notepad to organize my thoughts!*

With a sigh, I realized I'd have to buy a lot of things tonight, including a notepad. All the things easy to grab at home... the home I used to have, anyway. Thoughts bounced in my head like a ping-pong ball. More money to spend until I could gather these needed things at home.

I'd have to take a policeman to "supervise" when I went to the house for my things, they said. I guessed I'd just swing by the tiny Wellington station and get a Barney Fife. My head rattled with details of things I needed and where I'd keep them now... now that I was homeless. Thoughts spun so fast I couldn't catch them.

The deep pain, the heartache. I considered Stuart to be my soulmate, and I ached for him, needed him in all ways. *How can you do this to me, baby? I swear I didn't hurt you or do that to your face! I was just drunk, not dangerous! And we were having fun, a nice birthday celebration! Now THIS. What the hell?*

The more I thought about it, the hurt morphed into anger. Still spinning in my head, I shook with fury. *You set me up, scratched your own face, you sonofabitch! You like calling the police on people, you asshole! You're out to destroy me, right? Just like you screwed your poor ex-wife... now you've decided to screw me. Throw me under the bus. How could you? Don't do it! Please help me! I need you!*

I sat in the sand and cried. Sobbed. I wondered how it had come to this, what made him be so mean. I tried to keep the "sane side" of my brain at bay, but as I combed further into the past, I realized I should have seen it coming. Even before we first moved to Florida last year, in 1998, Stuart drank too much, got mean when he was drunk. And getting custody of

Jeremy was the last straw. How could a couple of drunks take care of a six-year-old, anyway?

Then came the "delusional side" of my brain, where I believed the problem was Stuart. I guessed maybe I drank a little too much, too. Sometimes. But that wasn't the point. At least I wasn't a former crack addict. At least I didn't like to hang out with prostitutes and those from the underworld, the lowest echelon of society.

My mother had taught me manners; I had that, and people told me I was fun to be with most of the time. Lela Fox was doing just fine, I thought. *But now I'm screwed. How did it come to this?*

Convinced everything was 99 percent Stuart's fault, I walked back to the van. Along the shore, I had come to several conclusions. First, I was screwed. Second, I had to find a place to live. Third, I couldn't afford a place to live. Altogether, I was double-screwed.

Mom couldn't get me out of this one like she'd "fixed" things for me many times before. I was desperate.

From the beach, I drove back to the 7-Eleven for an *Apartment Guide*, and two other rags with "for rent" listings. The A/C had cooled the hotel room nicely. I mixed a drink and made calls to potential landlords, scribbling a budget in the margins while on hold.

It didn't take long to realize there was no way I could afford a proper apartment on my own paycheck. Dejected, I called a few places with rooms for rent and made a note of the address, planning an expedition to see the bad side of town where I'd be living.

Oh, shit! What am I thinking? He's closed the savings account, too! It doesn't matter that all the money started out as yours, Lela! You have no money for a security deposit. Mom warned you about making those accounts joint, you stupid shit! Why didn't you listen to her?

I grabbed my wallet and counted the bills. A total of 218 bucks for ten days, and the damn motel room was forty a night! I realized I would be penniless before payday and that sent a roar of fury through my head.

I made the next drink strong then tried to find something to watch on the tiny TV. Within the half-hour, I poured another drink, knowing I was drinking too much but unable to stop. Another drink put me over the edge... overwhelmed, tripping over my thoughts, sloppy.

It was a drunk's idea that became easier to trust as the vodka flowed. The idea blossomed in my mind, becoming the ideal and ingenious way to move forward.

Around midnight, I was drunk enough to carry out my plan, bold enough to retrieve the missing piece that would restore my dignity.

DIVING FOR PEARLS
CHAPTER 3

I hesitated before I closed the van's door... thinking I could just go to bed instead of being so sneaky, but drunken wisdom won. I turned north on A-1-A, heading to Wellington. After scraping against the curb twice, and four times backing up and going forward to park parallel, I left my van two streets over in our neighborhood.

Stumbling crazily in the dark, I sneaked through the yards and carefully opened the side gate of our fence, entering our over planted backyard. Through the French doors of the house, the multi-color flickers of the TV flashed, and I wondered who was on the sofa watching the tube. The back screened porch light was on but nobody was outside. All was quiet.

Woof! I froze. *Oh, Murphy, my precious dog! I'm so sorry to leave you here with Asshole. I don't know when I can find a place for you and me, but I'll try.* A thought struck, and I hoped that Stuart would continue to give him the thyroid medication in my absence.

Murphy was a 52-pound Sheltie, while most are fifteen to twenty pounds. *Please don't bark, Murphy, not tonight. Don't let them know Mommy is here.*

A random thought crossed my mind and erased the reason for the trip. *Wouldn't it be cool to pee in the pool!* I didn't think it was a ridiculous thought at all. In fact, I considered it a challenge with a prize to be had when the deed was done.

I nearly fell while removing my shorts as I stripped naked and dropped my clothes in a pile. My purple-foam float was against the side in the deep end, and I scampered to pull it carefully to the shallows. The swishy sound of the water seemed so loud! I froze in place, making sure nobody could hear me. After a pause, I pulled the float into the well of the steps.

Whoa! The water is cold! With great care, I balanced on the float, laying on my stomach and making as little splash as possible. The fact that I could be caught never occurred to me; I was on a drunken tangent with no concept of consequences. Soon, I relaxed completely and peed in the pool. *Aah! Warmth.*

Relaxed and drunk, my head bobbled, and I stifled a giggle. Then I floated silently, thinking about what Stuart was doing inside, thinking about my dog, and wondering where I had hidden the pearl necklace. Everybody knew the necklace was valuable; thirty inches of fine pearls, a wedding gift from Stuart's well-to-do mother. Rich bitch Daphne. His high falutin' mother in Fort Lauderdale.

Weeks ago, I hid the pearls in the freezer, thinking it was a clever theft deterrent. I remember taking them out, but hell if I could remember where I put them next. With barely two-hundred bucks to my name, pawning the pearls was my brilliant solution.

I had never sold anything to a pawn shop and wondered where to go. *But maybe I should go to a jewelry store instead... with something honestly valuable like that. Yeah, that's it! Across the bridge into Palm Beach proper. I'll get all gussied-up and prance in as Daphne Weinstein-Graning would.*

Lost in the fog of my thoughts, I had drifted to the deep end and my head was under the diving board. I paddled slowly and aimed for open water, shifting my weight toward my shoulders.

Suddenly, I was in the water, sputtering. As quick as I could, I grabbed the float. Then I whispered a prayer, hopeful there had been no sound.

Reality struck with a wallop. *Why am I here, anyway?* My presence was a pure surprise to me. It was as if I had blacked out and came to in a rush. Surely I knew better than to think I'd be able to sneak inside and get the pearls! So what was my reason to come? I was 100 percent frantic and instantly scared shitless.

All he has to do is call the police and I'm in deep shit. Why am I here? I scissor-kicked underwater toward the shallow end, chiding myself for being so stupid. It was a tiny moment of clarity, cut short by a shout from the screened patio.

"Who's there?" Stuart's voice boomed. "The police are on the way! Show yourself!"

"Stuart, don't call the police! It's just me!" I didn't recognize my own voice, an octave higher than normal.

"Lela! Dumbass! You're busted now, you crazy bitch! You scary-drunk-redneck!"

"Wait, I just came to pick up some stuff, decided to have a dip first, baby! Let me in and get a notepad and a few other things, then I'll leave you alone."

"You really fucked yourself this time, my dear."

I ignored him. "And I need some money! Sonofabitch, you stole my money!"

"Ha-fucking-ha! Good luck getting money from *me!* Go away, crazy whore." There was a pause, and he spoke with excitement. "First, stay where you are!" He turned and rushed inside the house. A commotion. Our live-in maid Yona yelled in a frantic voice, then I heard the front door slam. Confused, I furrowed my brow. *What's he doing? Where's he going?*

Realization hit. The asshole had run to the side yard to move the cinderblocks and block the gate, the same barrier we had fashioned on the front gate. The sonofabitch had locked me in the yard.

Thigh-high in the pool with my hand on the purple float, I bent over to cry. Too drunk to make sense out of the situation, I turned on a dime and fantasized that Stuart agreed to let me stay and swim. Without a care, I climbed back on the float and paddled to the center of the pool, humming an old Jimmy Buffett tune from my high school days.

Jeremy appeared on the screened porch, wearing his Mutant Ninja Turtles pajamas and standing next to a dark figure that must be Yona. A tiny voice said, "She's here! Hide me!" I froze and felt a surge of Shame and intense remorse. *The poor kid is afraid of me! What has Stuart told him?*

Without pausing to think, I yelled, "Jeremy! Hey, little man, it's okay! No reason to be scared, honey! I won't hurt you! Because I *love* you, okay? You know I wouldn't be mean to you, silly! I'm just here for a swim." A motherly thought arose. "And what are you doing up so late, anyway? It's a school night!"

He ignored the question. In a voice that sounded painfully small and afraid, he said, "You can't *be* here! Daddy *said!*"

Shame overcame me. Oh, how I loved that sweet boy! Over the past few months, I had tried my best to be a good example, sometimes even skipping drinks during homework sessions. My heart ached for him, and I felt ashamed to have let him down like this.

"Jeremy, don't worry, honey. Everything is fine. Are you doing okay in school this week? Is Yona taking good care of you?"

"Go away. The *pleece* are coming and you're going to get in trouble. But I didn't do it! I didn't tell the pleece like I did with Mommy."

Two months ago, the poor child had been in the car when his alcoholic mom had a DUI wreck. She threw bottles of booze out the window; Jeremy told the police about it. That's when Jeremy left his unfit mother and came to live with us. As if it was better for him.

Through a veil of tears, I assured Jeremy of his innocence. "I know you didn't tell the police, sweetie. You're a good boy all-around. And I love you with all my heart, okay? Never forget that.

I had no answer to the question in my own head: *Lela, what the hell have you done?*

Murphy barked and my heart took another hit of Shame. *Please forgive me, sweet dog. I'll come for you as soon as I can.*

There was no siren, but I saw the rotating flash of lights from the front yard, casting shadows on the far side of the fence. "The police are here," I said out loud. Then, with confidence, "Screw it!"

As Murphy barked and Jeremy scolded me for using bad words, I flipped off the float and climbed back on, face-up this time. Defiance took over my ping-pong ball of thoughts. *If they want me, they'll have to come and get me.* I moved to the middle of the pool slowly, taking care to stay out of reach from the sides, paddling with cupped hands like a guppy.

Time passed, maybe five minutes. My frazzled nerves had disappeared in the quiet and, for some drunk reason, I felt calm and assured. *Surely they will let me go. How can they take a naked woman to jail?* Now confident, I closed my eyes and dozed a bit, I think, awakened by a gruff voice.

"Ms. Fox, you need to come with us."

"The hell you say!" I shouted back, sitting up with a jerk.

"You're in violation of a no-contact order, Ms. Fox. You're under arrest. Do you understand your rights?" The cop was a big, burly one with a buzz haircut, decked out in all the blue regalia. His sturdy legs, shoulder-width apart, stood firm on the edge of the pool, his beefy arms crossed on his barrel chest.

Like a smartass, I mocked him. "My rights? As an innocent citizen? Well, I forgot the exact words you used last night, mister sir, so you better say them again. You wouldn't want this thrown out for crappy police procedure, would you? Dumb ass cops!"

A female officer stepped into the light. With no inflection at all, she stated my rights, word for word. "Good memory, lady cop. You get an A."

The lady stepped back to the shadows as the big cop spoke again. "Get out of the pool, please."

"No can do. It's nice and refreshing in here. Come on in yourself! Enjoy!"

"Don't make me have to come to get you."

"Well, I guess you're gonna have to, mister big-fat cop, because I'm not getting out."

"Do you have clothes?"

"No, and you can't take a naked woman to jail. That much I know. I watch TV crime shows, see, and I know *all* about it."

Stuart spoke from the screened patio. "Sir, I'll get a blanket–"

I snapped at him, "Shut the hell up, Stuart! *You* caused all this! You're the one that oughta be going to jail! Crackhead-junkie-drunk-sonofabitch!

As I yelled to Stuart, I had jerked to a sitting position and the next thing I knew, the female cop was in the water, grabbing my arm with a yank to pull me off the float. I was too limber, too drunk to fight her. She put the handcuffs on way too tight, jerked me around more than necessary. Ms. Cop bitched me out with venom as she pushed me to the edge of the pool. The male cop pulled me out by the cuffs, leaving all my body weight against my wrists. It hurt like hell.

Later, I reasoned they needed to treat me roughly to justify adding "Resisting Arrest" to the charges. Drunk and swaying in the back of the patrol car, I blamed the cops. And Stuart. And Yona. Everybody and everything but me.

The car traveled east to my home away from home, the Palm Beach County jail, with a blanket covering me and my pile of clothes in the seat.

This time, there was nobody to bail me out. Nobody at all.

This kind of illogical behavior wasn't unusual at that stage of my drinking life, but the timing was bad and the consequences dire. I lived loose, moved by the swing of emotions and flashes of what I thought was brilliance. With no way to reel myself in, I reeled out of control like a kite in a violent July thunderstorm.

As wild tangents and absurd conclusions continued to drive my actions, the consequences stacked higher and higher. But this ridiculous stunt... it seemed I was close to defeat... and maybe I

welcomed that defeat.

I was tired. Disgusted with myself. Sinking so low... sick and tired of being sick and tired. And it disturbed me that I'd thought of suicide more than once. Actually, more than a dozen times.

I just wanted a way out of the mess I'd created... but couldn't accept the "defeat," which I thought would feel worse.

I could only see the short-term and what I saw was frightening. Sigh.

The quest for the pearls was for naught; I never got them back. Though I suspected Stuart Weinstein was determined to keep me in trouble, I seriously underestimated his tenacity and the evil in his heart. He wasn't finished with me yet, not at all.

But hope reigned eternal. That smart man promised to love and cherish me. And I believed he'd come around, eventually.

WHEN DENIAL DIES
CHAPTER 4

I don't remember much about that night in jail. Maybe I was getting used to being in such a place, maybe I was too drunk, maybe I was too much in my head with worry, or maybe all three. The next morning's hearing, however, is crystal-clear in my mind. I've replayed it dozens of times.

Like a dumbass, I flat-out told the judge I had no idea why I'd gone to the house for a swim. "I must have been in a blackout," I said, thinking it was an acceptable explanation.

Another bonehead move was the admission that I'd been too drunk to remember why or how I had beaten Stuart up the night before. "Honestly, Your Honor, I don't think it even happened! But I was too drunk to be sure."

I didn't see this as a bad legal move. Honesty was the best policy, I reasoned, and being drunk was an acceptable excuse for anybody, right? Sober, I was perfectly fine, and otherwise... well, I was just in the wrong place at the wrong time. Denial is not just a river in Egypt.

I pled for mercy and expected it; after all, I had my wits about me now. *When the judge finds out I have nowhere to go, a crisis by itself, he will surely want me to work that out first. He'd know staying in jail at such a critical time of my life would be counterproductive.* With confidence, I asked the judge to let me get settled then we'd follow up later.

Before I could properly present the idea, he had the bailiff pass me a piece of paper: a listing of about thirty halfway houses in the area. The judge asked me to choose one, then he'd release me with the promise to report there within 48 hours. The word "release" vibrated in my mind. That was the magic word, and all I needed to hear.

I randomly made a checkmark in a box near the center of the page. It meant nothing; I had no intention of going to a halfway house! All I wanted was *out* and to get to work before I lost my job. Besides, I thought a halfway house was like a charity, a place for the homeless. The fact that I *was* homeless didn't cross my mind. I just knew I was better than "those people," whoever they were.

Six cigarettes; that's how long it took for the taxi to pick me up from jail. When we pulled to the back cul-de-sac of Ashley Acres, I blew a sigh of relief to see my van still there, still parked crookedly. I didn't realize I'd blocked a driveway, but a quick check showed no damage or no snotty note on the windshield. *Maybe things are looking up for me. I have a plan.* A shower, and then I'd go to work... four hours late, but I'd get there.

First, back to The Blue Pelican, hoping they hadn't cleaned out my room though it was two hours past checkout time. No such luck. "Sorry, ma'am. We are strict about checkout times at The Blue Pelican!" The leather-skinned, gray-haired woman spoke with a proud grin that could only come from an owner.

"My things are in lost and found, then?"

"Yes, ma'am. Locked 'em up myself."

Everything was there except the bottle of vodka. *Sonofabitch! But wouldn't it figure? Maybe that's why the woman is so damn happy.*

I re-checked into the same room for the night and hauled my things through the rotting-wood door. The clothes in the tote bag included nothing appropriate for work; I wasn't thinking straight when I grabbed clothes the day before. "This will have to do," I said out loud, "wrinkles and all." I surprised myself with a voice that sounded stressed to the max. I needed a drink; that was the problem. On a day like today, I'd need two.

There you go again, dumbass. Maybe you should be thinking differently... like maybe vodka is the problem here instead of the solution. Wasn't vodka what started all this shit?

I dismissed the thought quickly; it made me nervous.

The Smyth Software office was six miles from my motel, and I found a liquor store within the first mile. I bought four one-shot mini bottles, two for now and two for later. The bottle of tonic I used for a chaser spewed on my shirt, dousing me. *Great... now I look as bad as I feel.*

☼ ☼ ☼ ☼ ☼

"Hey, Dale! I'm here!" I checked in with the boss a few minutes after two o'clock.

"Sit down." No smile. All-business.

Oh, shit. Here it comes. "Lela, this absence is not acceptable. At first, I was worried but now I'm angry, and so is the HR department. You've left us in a tough spot. There is too much work here for an unreliable employee."

"Dale, it's over now. The 'personal problem' is taken care of. No more absences. Trust me on that."

"Trust you? Lela, you told me yesterday you'd be here 'bright and early,' remember?"

"Right. Well..." I had no answer but tried another tactic without thinking. "But I'm staying late today. With nobody to bother me, I'll get a lot done after hours... more than make up for what I've missed, both today and yesterday."

Dale eyed me with suspicion and held the gaze for what seemed like five silent minutes. My heart beat like rolling thunder in my chest. *Does he know something I don't? Is there really that much to do? He's acting like I can't do it. Can I? Am I setting myself up to fail?*

Mostly, I feared he was ready to fire me, so I kept my mouth shut. Then Dale spoke through lips that barely moved. "Okay, one more chance, Lela, but this is strike two. Honestly, I had planned to fire you today. Just now."

I jumped in with a start. "But that would make the problems worse! I'll make it up, Dale. Give me any specifics you want."

He sighed. "Your inbox is full. Just do it all. *All* of it. And don't rush through as you do sometimes. You're a professional and now is the time to act like one." Dale blew a bloated *hmmph* and spoke to himself, "I can't believe I'm having this conversation!"

"No problem. I'll do it. Don't worry." *Maybe you should be the one worrying, dingbat.*

I scooted to my desk. Dale wasn't kidding about having a lot of work to do; there was a stack of papers and nearly forty emails projects. My stomach fell. *Yep, I should be worrying. No way I can get all of this done today.*

None of my coworkers greeted me or seemed happy I was there, not even Spooky Robert. I reasoned that Dale had told them something bad about me and now I was the outcast. But being an outcast wasn't a new thing for me;

I'd spent most of my life as a misunderstood drunk. But this was more personal, more hurtful.

The first two email projects were to-the-point but required deep thinking and studying things I didn't understand. I could hardly focus because my nerves were shattered.

Look at all you have to do! No way you'll finish! A panic attack started with a jerk as my feelings of being overwhelmed encompassed me. I felt afraid and inadequate. I knew now that I had over-promised and over-sold myself, another familiar feeling. But on that particular day, I was close to falling apart.

I hid my hands so no one would see them shake and stayed facing the monitor to hide my frantic eyes. *Breathe, Lela... breathe. In through the nose and out through the mouth.*

I managed to write a paragraph or two, but it took two hours to accomplish this easy "feat." I announced I was going for a smoke. Spooky Robert followed, so I darted to the left and headed to my van instead of the loading dock.

I had parked on the far side, next to the railroad tracks. I slammed the one-hit bottle and chased it with what was now *hot* tonic water. Bleck! The bad taste was a compromise with the warm glow that began in my belly and spread outward to relax me head to toe.

It was a cloudy day, not so hot, so I got out to sit on the bench next to the tracks. Since I started that job four months ago, I had come to like sitting there and watching the trains go by. It wasn't the first time I wondered what it would be like to jump across the tracks as the bullet-fast train approached. End it all. All my troubles solved in one easy step.

I wouldn't let myself use the word "suicide" because that sounded too scary. Instead, I used "off myself" and "take the short way home," sometimes "last call," which made me laugh.

With a sigh, I smoked and thought about my deep predicament. Lost in thought, I heard a group of employees leaving the building, laughing. *How can they be so damn happy? How dare they laugh and joke when my life is such a mess?*

I stomped back to my desk to see everybody was staying late. Half complained of too much work but two writers bragged about being almost finished. *Assholes! They must've been assigned the easy projects, fucking teachers' pets.*

Dejected, I realized I could never catch up, no matter how late I stayed. I couldn't finish "all of it," as Dale had specified. The drink had put me back in the driver's seat, though, and I plunged in, completing about ten projects in just a few hours.

As I slowly relaxed, I remembered what Dale said about doing things "half-assed, as I tended to do," and wondered what would make him say that. Had my coworkers complained of substandard work? Had the department heads ordered rewrites I didn't know about? I couldn't understand how he'd discovered my shortcomings.

Guilt ate at the bile churning in my gut. *Yep... here it comes, the full package. Guilt. Shame. Fear. Despair. My friends, my enemies. The hideous feelings that will kill me in the end. The end that's coming soon, Lela. Very soon if you don't get your shit together.*

A sigh. I straightened my desk and began anew. Deep into my work, I kept my head down, even when Spooky Robert said goodbye and leaned down to peck a kiss on the top of my head. "Stop it, Robert, dammit!" was my only response as the others tittered with nervous laughter.

Around eight o'clock, I dashed out for another cigarette and another shot. Again, I sat on the bench next to the railroad tracks and let the blasts of wind from the speeding trains blow my hair back against my head. *One day I'll be on that train, going anywhere but here. Going anywhere but nowhere, toward anything but the bare-bones room at The Blue Pelican.*

As I pondered my bleak future, the feeling of defeat consumed me. I knew I needed to go home, back to Mom and Dad in Tennessee, stay with them at the farm and wilt into nothingness. Just go to sleep and not wake up

My thoughts drifted to Bo, my sweet and probably confused seventeen-year-old son, and tears came to my eyes. Then, through a continuing fog of tears, I saw my father's smiling face, his silly grin, even thought I could hear his snorting laugh. And I envisioned my sister Karen, so eager to please, so loving toward me. Even my sister Jennifer was on my side if you forced her to choose.

I have people who love me so I'm not 100 percent bankrupt. But Lela, what you are is hopeless. Find a place to live and keep a job. Don't run from your problems, just straighten yourself up and now. Now, now, now.

After the fourth train passed, I stood to go back inside the building. In the sudden silence, I spoke to myself. "I can't work anymore tonight. I'm going home." But home was The Blue Pelican. Yippee.

I didn't say goodbye to my coworkers; I got in the car and drove away, stopping by the liquor store. With my hand on a bottle of Grey Goose, I thought about my thin wallet. *On second thought, I'm not too proud to drink cheap vodka.* I grabbed the Popov, barely above a generic brand.

As I drove toward the beach, I realized this had to be my last night at the motel. It was too expensive to pay a nightly rate. The problem was I had no place to go otherwise.

What the hell? God... or whoever you are... give me a sign, a direction. I think I need some help. But mostly, God, I need money. Can you arrange that?

A FRIDGE AND A HOT PLATE

CHAPTER 5

There were only ten ice cubes in my mini freezer. With a chuckle, I slipped the six-pack of Bud Light bottles into my new Igloo cooler, cardboard carrier and all, and dropped the pitiful ice supply on top. Outside, I locked my door, number 1 at the Homing Inn, a by-the-week motel on Highway A-1-A in West Palm Beach, a mile or so north of The Blue Pelican.

Ten days prior, I had moved to the Homing Inn, paying $100 a week for a room with a fridge and a hot plate. My plan was to save for a deposit on a "real" apartment, but the truth was I couldn't deal with the enormity of a plan, and certainly not a move. Anxiety ran high. I had barely been able to get through the days of work, had screwed up royally at most everything.

Last Thursday, just after my vodka lunch in the parking lot, Spooky Robert and I stood on the loading dock to smoke. He told me I was beautiful in his creepy, growling voice and for some dumb-drunk reason, I kissed him. On purpose. Full tongue with a little moan at the end. Then I said, "If you stop with the leering looks and snide comments, I'll kiss you again tomorrow."

I thought it would keep him away, but it had the opposite effect. After that kiss, I became his obsession. I felt naked when he looked at me, vulnerable and afraid of him in every moment.

More concerning, I'd been drinking more than usual, and, at times, it worried me. The familiarity of that worry concerned me even more; yep, I'd known for years that my drinking was a problem.

So how long have you thought alcohol may be a problem in your life, Ms. Fox? The way my mind said it was from the mouth of a knowing counselor of some sort. I pushed the vision away as fast as I could, but it ate at me, chewed at my stomach lining. I worried.

Today, however, I didn't worry at all.

The hotel pool was just a few steps away, and the weather was perfect that fine Saturday morning. It would be hot and sticky later; no one with sense stayed outside in the afternoon. Too hot in June, even this close to the breeze of the beach.

There was a crowd, mostly young singles with missing teeth and questionable hygiene. A few unsupervised Latino kids ran around the shallow end, so I spied a chair opposite from them and spread a black-and-white striped towel over the stretched plastic straps. *Oops, broken.* The chair rocked back and forth. *If I lay still, it will do.*

I twisted the cap off the beer and took a long, slow swig. An hour earlier, I woke up determined to make this day a good one. It had to be better than the hellish week I had endured. I had finished the updates at work, but not until late last night, a week late. I'd dropped the ball on several, doing what I knew to be wrong. There would be revisions, and probably a "talking to" by Dale.

The feelings of failure weighed heavy.

Work wasn't the only issue. I had plenty of problems happening in the so-called "new life" I'd been living.

My upset that morning wasn't the work, or Spooky Robert, or the sleaziness of my room at the Homing Inn. It was Stuart. He had called me dozens of times throughout the week, calling me nasty names, teasing me for being what he called a "homeless drunk redneck." When I quit answering his calls on my cell, he called at work, which was bad for many reasons. With evil glee, he threatened me with ruin, said he'd kill me if I tried to contact him again.

Yet when I asked him to stop contacting *me*, he laughed. "Never, bitch. I will haunt your dreams." *Crazy sonofabitch. How did I get hooked up with such a twisted man? Surely he's finished punishing me. What more can he do?*

The past Tuesday morning, he had a piss-poor selection of my belongings delivered to the parking lot of the Homing Inn. Stuart hired a tow truck through Ace Transmissions and haphazardly tossed my clothes and random personal effects on the back. No boxes or bags, no cover, and it was raining like a mother, a tropical-Florida downpour.

He wouldn't allow me to come to the house, even with a police escort, so I had to get a court order for what they called "timely delivery." Otherwise, I'd never have seen my belongings again. I ran back and forth in the rain, eleven times, carrying sopping-wet things from the tow truck to door number 1, on the first level of the building.

I guessed a lot of things had blown off the truck on the trip from Wellington, twenty miles inland. Maybe that's where the second shoe of nine pairs had disappeared, or maybe sending only a single shoe was purposeful; Stuart's idea of an evil joke.

The only good thing was he had sent my new juicer with all the bells and whistles. I bought a basket of fresh grapefruit from a roadside stand to mix the ultimate vodka-grapefruit, the perfect start to a day. To use the juicer, I had to turn all the lights and TV off or it blew the fuse in my room.

The delivery was but a pittance of what I had left behind. My tools were missing, my sewing machine, all of my craft supplies, purses, jewelry, so much more. Stuart had no use for these things; he would throw everything away but made a point that I didn't get them. Evil, spiteful man. Without a doubt, he knew how to punch every button I had.

Now he was harassing me, scaring me. How could I make him stop?

What will happen to me? How can I get far enough away for safety? Will I ever really be safe from him? Should I get the hell out of Dodge? I thought for a while about leaving Florida and running back to Tennessee. *Today, right now, Lela. Do it.*

My brain was too fried to conceive of the arrangements needed. Even the thirteen-hour drive was beyond my functional ability. *Face it, Lela Fox, you're having a hard time just getting through a workday!*

The anxiety and confusion had been building and had now turned into a full-blown manic chapter. The Bi-Polar monster roared. Grandiose thoughts, impulsive actions, staying up all night and spending money I didn't have. Of course, I had to buy replacements for many of the necessities I left behind, but this was not the time to buy perfume or a crystal keychain.

Commotion at the far side of the pool jarred me out of my bouncing thoughts. I opened another beer and sat up to see who was making all the noise. Two couples at the back-corner table, one man talking to an incredibly pregnant woman.

Preggo was bitching out her man, I supposed her Baby-Daddy, pecking her finger at his tattooed chest to emphasize syllables here and there as she shouted. Even straining to listen, I couldn't hear every word, but her anger rang through. I heard the word "asshole" several times, plus a great variety of cuss words. Baby-Daddy put his hands up in defense.

Suddenly, Preggo screamed, "You suck!" and slapped the hell out of him. Full hand-across-the-cheek. The man ducked, but the contact was complete, a *pop* audible to everybody at the pool. All heads turned.

Preggo turned and waddled off, got inside an old sled, a blue-and-Bondo Chevy. As the sun beat down on her, I could see beads of sweat on her forehead.

Baby-Daddy ran to the fence and yelled. "Carmen, dammit, get back here! You don't know the whole story!" She flipped him off and sped away. The smell of burnt oil wafted over the pool area.

The Baby-Daddy man shook the posts of the fence surrounding the pool and stepped back, almost pushing the fence forward. He put his head down and mumbled loud enough for me to hear. "Goddamn hormones!"

He stood there a minute, shaking his head and flexing powerful muscles. Surprised that I would find a man like that so sexy, I looked away. But I sneaked to look back and found him staring at me. He grinned, showing a cute gap between two ultra-white front teeth. *A gap like my Momma's teeth. How fucking charming is THAT?*

Looking away again, I focused on the other couple at the back table. They seemed oblivious to Baby-Daddy's drama at the front side of the pool. The woman, about thirty and painfully thin, sat on the lap of a scraggly haired man of the same age. The man was shirtless but wore full-length blue jeans. *Damn, he must be hot... uh... temperature-wise, definitely not sexy-wise.*

He had "summer teeth" – some were here, and some were there. Snaggle-Tooth. Streaks of bright-blonde hair ran through the tangled mess of greasy brown; they looked painted-on as if someone had attacked him with a stubby yellow paintbrush.

The bikini-clad woman on his lap was singing, the song unknown, but she was into it. Head back and rocking her body, holding an invisible microphone, unaware to all happening around her.

Baby-Daddy walked back to the table, fidgeting. He picked up his beer, Coors in a can, and turned it up. Then he set the can on the table and squashed it flat with powerful force. There was a sound, a combination of a belch and a chuckle, an angry release of air, as he threw the beer can over the fence.

Lap-Dancer continued her dance, unconcerned. Snaggle-Tooth appeared to be listening to Baby-Daddy, but he also patted his foot in time with Lap-Dancer's non-existent music.

As I gulped beer and fidgeted, my manic, racing thoughts turned to the creative side. In my mind, I concocted their story. *Baby-Daddy lives here in the motel, works as a carpenter, and drinks his money away. He doesn't intend to support the upcoming baby... twins, actually. And the mother, Carmen, is working two jobs, just a month before her due date.*

The other two have been at the pool for hours, both already drunk and will later gather coins and crushed dollar bills to buy more beer, more Coors. They are passersby, from Canada or somewhere like that, on an adventure to find the best and sunniest party in North America.

They're in the right place, I thought. Right here at the Homing Inn.

As "my story" expanded, I began to feel close to them, as if I knew them intimately. The third beer helped my thoughts slow a bit, but I became curious, needing more information before I could conclude the story. The trio gathered their things, ready to leave. *Damn, it was just getting good!*

Baby-Daddy caught my eye and didn't look away. *Wow. Look at those baby blues!* No doubt, I had noticed his tanned muscles before, but they now glistened with sweat and the veins in his arms became more prominent. As he walked forward, I saw a close-up of his tattoo against a hairless chest, a stylized dragon. Well-done, in four air-brushed colors.

"Hey, pretty lady!" he sang. The smile was pleasant and kind. He seemed to be the opposite of the worthless Baby-Daddy I had created in my story. "Do you need a beer or something? We're going to 7-Eleven. You want to come along?"

"Why not?" I answered, also wanting to know if the story I had created was true. In my four-beer state with an underlying manic attitude, there seemed to be no danger in getting in a strange car with strange people. I didn't question my judgement.

In the backseat, Baby-Daddy put his arm around me and tried to cuddle up. I scooted away. "Don't do that, dammit, we're just getting beer, and you're *not* getting laid. Besides, you have a baby due soon."

"*Two* babies, twins," he said. *I knew it! I was right! Could the rest of my story be true?*

"Do you work construction? Are you married to Baby-Momma?"

"Whoa! Is this an intervention? An interrogation?" He laughed. "I work when I can get it. I'm an electrician, non-union, so it's hard to find work. And I'm not married, not even sure if the babies are mine."

He cocked his head. "And can I ask the same personal shit about you?"

"No." He huffed a chuckle, which I ignored. "See... I invented a story about y'all from my chair across the way."

"*Y'all?!* Where the hell are you *from*, girl?" Baby-Daddy cackled.

"Hey, watch it! I'm from Tennessee and damn proud of it, so shut your pie-hole!" I laughed, but to be frank, I was miffed. Sure, people made fun of my accent, but rarely made it so personal. This felt derogatory, too close for comfort.

"Do you wear shoes? Did you marry your cousin?" Baby-Daddy laughed, determined to piss me off.

I'm sure he didn't understand my answer, but I spit it out. "Would'a been better off if I *had* married my cousin!" The man raised his eyebrow but asked nothing further.

I shouted to the couple in the front seat. "Are you two from Canada?" The girl laughed but didn't answer. Snaggle-Tooth snorted, "Kansas. But we're just passing through. We'll probably turn around after a week or two in Miami, back to the Kansas cornfields." Snaggle-Tooth continued to laugh through his nose. *And they think I'm the one with an accent? Jeez! The Kansas nose-snort?*

With my dwindling bundle of cash, I bought another six of Bud Light while the others were combining change to buy just a six-pack of Coors. "Here, man, I'll chip in." I only had a five and laid it on Baby-Daddy's open hand. Lo-and-behold, Snaggle-Tooth "found" two crumpled dollars. Miser. Now they could afford a twelve-pack but stuck with Coors. Cheap, rot-gut beer, in my opinion. Not that Bud Light was any better, but that was my business, not theirs.

Back at the pool, I saw someone had stolen my towel and cooler. Shit. *Asshole criminals around here!* I went to the back table, still available, we all sat down. "That's what you get for leaving it here," said Baby-Daddy.

"I keep forgetting this isn't Tennessee. Or Wellington," I answered.

"Wellington? The fancy town west of here?" Baby-Daddy seemed to know the area.

"That's the one." I gave a condensed, matter-of-fact version of my situation and, explained so simply, it sounded even more ridiculous. *What the hell has happened to me?* I got lost in that thought and came close to blaming myself. "I don't know what to do, really, I'm stuck."

"What you'll do is stay stuck right here and get drunk with us!" Snaggle-Tooth raised his beer for a toast. We all clicked in the toast, even Lap-

Dancer, who hadn't said six words. The four of us sat back and drank with a thirst only a drunk can have, watching the pool crowd thin out to just a few sleeping obese women.

Two men with beady eyes, from the Middle East somewhere, threw their towels over the fence and dove in, swimming the length of the pool and splashing us all. Baby-Daddy opened his mouth to yell at them but stopped short when one of the young men shot a look that could kill. There was a distinct *slap* sound as Baby-Daddy's mouth closed. He leaned in to whisper to us all, "Don't look now, but these guys look like terrorists."

"No turbans, though," I said. Snaggle-Tooth snapped his head up, shaking "no," and put his finger to his lips to shush me. The men talked to each other, nodding toward us. Goosebumps rising, I got the creeps. Were they talking *to* us or *about* us? I wanted to sink into the chair, shrink to the size of a pea.

"Just ignore them," whispered Snaggle-Tooth. "They're probably harmless." The men swam laps, with awkward touch-turns at each end. Shrugs from me, but Baby-Daddy watched them with suspicion.

"Quit it, man. Be cool. Quit looking." I wasn't kidding. Despite my objection, Baby-Daddy continued staring.

A car drove by. The driver yelled at Baby-Daddy, calling him "Pooh." I realized I didn't know their real names, nor did they know mine. Just as well... drinking buddies don't have to share intimacies, I thought. Baby-Daddy squeezed my bare shoulders as he walked to see the guy who called him Pooh.

His head disappeared inside the driver's side window of the visitor's Toyota. *What the hell?* Then his body stuttered as if trying to hold an extra-large hit of a joint in his lungs. At long last, Baby-Daddy withdrew his head, waving as the car pulled away.

He turned to rejoin our group. *Oh my god! Look at his eyes! So bloodshot! Baby-Daddy, bad boy! What kind of weed was that? Or was it something else altogether?*

A moment of fear passed, wondering if the "weed" was a rock of crack like Stuart had smoked... the crack that made him crazy. *No, Lela, be honest. You smoked it, too, even though you didn't know what it was. Crack is bad. You don't want to spend one minute of the day with these guys if they smoke crack.*

The Middle Eastern men got out of the pool at the opposite end, after swimming laps for a half-hour. They dried themselves with brisk strokes, including the crotch, reaching inside their Speedos. The men were talking loud with their guttural accents as they donned flip-flops and hurried to the back side of the building.

Not long after they left, I said goodbye to Baby-Daddy and the pool crew and sauntered back to my room, sweating in the Florida heat. A nap was in order, I thought. But I didn't yet know why it would be so difficult to stay asleep.

As later reported, the two 9/11 pilots stayed at the Homing Inn while enrolled in flight school. The timing would have been exactly right.

While I have no proof the two men at the pool were part of the terrorist team, I felt a convincing chill that day, a vibration of evil, even as they swam. It's unsettling to this day.

Perhaps I should've had the same suspicions about Baby-Daddy and friends.

HOODWINKED
CHAPTER 6

I lay on the worn-out twin mattress, tossing and turning. The window air conditioner churned and groaned, trying to cool the filthy room but the attempt was unsuccessful. Sweat gathered on my upper lip as I lay on the stained sheets. Even a cool shower didn't stop the blistering heat radiating from my body.

Sleep eluded me and the beer called. "Why not?" I said aloud, uncapping my last beer. "And for later, the dregs of the vodka bottle. It'll do." Perhaps simple drunkenness put me out, but I managed to stay awake long enough to finish the beer.

I don't know how long I slept, but the phone awakened me. A surprise, because my cell phone seldom worked in the dungeon of my room.

"Hello," I said. It was a drawn-out, sleepy salutation.

"Hi, there!" Stuart chirped in his charming way.

Instantly anxious, I sat up with a jerk. "What do you *want?*"

"I want *you*, baby. I miss you."

I froze in place. *Why is he saying this? Could he be telling the truth?* I answered, "But you've said such horrible things, Stuart. So mean!" A river of tears flowed freely now, dripping from the bottom of my jaw and landing on my sunburned thighs.

"So sorry, baby. I just get weird sometimes. I didn't mean a word of it, you *know* that. The truth is... I love you, Lela. You're my wife! More than anything, I want us to have a happy marriage, be a family with Jeremy. He misses you, too, by the way."

"I miss *him!* And *you!* So much, dammit... but–"

"But nothing, Lela. Let me take you to a nice dinner tonight, make you feel like a million bucks. I don't want us to be enemies."

A buzz of excitement built behind my ears. Back to being a couple? Back with my soulmate? Yes! Please let this be true! A few deep breaths brought my blood pressure back to normal and a barrage of tears began with a buzz between my temples.

"I've been so lonely without you, Stuart."

"This house echoes without your bare feet on the tile, without your bad singing. I miss you terribly."

Before I let myself smile, I had to get a few things straight. "Why have you been harassing me, ruining my things? I need the truth."

Stuart's smooth, pouty voice spoke... the one that made my heart flutter. *Don't be gullible, Lela! Don't let him con you! Find out what he's up to!* He purred in a heartfelt tenor, "Truthfully, baby, I don't know *why* I've been so ugly to you. I've just been so upset, so freaked out about all this... mess. I didn't know what to do. Can you forgive me? Please, sweetie! I am sorry, so sorry it hurts me. And the last thing I want to do is hurt *you.*"

"Another question, then. Did you tell Jeremy something bad about me? He was, like, scared of me last week when I was in the pool."

"Forget about last week. All a mistake. Let's think about the future. You and me. Lela, we're meant for each other."

"But you..." I searched for a word. "You *betrayed* me, Stuart! You had me thrown in jail *on purpose! Twice!* Why? Please tell me why!"

"Honey, I'll tell you all about it tonight. Let's go to The Limelight, your favorite." The Limelight *was* definitely my favorite, my hangout when unemployed. I knew the bartenders and servers well, and they knew me. It was the kind of place where a vodka tonic appeared before I even ordered.

I played my mind's film of being at The Limelight with Stuart. *Could I trust him? I swore "never again," but... he really sounds sincere right now.* He spoke again as if hearing my doubts. "Don't be scared, Lela. I've thought long and hard about this. I'm serious about us getting back together. As soon as possible, sweetheart."

"Well, I'm not sure you–"

"*Please* be sure. Please say yes! And we can get some yummy, sexy Love Pizza, baby!" He referred to the mozzarella-and-sundried-tomato specialty at The Limelight, a dish that spurred raucous lovemaking for us every time.

Stuart proceeded to tell me how he would ravage my body, make me scream for more, using all the right words with the right low-growl whispers, meant to turn me on.

It did.

He asked, "Six o'clock. Can you make it that early?"

"Just barely, but I'll be there."

"Hey, wear that sexy dress I like, the purple-ish one."

"Oh-la-la! A sex-starved soldier-man, huh? Should I leave the underwear at home, too?"

"Always. I like to imagine what's under the table."

I arrived at 6:25. Late. Stuart was waiting at the bar, his knee bouncing up and down as if he was nervous. I pecked him a kiss. "Oh, that's not good enough," he said and pulled me between his legs as he sat on the barstool, kissing me deeply and moaning loud enough for others to hear.

"Damn, dude! You want me, huh?

"Like the devil wants ice water." Stuart flashed a wide grin. Without taking his eyes from me, he said, "Bartender! Vodka-grapefruit, a double, for my lovely bride." I giggled; it felt great to be wanted.

Throughout dinner, we flirted like teenagers, feeding each other forkfuls of Love Pizza, complete with accompanying *mmm's* and *ooh's*. I was over the moon with love and delight.

Wanting all-possible assurance, I asked, "So do you still love me?"

"You blow me away."

"I still rocket you to the fourth dimension?"

"Absolutely."

"You're so silly. I love that phrase."

"It suits us, don't you think? Just exploding with love and lust... beyond the limits of the real world."

"Yeppers! That's us. Out of this world. In the fourth dimension." I bopped him on the nose. I knew he hated when I did that but he didn't tell me to stop; obviously, he was really into me. And it felt fantastic to be wanted!

He ordered doubles for me all night. Each time I tried to bring up serious topics, to question what had happened over the last few weeks and his cruelty toward me, he changed the subject. Eventually, I quit trying to "force him into a corner," as he said.

When we finished the pizza, including the crispy crust, he signaled the server again. I warned him, "No need for a double now. Baby, I'm smashed."

"No such thing as *too* smashed, right?"

"Then why aren't *you* drinking? What's up with straight Pepsi?"

"I'm driving, girlfriend."

"Bullshit! That's never stopped you before. Besides, it's just a few blocks."

"Stop worrying and drink up. I want to go home and make you scream. Baby, I need to see what's under that dress."

"But I'm not supposed to go to 'your' home, Stuart. The restraining order, remember?"

"Oh, that damn thing... *psspht*. Don't worry about it. I'm going to see if I can cancel it, anyway. And another thing, I don't want you living in that terrible place. The Homing Inn, for God's sake!" He blew a sarcastic laugh. "What are you, a pigeon? What you need to do is to move back home and live happily ever after with me and Jeremy."

Both sporting smiles, we toasted. I felt like a Southern Belle when he pulled my chair back like a gentleman, to help me up from the table. Good thing, because I stumbled. "Whoa! Damn! I'm drunk-Lela tonight, baby."

"Daddy-Stuart will take care of you. Count on that." I thought the evil laugh was a prelude to a long session of lovemaking and I melted inside.

He walked me to my van, his hand on the small of my back, and opened the door, helping me settle in. I felt special, wanted, even *adored*, and so happy that Stuart had seen the light about continuing our relationship. "See you there!" I said and eased onto Wellington Boulevard. In less than a mile, I turned into Ashley Acres.

When I reached our driveway, Stuart wasn't behind me as I expected. With the AC blasting in the van, I sat there for five minutes or so, waiting. Then Stuart's dog, Rock-Bob, barked, and I wondered why Murphy hadn't done the same. Aloud, I said, "I miss my dog, dammit. What I need is a fat-dog kiss!" With that, I walked to the front door, digging in my purse for the key.

As I struggled, Yona flipped on the porch light and I shouted through the door, "Thank you! I can't see the keyhole!" When I walked inside, her eyes were wide.

"You're not supposed to be here, Mizz Lela! Go away!"

"Relax, Yona. Stuart's right behind me." Scanning the sofa, I noticed Murphy's typical sleeping spot was empty. "Where's Murphy?"

Yona didn't answer, still standing with a stressed expression and her mouth agape. "He... well, uh, Mister Stuart took... uh... Murphy is not here."

"Where is he, then?" I asked.

"At the pound, Mizz Lela. Unless somebody has adopted him."

I furrowed my brow, *"What? Why?* He's *my* dog!" That's when the police pulled to the front of the house, Stuart's Lexus close behind. Perplexed, I looked at Yona. "Did you call the police?"

"No, Mizz Lela, but I *should* have. You're not supposed to be here!"

"Then there must be a mistake. This can't be right." My drunk mind couldn't wrap around what was happening, and never in my wildest imagination could I conceive of what was getting ready to go down.

Stuart walked inside the house and took my hand. With an exaggerated look of pity, he said, "Time for you to go now, dear. I know you're thinking of suicide, or thinking about hurting someone else, so now you get help for your mental problems."

Confused, disoriented, in awe, I let Stuart lead me to the front yard where a Wellington cop pushed a piece of paper toward my face. "Relax, Ms. Fox. You can get help now."

"What the hell are you talking about? Help for what?"

"Says here you're a danger to yourself and others. Your husband has filed a petition, the Mental Health Act, or the Baker Act, most people call it. Only Florida has it. We're here to take you to the hospital."

Silence. *The Baker Act? Involuntary commitment for crazy people! Has Stuart really done this? He got me drunk so he could do this? How could he? Oh, I'm ruined!*

Stuart continued in his sickly sweet, purring voice. "It's for your own good, dear." He patted my arm. "Everybody knows you're a little off your rocker, right? A bit out of control, honey. This will help you, and Jeremy and I won't be scared of you anymore."

"Like the Baker Act says, ma'am, 'a danger to others.'" The cop chimed in, wearing a syrupy smile like Stuart's.

My mouth hung in a permanent "O," stuck there in absolute confusion. "But I'm not–"

Stuart interrupted. "This is all for the better, hon. Thanks to the state of Florida, you can get help now, and everything will be *all* better. I love you, sweetheart. And I want to see you sane."

The realization hit like a hurricane. "You sonofabitch! You tricked me! God *damn* you! And you stole my dog!"

"Your dog will be just fine," Stuart said in a calm and exaggerated soothing voice.

"Crazy-crackhead-junkie-asshole! *You're* the one with a problem!" Tears erupted from my eyes. "The damn Baker Act! You've been studying ways to get me, to hurt me as much as possible! And you *tricked* me! *How dare you?*" By this time, my words were screams.

The cop put a finger to his lips to shush me. "Now, now, Ms. Fox. No need to get upset." Incensed, I scoffed at him. Then he reached into the depths of his belt and a pair of handcuffs appeared. "But, ma'am, I need to put you in loose handcuffs for the ride to the hospital. Everything seems in order, the paperwork is right here. You'll be evaluated within 72 hours. That's part of the law."

"Evaluated? Seventy-two hours! *What the hell?* I'll lose my job!" I turned to Stuart as tears exploded from my eyes, suddenly sober and on high alert. "How could you *do* this, Stuart? You're taking away any hope I have left.

"Deal with it, Lela," he said, not so kindly this time. Without thinking, I growled and lunged for his throat in a sudden move, but the cop moved faster than I did. Before I blinked, my wrists were in cuffs. Stuart blew an evil laugh.

"Gotcha!" he snickered. The cop shot him a questioning look. Stuart must have felt the cop's suspicion and changed his tune. "Gotcha... some help, baby. I wish you would have done it on your own, but your therapist agreed with me. Gloria signed the papers with no question. It's all for the best."

"You paid her off, then! This is all a set-up, dammit! Love Pizza, my ass!"

The cop whispered details to Stuart. I heard bits and pieces, enough to know my van would go the impound lot, and I would go to South County Center in Delray Beach. My mind reeled.

I remember little about the ride to the hospital or checking in, but I remember going to bed. Exhausted. Physically and emotionally. I slept through the night, awoke with the sun in my eyes, slept some more, and then stumbled down a hall to find water.

Feelings roared through my heart. Fear, despair, confusion, anger, and more despair. Guzzling the water, I went back to bed and slept more, woke up in the dark, rolled over, and fell back asleep. Through the two-day stay, I have a just a few flashes of memory: a female nurse shaking my shoulder and a man holding a clipboard loudly clearing his throat. Still, I slept.

When I wandered into the hall for another bottle of water, a nurse stopped me at the entrance to my room. "Ms. Fox, you will see Dr. Pulton in just a few minutes. Good time to wash your face, brush your teeth, whatever."

"Screw you," I said.

No reaction from the nurse, but a female voice down the hall yelled, "You tell her, girl!" Had to be another patient. *What kind of place is this? How am I going to get out of here? Do I need bail?* No, it wasn't jail, I remembered, even though it felt like it. I wondered how long I'd been there... seventy-two hours yet?

And who can give me a ride home? I cried when I realized the Homing Inn was "home" and the only person who may help was Baby-Daddy. Not only that, Baby-Daddy didn't have a car. *But Snaggle-Tooth does! Maybe I can call the Homing Inn and get his name and number. Surely they will know who I'm talking about. I mean, Baby-Daddy stands out from the crowd.*

As my thoughts wandered, I tried to imagine where the impound lot would be and how much it would cost to get my van out of there. And I wished I would have worn underwear. Chiding myself, I marveled at how I could have fallen for Stuart's deceit.

How could I believe he still loved me and wanted me to come home? How can I be so stupid? With a shake of my head, I blew a laugh at myself. *Well, vodka is one reason you're always so stupid. Lela. You're drinking 24/7 now. And now you need someone named Baby-Daddy to rescue you. That's the only person you know. What's wrong with this picture?*

The longer I sat in the room, the angrier I became. Angry with myself, with Stuart, with the world. I gripped my hands in tight fists and punched the mattress a dozen times, tears and snot flying. I collapsed and, slowly, my thoughts turned to matters more practical.

No job now. Two more days of no show-no call. *So what? I hate that job anyway. Dale and... everybody... they made me feel so inadequate. The assholes!*

It hadn't occurred to me I would have been inadequate in *any* job by then. The time had come where I couldn't function in society, such as my "society" had become. *But it's not my fault! It's THEIR fault! They're assholes, every one of them!*

I felt sticky between my legs and rushed to the bathroom to check it out. Yep, I had started my period. No underwear and only the baggy, "prison issue" scrubs they gave me at check-in. Humiliation on top of humiliation. I wobbled to the nurses' station to ask for a Tampax.

"We only have pads," she said. Great. Now overwhelmed, I tried to explain the problem with having no underwear and baggy pants but there was no convincing her. "We only have pads," she repeated with a snap. "I'll bring one to your room in a minute. And no more whining!"

Back to my room. The small rectangle looked like a jail cell except for the window. The bed was bolted to the floor, the bedside table was a shelf bolted to the wall, and the paint was that "calming" shade of yellow. A sigh escaped my lips and tears flowed: big, crocodile tears with racking sobs.

A crazy circle of thoughts crowded my mind. I felt utterly defeated. *Oh, God, I am so screwed. How am I going to get out of this? The bad thing is that maybe I am crazy enough to be here for real. Maybe I should stay, sleep more, be a nobody, a number, a ward of the state.*

Then I thought of my stuff at the Homing Inn. I didn't want it thrown in the dumpster because it was all I had. *Pitiful, Lela. Pitiful, pitiful, pitiful.*

A young nurse tiptoed into my room, the one who sat beside the fat one who offered nothing but a maxi-pad. She held a wrapped Tampax and slid it under the covers in a stealthy move. "I didn't give this to you. Do you understand?

I whispered a "thank you" with my head low. The nurse turned on her heel and scurried out of the room. *Thank God, there are still people who see me as a human... a pitiful human maybe, but a human.*

☼ ☼ ☼ ☼ ☼

"No sir, I'm fine. I have meds and I take them regularly!" Somehow, I had managed to fill out a medication list on their paperwork, though I struggled through the other questions.

Dr. Pulton spoke calmly and with care. "Ms. Fox, you take five medications for Bi-Polar, at high doses. I'd like to substitute another for the Prozac. There are many better ones now."

"No! I don't want to change anything! And I don't want or need to *be* here! I just want to go home and go back to sleep. Listen to me!" I stood and paced the room. "See, it was my deceitful, lying husband who said I was a goddamn 'danger to myself and others' because I'm *not!*"

More pacing. "Baker Act, my ass! Stuart did this to *hurt* me, not to *help* me! We're in the middle of a divorce, and he's an asshole." I had never thought of the word divorce as it related to Stuart. The words shocked me, and I guess the shock was noticeable.

"How does that make you feel, Ms. Fox? Frightened?"

"Jeezus! Quit the kind-doctor act!" I snapped. Then silence. Defiant and angry, I would say no more. He probed me with questions that I refused to answer. After five minutes of his attempts to prompt me, I said five emotionless words: "I want to go home."

The doctor stood up from his desk. In a voice as terse as mine had been, he said, "Fine. Home you will go. I'll have the nurses begin the paperwork as soon as possible." As I opened the door, the doctor said, "Lela?" I turned. "Do you remember who I am?"

"Am I supposed to?"

"We were friends once. In Rockville, years ago. Don't you remember Jilly?" *Jilly. Of course I remember Jilly!* Our crazy duo partied hard on the lake, all over town, for that matter. That was during marriage number two, toward the end when everything went to hell.

The doctor continued, "I used to work with her and the three of us became hang-out friends, played the game Password sometimes."

"Okay... so?" I did remember the name Pulton; who wouldn't? But why would Joe Pulton be in Delray Beach, Florida?

"One day, you, me, and Jilly... we had a picnic together. You were drunk. Trying to be funny, you smashed your face into a bowl of potato salad.

I felt busted, hit with the reality of how long my drinking had been a problem, how I'd been ridiculously drunk for years and years.

There was no appropriate response. Head down, I walked back to my room, feeling like an outcast, depressed by the whole scenario. I found my dress in a drawer-cubby bolted to the wall and changed clothes. As I watched through a fog of tears, my hands shook.

Man-oh-man, do I need a drink!

The Shame of that thought brought more tears; I crashed into the sheets of my bed, rocking with sobs. If my legs had been longer, I could have *literally* kicked myself in the ass.... I was doing a pretty good job of it with the thoughts in my head.

I knew there was no sense in pretending anymore; I was a dumbass, worthless person... an alcoholic of no use to the world at large. Tears couldn't rinse the truth away.

About an hour later, the young nurse who gave me the Tampax arrived with a clipboard. Check-out papers. The process took nearly an hour as I signed my life away, or so it seemed. In the end, the nurse set out four shiny quarters so I could make calls from the bank of payphones at the front of the ward.

The first call was to my Mom, collect, though there was nothing she could do. Maybe I just needed to vent, to pour the brimming emotions to someone who loved me. I ended up making her cry, too, and instantly felt like an ass. In a rush, I back-pedaled to say getting a ride would be easy, blah, blah, blah. All was well; I'd just over-reacted.

"But who is this Baby-Daddy character? That's an odd name, honey. Are you sure he's honest? Maybe Stuart paid him off, too."

"No, Mom. He's..." *How can I give the real answer to my Southern Belle mom, the woman who crosses her ankles just-so?* "He's just a friend. I met him at the pool. And surely Stuart's reach doesn't include the Homing Inn. He's cool. Don't worry."

Then I worried. *What if it's true? What if Stuart offered Baby-Daddy cash... payment for his promise to turn me in... steal my stuff... something to betray me?* I knew Baby-Daddy would take the money; people like him will do anything for money. And as for Stuart, I knew it wouldn't be beyond his reach or outside his moral compass.

I begged off the phone with Mom when she asked if I wanted to speak to my father. I couldn't bear to break his heart, too.

A phone book hung beside the payphone. The front desk person at the Homing Inn, a woman with a Jersey accent, knew Baby-Daddy by description. She asked me to hold on, said she'd check to see if he was at the pool. Six minutes later, a gruff Baby-Daddy said, "Hello?"

I began a long story of explanation.

☼ ☼ ☼ ☼ ☼

It cost $189.16 to get my car out of impound and I paid Snaggle-Tooth twenty to cover the gas for the long ride. I asked for a stop at the 7-Eleven first thing and bought a full case of beer for the group. The least I could do. Three beers later, I felt better.

Back at the Homing Inn, Baby-Daddy wanted to keep up the party, and I joined them at the pool though my heart wasn't in it. I felt about two inches tall, despondent and hopeless. And now I was unemployed; what was I supposed to do about that?

"You'll think of something," Baby-Daddy assured me. "You've made it this far, Tennessee, and like a cockroach, you'll survive."

"It's not death I'm afraid of, man, it's living. I mean... living like this."

"Shut up and have another beer, girl," said Snaggle-Tooth. "It's the last one, but you have money for more, right?"

GLASS IN THE CINDERS
CHAPTER 7

The train was at full speed, blowing my curls back in the wind and filling my ears with the sharp scream of the horn. I had my "Big Gulp" cup full of vodka-tonic, sitting on the bench next to the train track that bordered the Smyth Software parking lot. A Thursday, late evening and still steamy hot. I wiped sweat from my upper lip with the strap of my tank top as the last of the rail cars passed.

Okay, the next one. And take your drink just for good measure. Afraid to lie down on the tracks and wait, I thought they might see me in the distance and stop the train. *Wouldn't THAT be embarrassing?* No, I'll wait and jump just before it passes.

Another horn blew in the distance and I took a few steps forward, then another step onto the cinders next to the tracks. On high alert, I felt my racing heart from every inch of skin, felt the hot moisture of my sweaty palms, heard my own silent screams. The train was in view. *Wait, Lela. Be patient.*

Frozen in fear, I let the train pass, twelve inches from my nose. Black soot shot like a cannon blast, filling my eyes with a film of power. I naturally reached to wipe them but found them full of tears. *Fuck. You lost your chance.*

I collapsed, sitting cross-legged in the cinders. *Chicken shit. You big fucking chicken shit! Your life sucks and you're still here. Can you find one good reason to NOT jump in front of that train?*

The glass within the grit of the cinders ate at my butt and prickled the back of my legs, and it felt as good as it did bad. I squirmed to push the glass further into my skin, punishing myself as much as possible. *A dirty, painful reminder of how despicable you are, Lela Fox. A lousy, worthless drunk.*

The flash of a memory hit me… sitting in the gravel alley drinking my first beer when I was thirteen and happy to be drunk. Broken green glass. *How did this glass get here? Green, amber, clear chunks with sharp corners meant for me. Maybe sitting in glass is like laying the gutter.*

In the distance, the third train blew its horn louder and longer than the others had, it seemed. I leaned forward, ready to pounce when it came within ten feet of me. *Or is ten feet too close? I don't want to be… halfway.* I found myself morbidly chuckling, thinking there was probably an algebraic formula for where I should spot it. Maybe my nerd boyfriend from high school would have known, but that was a dozen lifetimes ago. Years and years before it all went to hell

Okay, twenty feet. How far is twenty feet? I stared at a spot on the tracks I guessed to be twenty feet away. Suddenly the train was there, too soon. Too soon. I wasn't ready.

Hot wind from the train blew against me like a hurricane, smelling like pure diesel fuel. The acrid, industrial smell wafted behind the train, dousing the hair in my nostrils with its rancid dirtiness.

More soot washed my face. I squinted as the hot-hazy view of the train's rear end disappeared. *Dammit!* Again, I had missed my ride to freedom.

Okay, the next one and I'll be ready. I turned my drink up and guzzled three swallows. Glunk, glunk, glunk. Effervescent tonic water ran down my chin and I let it drip. I sucked on the sour taste as I waited. Tears carved rivers through the dirt on my face and hiccups of sobs shook me at random intervals.

The unnerving time and silence between trains stretched to *years* between. I thought maybe an engineer had radioed ahead to tell the boss there was a crazy woman sitting by the tracks. *No, please, just shut up and do your damn job.*

The next train seemed to slow as it approached. *Am I imagining that?* In an instant, all sound stopped, replaced by an echoing scream as I looked at the thirty-foot spot I had chosen, then back at the incoming train. *Ready? Go!* I dropped my cup in the cinders and squatted to gather power for a lunge. As I stared at the spot, the train passed over it. *Shit! I can't get the timing right. I can't even kill myself right!*

54

Closing my eyes, I screamed a growling frustrated sound, throwing my head back and clenching my fists. I screamed through the roar of the train, a short one this time, and when it passed, my scream echoed in the silence.

Then I heard a whistle, like an umpire's whistle. *What the hell?* I turned to look over the hedge behind me, the row of Lantana bushes that separated the train track from the parking lot. I could only see a hat and a forehead. A cop. Blowing a whistle and waving his hands in the air.

"Get out of there!" he screamed. With a nervous and defeated sigh, I stared at him for a while, reorienting myself to life on the other side of the bushes.

I grabbed my "Big Gulp" and headed toward the parking lot. *Jeezus, Lela, you chicken shit, and now you're gonna be arrested! You fucking idiot!*

The uniformed man shouted at me, though the scene was quiet. "Ma'am, it's against the law to be within twenty yards of the tracks. That bench is right on the line so stay there or leave."

In a matter-of-fact tone, I yelled back, "No problem! I'm just here to kill myself, sir." I shrugged. "Turns out, I'm a bad judge of distance."

Why did I tell him what I was planning? Was I wanting help or being a smart ass? Not sure. It did feel good to admit my intent out loud. Somehow, it made my actions seem ridiculous, even to me. But for the cop to ignore my honest drama was a slap in the face. I'm not sure why... because by that time, the drama had lost its power. I was tired of crying, tired of feeling anything at all.

The policeman cocked his head as if studying me. "Are you okay? I could call the Mobile Crisis Unit." Then his radio squawked, and I jumped back, scared that he'd already called somebody.

Panicked, I ran to my van and opened the drivers-side door. "No, please no, sir. I'm fine. I'm leaving now."

"No, you're not."

"Yes, I am. You can't stop me. There's no reason for your concern."

"You're not leaving with that drink, ma'am, and not until you talk to me."

"Oh." I looked down at the insulated cup. "Uh, sir, it's just Sprite. Why would that make a difference?"

He hiked up the right side of his belt, leaned to the left. "Then let's do a field sobriety test before you get behind the wheel." I froze in place as his eyes pierced my soul. "If you know what's good for you, ma'am, you'll shut that van door."

I slammed it hard. *Think fast, Lela. Explain why you're here... why would a normal person be here?* "Maybe I'll just go back to the bench and keep thinking about the poem I'm working on. I'm a poet, sir, a published poet. My notepad is in the van... can I at least get that?" *What a stupid excuse, dingbat. A poet? Jeezus.*

"Stay outside of the vehicle," he said.

"Look, it's in the *back* and I can't drive from there!"

The minute of silence before his answer sent my heart rate to the max. "I should take you in," he said, enunciating each syllable.

"Why? You have no cause!"

The cop's stare, as piercing as a missile, seemed to last an hour. *What is he thinking?* Finally, he spoke. "Okay... get your notepad, ma'am, but don't go any closer to the tracks. And don't do anything stupid." I didn't realize I'd been holding my breath until I blew it out.

The cop continued, "Tell you what... because I have paperwork to do, and this seems like a great place to do it, I'll be right here while you..." He cleared his throat. "While you write your, uh, poem."

Almost disappointed, somewhat flabbergasted, but giddy that he wouldn't arrest me, I nodded. As confused as I was, I knew the last thing I wanted was to go to another mental hospital. Thankfully, I got away with the lie, finding a ragged notepad in the backseat. I dug through my purse for a pen. "Okay, I'll be over here... on the bench... writing my poem."

"What's the poem about?" he asked.

"Suicide." Tears came to my eyes, and the cop looked away. "Suicide and being chickenshit."

Notepad in hand and still armed with a half-drink, I sat on the bench and thought about being dead. I begged for it, begged for lighting to strike me then and there. Closing my eyes, I envisioned being a hollow shell. I could see the veins shrinking, disappearing, no longer needed. I could hear the echo.

Why did I need a body for the soul-less, heartless, hollow shell I had become? I had nothing to offer life and nothing but more pain for the future. *So I'll wait for the cop to go away and finish my task. He can't stay there all day, but I can stay here forever. I have nothing else to do.*

Overwhelmed with emotion, I burst into tears, dripping on the notepad's scribblings. *Yes, you're a drunk, Lela Fox. You can't stop drinking, so why not just drink more and more and more? Force yourself to stay awake and drink even more than that!* Tears flowed as I realized I was ready for such a deadly feast and a no-matter-what release. *God save me from this PAIN! Let me dissolve, sink into the sand around this bench, turn to jelly and melt like the Wicked Witch. Get me out of this hell I'm in!*

Sobs began anew as my head pounded... boomed with every heartbeat.

☼ ☼ ☼ ☼ ☼

I raised my head when I heard a cough. The policeman walked toward me with purpose and a face full of worry. *Is really he trying to help a shithead like me? Why, dammit?*

"Ma'am?"

"Yes, sir."

"Here... take my card. I received a call and must go. But if you need help..." He wrote on the back of the card. "And there's a number on the back, too. Many people can help you."

"I'm fine," I said, hoping my lie wasn't as obvious to him as it was to me. "Just working on my poem here..."

"Okay, then. Take as long as you want, just don't go close to the tracks, do you understand?"

"Got it."

"I'm serious."

"I understand."

With a look that reeked of pity and sadness, he turned to leave. I watched the car turn right and heard his siren as he raced down Boca Boulevard. *Thank God, he's gone.* Racks of sobs returned, realizing I was alone.

Knowing what I must do, I walked back to the cinders beside the track. I chided myself when noticing that I'd mistakenly brought my cup and notepad with me, then stopped to read what I had written. It was like the suicide note I swore I wouldn't write. *But maybe people need to know, in case they think it's an accident.*

With my butt smashed in the cinders once again, I let three other trains pass, each spitting tiny rocks that pricked my skin. Each left a trail of black exhaust that mixed with my sweat to create a gray swirled complexion. Between trains, I sipped my drink and cried, mumbling.

In the silence between trains, as if in a trance, I flashed to a vision of a redneck railroad crew scraping my body off the tracks. The blood. Guts. My face, my eyes, looking up at... *oh my God! MY SON!*

Bo's last vision of his mother would be blood and guts, a messy glob of a has-been. *Dead by her own hand.* He'd be scarred for life and feel the guilt us Fox folks feel even when it's not our fault.

I collapsed, falling forward with my head just inches from the tracks, crying from the core of my soul. *I can't! I can't! I can't do it! Dammit!* A train horn blew in the distance and I scrambled to get back to the bench.

I turned my back to the train as I crouched, feeling as small and weak as a sparrow. I tried to think of another reason to live but couldn't. So I found myself thinking of other ways to die, trying to take Bo out of the picture.

How could I make it look like an accident... drive into a bridge abutment or something, drive off the side of a bridge to the highway below, drive into the Everglades to become the alligators' midnight snack, drink myself dead?

That's it! Drink myself dead as if it was an accident. Everybody will believe that! It will make perfect sense! So... okay... I'm ready.

Why not start now?

I stomped to the van, feeling bold and bitchy. On the way home, I pushed the vehicle to its maximum speed, weaving in and out of traffic as if I had nothing to lose. Because I didn't.

WE GOTTA GET MORE
CHAPTER 8

I drove home recklessly and when I arrived in one piece, I cried in the parking lot thinking I'd failed at yet-another attempt to end it all.

So with a renewed determination and overwhelming sadness, I drank most of a fifth of vodka that night and cried a bucket of tears. Around three AM, I passed out with a drink in my hand and woke up groggy, definitely still drunk. *You didn't die, dammit, you disgusting piece of chicken shit.*

Then I had a long talk with myself and realized my plan for suicide, whether by train or by drinking myself to death, would be too much for me. Too much trouble. *I'm too tired and too lazy to even try suicide. Maybe that means I want to live or maybe that means I'll find another way to relieve the pain.*

Too much work. I envisioned myself putting that idea on a high shelf for later. Aloud, I said, "I'll live another day, but just *one*, dammit!" As I'd heard somewhere, "One day at a time." I had no idea what it meant, but "one day" was something I could swallow.

Okay, just treat today like a normal day... get beer, go to the pool, same as always. And don't tell a soul what you tried to do. I didn't want people going goo-goo on me about I had so much to live for, blah, blah, blah. *Fuck those people!*

After a brisk shower, I felt better. I jumped in the van and headed to the 7-Eleven.

Though it was early, Baby-Daddy and the gang were at the pool with their own twelve-pack. We laughed and made fun of the people coming and going, as we always did. We giggled like children, louder and louder as the beer inventory lessened.

At sweaty three o'clock, I sauntered back to my room with Baby-Daddy in hot pursuit. At the entrance to my room, I turned, and he was standing *this close* behind me. "No man, I'm taking a nap. Go away."

"But I've got a treat for you later if you'll give me a ride," he said. As he rubbed his chest, the dragon tattoo rippled, winking at me. The smile, a temptation.

"What kind of treat?"

"You like to get high, right?" I nodded. "It's a surprise. Come back to the pool around dusk and we'll talk about it." Baby-Daddy winked and locked his eyes on mine. Interested, I wiggled my eyebrows. I hadn't smoked a joint in a while and it would be a nice change.

"Okay, man. I'll be there." Drunk-talk, maybe, but there was something irresistibly adorable about this muscled man. Just getting high would be no surprise, so the "treat" must be something different. I guessed he was a lightweight, maybe, and it was just kick-ass Columbian or something. Hopefully, it wouldn't be that laced weed like Stuart had in the Bahamas.

"Have a nice nap, Baby-Daddy," I said, putting the key in the lock.

He blew a huff as if exasperated. "My name's Larry, girl. And what's yours?"

"My name is Tennessee. Let's keep it at that. And I'm calling you Baby-Daddy whether you like it or not." With the gaffe of a drunk, he stepped forward to kiss me, but I slipped into my room. The sound of him falling against the door made me laugh. "Go away, Baby-Daddy!" I yelled through the door.

When I awoke, feeling serene and sexy as if I'd dreamed of a porno fairytale, I saw the sun's angle and knew it was close to dusk. I stretched and yawned, moaning loud enough for a passerby to hear.

Though I knew the answer was no, I got up to look inside the mini-fridge. No beer. On the dresser, no bottle of vodka. I'd have to go out. A few cigarettes later, I took a shower.

At dusk, I meandered to the pool. Baby-Daddy was alone, sitting at the table that had become "ours." The air barely moved; it was still hot and sticky. "Hey there, big guy. What's shaking?" was my cheerful greeting.

Baby-Daddy wasn't interested in small talk. "Let's go." At his urging, we rushed to the van. "It's not far. Here, turn left. Keep going 'til I say stop." It was a short drive, meandering through a bad neighborhood on a rare rise in the landscape. "Drop me off here. Drive up to that white house and wait." He was all business, and I got anxious.

"Is this okay to do? What *are* you doing? Why such precautions?" I thought this was an ordinary weed purchase, but he was paranoid to the max. *What the hell is up?*

Less than five minutes later, Baby-Daddy jumped in the van and spoke as soon as his butt hit the seat, with a powerful tone, yet it was a whisper. "Go! Get the hell out of here! There's a cop cruising, right behind you! Go!"

The van's engine was still running, air conditioner on full blast. My foot stepped on the accelerator hard, but not hard enough to sling gravel under the car. The cop car reflected in the rearview mirror, shining a bright light left and right onto the houses that lined this seedy street.

"Why the cops? What the hell is going on? What are you up to, man? Are you in trouble? Am *I* in trouble? What the hell?" My heart rate increased with each question mark.

"Just shut up and drive. Don't let him follow," he said, looking in the side mirror.

"I can't stop him from following, for God's sake! You gotta tell me! Are we about to get busted or something? Why? Is this the 'hood?"

"Just drive! The speed limit, dammit." Full-volume tension filled the van. I gripped the wheel and felt instant sweat build on my palms. Baby-Daddy licked his lips nervously and his hands shook. The anxiety transferred to me, it seemed. My stomach was in a knot, cramping.

With my eyes focused on the rearview mirror, I saw it all. "Oh God! Wait... he stopped! The cop's not following us! He's shining the light on another house, stopped. What kind of neighborhood *is* this, dammit?" Baby-Daddy didn't reply. Soon we were back on A-1-A, with no car behind us.

"Pass the motel one time, go up there and turn around, make sure we weren't followed." His eyes darted back and forth from the side mirror to the windshield. A nervous wreck, he wrung his hands now.

"I'll turn around at the store and get some beer, okay? Act like normal."

"NO!" He freaked, his whole body a jackhammer.

"Damn, man... chill! Nobody is following us!" When I passed the Homing Inn, he visibly relaxed. "They busted the house, not *us*," I said. "So I'm getting beer and fuck you if you don't like it."

"Okay, thanks, man. Thanks."

"For what?"

"Just shut up. Vodka would be better, go on up to the liquor store instead."

I decided he was right, and when I returned with the bottle, Baby-Daddy wouldn't look at me. He sat on his hands, saying nothing.

As we entered my room, Baby-Daddy ordered, "Don't turn on the light until the door is closed." Inside, the darkness held silence for ten long seconds. "Okay. We're cool."

I turned on the light and got a clear look at Baby-Daddy's face. *Oh, my God!* "What kind of drugs are you taking, man? You're as red as a crayon." The man looked at me with an innocent smile, but his anxiety was obvious. He jerked to sit on the bed, like the rehearsed move of an acrobat. His bouncing heel vibrated his knee up and down. And with his elbow on his knee and his hand on his face, his whole body vibrated with an unheard beat.

I thought of Stuart and his annoying fidgets. *Oh hell, maybe this "treat" is crack... causing the hyper bullshit like it did in Stuart.*

Crack. C-R-A-C-K. The word seemed to roll off the tongue, not near as scary as it'd been in my former life when I loved and trusted Stuart Weinstein.

"Just a little crack, baby. Got us a nice rock. Sit down. I need a can... beer can or a coke can, you have one? Gotta make a pipe."

Crack, just like you thought. Here's your opportunity, Lela. This will be the end of you. That's what you wanted, right?

As I poured a half-and-half vodka-tonic, I realized I didn't care one way or another. I would fake concern for the sake of propriety but what the hell... I was already so low; I couldn't go any lower.

My tone was flat, emotionless. "Crack? Oh, my! That's not cool!" Then a heartfelt statement: "I don't want to be as paranoid as you."

Baby-Daddy spoke fast and in choppy sentences. "It's okay, baby. I'm just crazy about the cops. This guy, who I bought it from, got busted not long ago, just out of jail. I felt the fuckers *this close* behind me." He held his fingers up, an inch apart. "The one hit I took in his living room... Jeezus, my heart went racing. That's not normal. But it's cool now. Don't worry and I know you'll like it. Where's the can?" Rat-a-tat-tat talking, and his heel was still bobbing up and down.

Baby-Daddy fidgeted more than Stuart did! Then the thoughts and second-guessing started in my head. Stuart... smoking crack... the

Bahamas... what I thought was just laced weed. *So now you know the truth, and you're going to smoke it on purpose now? Before, it was just an accident, an innocent accident. Felt damn good, though... didn't it, Lela?*

I snickered; Baby-Daddy looked at me with a devilish smile as if reading my thoughts. But my thoughts were swirling, never-ending.

I wondered how long it had taken Stuart to get addicted. I guessed it would take years for that to happen. *But what would it matter for YOU, Lela-Loser? Maybe it's my chance, my suicide technique.*

I had said nothing, standing frozen and trying to justify what I was getting ready to do. I looked at Baby-Daddy for a long while before I moved. I guess he felt the tension, so he laid back on my bed and tried to change the subject. "Where in Tennessee? I mean... you seem okay, not like a barefoot hick. So maybe you're from Nashville or something, a bigger city?"

Again, I said nothing, knowing he was trying to divert the tension. A long silence was fine with me, knowing it may be my last moment before taking a U-turn to Hell's special path for addicts. I waited three full minutes before reaching into the trash can for an empty can. "Is this what you need?" With a smile, he popped up in a sitting position.

"Yeah, exactly what I need, babe." Baby-Daddy pulled a packet of aluminum foil from the front pocket of his shorts and opened it. The rock looked like a crystal, milky-white, shaped irregularly. He set it on the side table carefully and smoothed out the piece of the foil. A pocketknife appeared from within his shorts, and he punched a hole in the can, and then maneuvered the foil into a bowl shape.

I had seen bowls for smoking weed made this way, but he was fast, and it looked a lot more professional than any I'd seen. I said, "You're damn good at that, man."

He looked up through his eyelashes with a grin; obviously, I'd pleased him by saying that. "Practice makes perfect, ya know."

Baby-Daddy put the rock in the bowl and struck a pink lighter. He took a long draw, snorting as the smoke expanded in his lungs. Ten seconds later, he motioned me toward him, gesturing for me to inhale his exhale. *Just like Stuart did.*

I felt the smoke hit my lungs... and radiate through my brain, setting my extremities on fire. *Oh my God! What a rush!* "Instant happiness" is the only way I can describe it. With lungs on fire, I held the smoke in as long as I could. Baby-Daddy motioned for me to exhale into his mouth this time. I did and then cracked up laughing.

63

"Third-hand smoke?" The tattooed man smiled, still holding his breath. Being inexperienced, I wondered if it would be fourth-hand smoke and got ready, but he waved me away. His exhale appeared to be nothing but air.

The two of us sat still, gazing at each other, smiling wide. The want for another hit was instant, overwhelming. I felt anxious, nervous, yet the feeling was indescribably serene. Somewhere between good-frantic and bad-frantic. Baby-Daddy passed the pipe to me.

The process repeated, but this time I got two hits, the original and the third. I was beyond stoned, beyond happy, beyond excited, and aching for more. The addiction, if that was the word, was instant and against my will.

Three more rounds and the rock was dead. On my last hit, still holding my breath, I turned feverish and said out loud, "We gotta get more, man, *right now.*" At last, I exhaled. "Can we go back? We gotta get more."

Baby-Daddy laughed. "I told you you'd like it."

I stood up to dance and twirled in a circle with my head back. What should have made me dizzy made me laugh. I felt ultra-light on my feet, totally uninhibited. *Free!*

Baby-Daddy lay back on the bed to watch me dance, which prompted a dirtier dance. With a flourish, I took off my top, showing my braless chest. He cheered from the bed, urging me on.

When the provocative striptease was complete, I climbed into bed with Baby-Daddy, growling. I can say without a doubt it was the best sex I'd ever had. Each sensation felt amplified, multiplied by a gazillion.

I teased him without mercy; Baby-Daddy loved it. I felt powerful, sexually powerful, for sure, but also powerful in strength, stamina, and pleasure. I imagined I was, literally, on top of the world and that nothing would stop me from feeling this incredible euphoria. Even a massive orgasm didn't exhaust me, though Baby-Daddy was breathing hard, prone and still. I started the dance again.

A half-hour later, we drove back to the bad neighborhood. This time there were no cops. The smoking process repeated in my room, including the striptease and the phenomenal sex.

It was a good day and an even-better night. *And to think you wanted to not be around for this! Just yesterday you were ready to check out. Kick the bucket. Throw in the towel. Aren't you glad you waited just one more day, kid?*

A BOTTOM IN THE MORNING
CHAPTER 9

I woke and rolled over to look at the tattooed man in my bed. I had no hangover, but an eerie feeling, a buzz between my ears. It was like floating on the ceiling, looking down at myself, watching each move and noticing each detail of my surroundings, seeing the hairs on my goose-bumped arms.

Baby-Daddy hadn't roused. I got up to pee and, passing by, looked in the mirror. What a shock! Dark-brown ovals under my eyes, a haggard and splotchy face, and thin, spindly arms. *When did I get so skinny?*

Suddenly, and it felt completely real and normal, a voice from far away whispered to me. My father. "Lela, honey... please." I closed my eyes, and the voice turned into a wavy vision pushing hard against the back of my eyes.

Surely a delusion, but it also seemed convincingly real.

I saw a flash of Daddy's face, a pleading and caring expression. My face became a river of tears, a sunken and sad face that didn't look anything like me. *A stranger. I've become a stranger. I hate this. I want out. I want OUT! God! Get me out of here!*

The pressure against my temples pounded at a frantic pace. *Help! Oh hell, no. This is not me! This is hell. I'm in hell!*

I blinked the tears away, and with a 360-degree turn, I scanned the ratty motel room... the pile of clothes on the floor, the small refrigerator with a broken handle.

With new eyes, the hole in the paneled wall was bigger, more jagged. And the man. Tattooed. Shaved-bald, scarred on his face and arms. With his mouth open and drooling, I saw rotting teeth I hadn't noticed before; what I had thought was a cute little gap in the front was actually a missing tooth. *Eew! And I kissed that!*

I closed my eyes, swaying with weak legs. As I rested my head on the door frame, thoughts screamed in my head. *Lela! Listen! What the HELL are you doing here? You've been reduced to THIS? Smoking crack in a by-the-week motel with a man your mother would run from?*

I looked again at the man in my bed, a pitiful human being. Dirty, smelly, ungroomed, a 'round the clock drunk and fucking crack addict. A loser. *But look who's talking!*

I ran back to the mirror, giant tears streaming off my jaw onto hot, clammy skin. I pleaded with my reflection. *Open your eyes to what's happening, Lela Fox! Are you trying to kill yourself? Become the lowest of the low? Why? ANSWER ME! WHY? You don't belong here! Get the man out. Get your shit together. Call somebody! Get help!*

I thought of my parents, my poor parents. They must be worried sick. *They love me. No matter what, they love me. They've never turned their back, though I've given them every reason. Call them now! Ask for help. Get out of this Godforsaken place!*

The reality of this inner plea hit home. Fear washed over me like a tidal wave. Fear, doubt, disbelief, defeat. *You can't just stop drinking by yourself. You're fucking addicted, an alcoholic, just like the bum in the street. You can't do it alone. Just kill yourself.*

I had never felt so beaten, or so alone. My chest was bursting with sobs as my thoughts continued to bounce in my pounding head, vacillating between "yes I can," and "no, I can't." I chided myself, then encouraged myself in the next breath. *But I CAN stop drinking. I can get help. I can! I need it. Oh, my God, maybe I even deserve it. Oh, my sweet Daddy! Yes! Daddy, help me! Please!*

I looked down to see my hands shaking and slowly sunk to the floor, naked on the filthy, threadbare carpet. My throat had shrunk to the diameter of a sewing pin; I could barely breathe.

God, don't let me die by choking to death, please! I forced myself to relax, to relax my throat... which removed all energy from my body. Weak, I barely moved as I racked with sobs, but the moans were loud enough to rouse the tattooed man.

Baby-Daddy rolled over, flat on his stomach. Though in an abysmal state, I noticed another tattoo on his shoulder, a small one: an eye with teardrops falling. *I think that's some kind of jail tattoo, isn't it?*

With my eyes focused on Baby-Daddy, I felt horrified yet somehow satisfied. I remembered the great sex, the euphoric feelings of last night. The other side of my mind spoke. *Baby-Daddy is the best you can get, Lela. This is it and it's fine. You can't get out of here! And why would you want to?*

I banged my head against the concrete floor in a slow rhythm.

Thud, thud, thud.

My mind screamed with self-hate and self-doubt. *You're a drunk and will always be a drunk. A lousy drunk at that. You can't and won't stop. That's why you smoked crack with a worthless man. That's why you drink with a bum and a snaggle-tooth. You are worthless. And stuck. Stuck.*

Again turning on a dime, the rationalizations began. I thought surely I wasn't that bad. Not so far gone that I was stuck and hopeless. I could easily find another job and it would just be a matter of time before my life shaped up and all would turn out peachy. *Peachy, right?*

Then the tears started anew. *Shut up! You're beyond help! Go down with the best of them. Nobody cares. Live on your laughable retirement money until it's gone. Face it, dumbass... you'll be dead by then, anyway.*

I didn't know which voice to believe. I asked myself "yes or no?" over and over. Do or die? Fake or real? Love or hate? You or them? Good or bad? I thought of dozens. The back and forth reminded me of being Bi-Polar. Up or down? Which one today?

The conclusion: I was losing my mind. Thinking of kicking my feet in a toddler fit, I laid on the floor full-length. *Am I having a nervous breakdown? Like when Bo left with his dad? Oh, what a shitty life I've had! Help me, God! I can't go down in this ratty room with this loser in my bed!*

I sat up. *No, Lela. You've got to do something. You've got to move forward with something good. You can't stay stuck in this room, going nowhere. Unemployed and unemployable. Do something!*

With a jolt of sudden determination, I stood and threw the threadbare sheet back. "Get out!" Baby-Daddy jerked awake. He looked shocked, but his immediate reaction was to attack, which scared the hell out of me. *He's been attacked before. Because he's a LOSER!* I stood ready for an assault, and repeated, "Get out! Get the hell out!"

"Jeezus, girl. What's wrong?" He sat up but didn't make a move to get out of bed.

"*Out!* Get out of this crappy room! Get the hell *out!*"

"Okay, okay, Jeezus! Calm down!" He sat up and swung his legs over the side of the bed, reaching for his shorts. "Why are you being such a bitch? What's *wrong* with you?

"Let me tell you something, *Asshole*. There's *nothing* wrong with me. What's wrong is *this!*" I spread my arms wide, spanning the room. "And *this!*" I pointed to him and then to me. "Everything! THAT'S what's wrong! Just get *out!*"

"You're messed up, man. I'm going to stay far away from your scary ass," he said while zipping his fly. "So you don't say, 'Thanks for getting me high?' or 'Thanks for the best dick I've ever had?'"

I had no words. Exhausted. *Maybe he's right. Maybe I should be thankful, smoke more of that awesome rock, have another roll in the hay...*

Baby-Daddy saw my change in attitude. "Come on, let's go to the pool, sweat a little, have a beer, see what comes up." I looked at him as he flashed a mischievous grin.

A sigh. A deep breath through my nose. *No! No! No! No! No!*

With renewed resolve, I opened the door. "Out. NOW."

He whined, "Oh, man! Don't do this. Don't ruin a good thing, Tennessee."

"Don't call me that! *Get out!*"

"Your loss, *bitch*." Baby-Daddy walked out, and I slammed the door, leaning against the back. Emotionally exhausted, I sunk to the floor, but I had no tears. I felt resolute. *You can do this, Lela Fox.*

Though I had no idea how, I knew I would change. I knew I could stop drinking. And I knew I would start that very moment.

It's time. YOUR time. Call your parents.

I felt something eerie within me, something that opened up the buzz clogging my ears, something that felt like puffy white clouds, something like... hope.

HELLO? HELP!
CHAPTER 10

After my outburst at dawn, I didn't cry much. Maybe there were no tears left. My heart was broken into a dozen pieces, but instead of falling into my usual emotional pity-fest, I was on a mission.

Determined, I scoured the phone book and made a list of rehab places. Surprisingly, I learned West Palm Beach was the recovery capital of the Eastern Seaboard, the destination for junkies and alkies from Boston, New York, and beyond. One place dubbed itself "The Malibu of South Florida." That one, I knew, was too pricey for a working-class girl, no matter how much her Momma had inherited.

Many were "dual diagnosis" rehab centers, treating mental illness *and* alcohol or drug addiction. In the margins of the Yellow Pages, I drew a star beside those places.

As usual, my cell phone didn't work in the dark dungeon of my room. With a sigh but staunch resolve, I stepped outside and sat on the low wall and lit a cigarette. Procrastinating, I played with my phone, studied it, scrolled through the contacts, and fiddled with the yellow scrap of paper where I'd written a local phone number. A place called Recovery Resources.

I held my breath and dialed the number. When a chirpy voice answered, I hung up the phone. *How can somebody be so cheerful when this is so damn serious? Some candy-ass attitude.*

Tears burned in my eyes but I knew there was no choice; I had to make that, ready or not. All I wanted was basic information; wouldn't give my name or anything. All anonymous, right? That's what the ad said.

I flipped my dead cigarette into the parking lot and found the resolve I felt earlier, a few hours and a lifetime ago when I lay naked on the floor crying. The redial button looked tiny, like I'd need a sewing needle to press it, but my stubby index finger found it and the phone rang.

My heart thumped outside my chest, it seemed, even pulsating the tip of my nose. The same chirpy voice answered, paused when I said nothing, and then urged, "I know it's hard to start, but I'm here to help you." *Well, at least the chirpy voice can be understanding, too.*

"Uh... I need to go there."

The voice turned more empathetic, softer, with a tinkling tone. "Sure! We're here to help, so let me transfer you to Laura. General information, right?"

A squeaked "yes." A burst of fear beat double-time in my temples.

"Sorry, but it's crappy elevator music while you wait. Please don't hang up, okay? I'll get her on the phone as quickly as possible."

I mumbled an okay until a click brought the crappy elevator music she promised. My mind reeled. *Will this be an interrogation? A soul-baring confession? Should I hang up the phone? No, no, she told me not to hang up. I guess many people do.*

Before my thoughts were complete, Laura answered. Friendly like the receptionist, but with an all-business undertone. Laura was the intake manager, she said, the one to set me up for admission and help me through the red tape.

I guess I was expecting a lecture. "Why have you let yourself get so low? Don't you know better than that!" But that wasn't the case at all. The other possibility I imagined was the mealy-mouthed counselor type, forcing me to talk about my "Daddy issues" and it would be either an argument or an emotional purge.

But Laura was upbeat and kind, said she knew I must be suffering and that she'd do anything to make my worries disappear. I didn't even cry.

We talked for about ten minutes. Although she used the pronoun, "you," she spoke as if the "patient" was a third party. I kept my shit together and knew the credit went to Laura; she put me completely at ease.

I flashed to a vision of a Hollywood director giving instruction to an actress, *certain* she would excel in her role. It seemed Laura assumed I was a responsible person, and I felt obligated to prove her right. *Maybe that's her trick... make 'em think they're smart.*

She also covered details about insurance, the length of an inpatient stay and the expected follow-up of Intensive Outpatient care. The location, surprisingly, was in a shopping center, about two miles from Smyth Software and next to a fitness center. Patients stayed in the apartment complex behind the building, she said. I knew the complex because I used to swing around the corner from work and have a drink there. Palm Place, they called it. A nice one, probably expensive.

Laura quoted the price. I don't remember the exact figure but something like ten-thousand comes to mind. *Holy shit!* She clarified. "That's for thirty days inpatient. Then half that for sixty days outpatient."

I had nothing to compare it to, of course, but that one sentence sent my mind into a continuous, vibrating loop. *Thank God I have good insurance, but oh, hell!* Suddenly, everything seemed way too real.

As anxiety rose, my palms itched, a common symptom when feeling stressed, and a good clue that I should try to settle myself. *Breathe in through your nose, out through your mouth... Slow, Lela, do it slow.*

The tactic didn't work. My heart beat too fast and the reaction was an overwhelming need to get off the phone. It was too much, too much change, too much fear, too much unknown, too much money, too much for my fragile frame of mind.

Though it was only a few paces, it seemed I ran back inside. The neon paper of the Yellow Pages glowed in the dark of the dungeon and drew me back to the book, seeing the dozen other places I had marked with stars.

But my vision blurred as tears began anew. Overwhelmed, my mind shut down. I couldn't handle any more calls. My first choice would be "the one," even if there was something better out there. No comparison-shopping for my future. No way. Too much trouble.

The next phone call would be the hardest one, anyway.

On the sixth ring, an out-of-breath Daddy said, "Hullo?"

"Daddy! Daddy-Daddy-help! Oh, Dad, I need you."

There was no hesitation. "What do you need, baby? Tell your Daddy." He was serious, must have heard the desperation in my voice.

"I'm a drunk, Daddy. I need help. Drunk like... scum, like a loser. I did *bad* drugs last night, Daddy! I'm scared, falling... down a hole.

"It's okay, baby, talk to me."

"I want to die, Daddy, and I'm afraid I'll do it. Please! I almost jumped in front of a train! I want to die but I *can't*. Because of Bo! Oh, God! Can you come to get me?"

"Yes, we'll come right now. But hold on... let me get your mom on the phone." He yelled "Margaret! Hurry! It's Lela!" Daddy kept talking, cooing a litany of assurances and promises.

When he said they would bring me home to Tennessee, I interrupted. "Daddy, I need to go to a treatment center or something. I'm an alcoholic and I'm crazy as hell. So scared, so upset, so embarrassed." A rack of sobs caused a pause in my ramblings. "Oh, God! Daddy, do you even still love me? I've been so terrible... for so long! And I'm so alone here and I'm—"

My father interrupted. "Of *course* I love you, darlin'. You're my favorite baby daughter! And you're *not* alone. We are on your side, always, and we'll help you get through. No questions. Hey... here's your mom. I'm gonna get the suitcases."

Mom took the phone. "Hey, honey. I'm here." In the background, I heard Daddy talking to Mom, snippets of "alcoholic" and "rehab" and "suicide." Mom's voice took a new edge. "Yes, Lela, we can help get you into a rehab center. And you have no idea how long I've waited to hear you say that, baby. I love you so much! We'll be there as soon as we can. What do you need?"

"Hell if I know, Mom. But thank you, I love you, oh, my God..." Words faded into sobs again. My throat had never been so small in diameter. I felt like I was choking.

"Exactly what can we do, Lela?" I couldn't speak because I was crying too hard. Though I didn't know who I was praying to, I thought, over and over, *Oh, thank you, God, for my parents.*

Mom asked, "Lela? Are you there?" I squeaked a "yes."

"Talk to me, baby. I can help you find a treatment center. We'll do this together, all three of us. I want to hug you so hard right now!" She cried, and I envisioned tears plopping on the phone's handset.

I finally spoke up and made sense, or so I thought. "Just come to Florida. I can't seem to do anything myself. I'm like a bowl of Jello. A stupid cow."

"Be kind to yourself, dear."

"Stop it, Mom! There are things to do and I can't do them. I can't get my shit together!

"That's where I come in, Lela. Your father and—"

I interrupted. "Because first, I need to get the rest of my stuff from Stuart's house before he throws it away. Can you bring a truck or something?

Will you stay here, with me? In this motel?"

"Anything to make it better, Lela. Anything! I'm so glad you called, that you saw the light. Thank God and Jesus! Now you can quit drinking and have a good life."

"I don't know if I can do it, Mom!" The sobs had returned.

"They'll teach you how, baby. All you have to do is show up."

"I'm sure there's more to it than that."

"I'm coming to help you."

Mom stayed silent while I babbled for a while, talking as my thoughts bounced like ping-pong balls. I calmed enough to light another cigarette, and I said, "One thing I know..."

Silence from both ends.

"Just one thing?" She tried to make a joke, just enough of a stop in the drama to open my eyes to the real possibility of moving forward.

"One thing I know is... somebody who can help you load my stuff from Stuart's garage. It's a guy named Snaggle-Tooth."

"Whaat? Snaggle-Tooth?"

Another laugh, a cleansing chuckle with Mom joining the light moment. "I don't know his real name. But him, and maybe his friends... they have muscles. The police will have to go with you, too, ya know? Can you handle that kind of stupid shit, Mom?"

"I can handle anything if it gets you out of that hell-hole!"

"Mom! Watch your language!" I'd done it; I made a joke. But laughter morphed to more sobs, and feeling utterly defeated, I dropped my head into my hands. More sighs, more tears, and a deep breath. *Get your shit together, Lela.* I wiped my face on my t-shirt and lit another cigarette.

Down the way, the two Middle Eastern men from the pool walked into the laundry room, barking in their angry-sounding language. It was the final straw. *Oh God, I gotta get out! There's no staying in this hell, not the kind in my head and not here at the Homing Inn. Get sober, now, while you still can.*

Mom shouted at Daddy with the phone away from her mouth. As if there was no break in the conversation, she spoke, now all-business. "We'll put your things in storage, no problem. Have you called a treatment center yet? Don't worry about insurance. I'd pay a gazillion dollars to see you well."

"The treatment center said I'd have to get a referral from a therapist before insurance would cover it. God, I hate that therapist, Mom! Stuart paid her off for the Baker Act thing."

I knew Mom didn't know what "the Baker Act thing" meant, and I didn't want to explain. So I was happy when her thoughts took another path. "Never mind Stuart," she snapped. "Call your therapist, Lela, within the hour. It's important. We'll see her together."

Mom was in planning mode, I could tell, but I was winding down, too exhausted to cry or think. "Hurry, Lela. Please promise you will call this morning."

"You mean like Daddy would say, 'Immediately if not sooner?'" I laughed, trying to make a joke. The laughter felt awesome, like there was still a reason to live, a way to fight the demon sucking the life and power from my core.

Mom interrupted my wondrous feeling. "Lela, I'm off to pack, do laundry. Sweetie, I'll call again after you've called your therapist. Make an appointment for tomorrow afternoon. The plan is that your father and I will leave before dawn. So we'll be in West Palm Beach around two. Make a room reservation for us. Is it a safe place?" I thought it was best not to answer that question.

"Do you want to talk to your dad again?"

"No, I want to collapse," I said, taking another swipe at my tears. "But I'll call the damn therapist first."

"Please watch your language, even now, okay? But Lela, if you want this to work, if you want to go to rehab, then call her. And I'm so glad you will go!" Mom seemed giddy with excitement. "You'll be fine, Lela, and we'll all be so happy! Can I tell your sisters?"

"Yeah. I'm sure this will surprise Karen."

"Oh, this will surprise *no one*," she said flatly. "We all saw what was happening to you, Lela, for *years*. The surprising thing is *you* can see it now. A wonderful, happy surprise! Be strong, dear. I'll call later."

There may have been a better treatment center for me had I made a few more calls, and certainly there would have been a cheaper alternative. What mattered, I thought, was my attitude, not the locale or specifics, and I felt ready. More than ready.

Disgusted with myself, I stepped into an unknown world, guided only by hopelessness. I had met my bottom and this time I stopped digging.

Years later, I realized my bottom wasn't "high" like some asshole

AA's accused; it was a spiritual bottom that left me hollow and dead inside.

I wish all people, alcoholic or not, had the benefit of a loving family. I realize how lucky I am, and my gratitude for them explodes in my heart, still sending me to the stratosphere with all the good stuff life and love brings.

I also know that without my parents, that day would have been my last. But Dude had other plans.

THE BEGINNING BEGINS
CHAPTER 11

It was a work-in appointment, but we'd already waited for more than an hour. I went to the front desk to make sure Gloria, the therapist, knew we were still there. The uninterested staffer said, and I quote, "Cool your heels, Ms. Fox. She's cutting other patients' time short just to see you." With a sigh, I sat down and fidgeted with the hem of my shorts. Mom looked exhausted, and I felt guilty for putting an old lady through such stress.

That morning, I thought it best to skip my usual first-thing activity, so I hadn't had a drink. Now I regretted it, feeling my anxiety rise like a nuclear missile. A gnawing contortion filled my mind and churned in my stomach. "I'm sorry, Mom," I said, leaning on her soft shoulder and closing my eyes.

"Nothing to be sorry about, honey. I love you and I'm proud of you." I wished she would stop saying that. *Proud? Ha!* Who could be proud of a lousy drunk? A pitiful drunk who brought a man like Stuart Weinstein into their lives? An out-of-control drunk who caused all varieties of chaos and reasons for worry. Who could be proud of that?

I felt sick. Nauseated. And my hands shook like I held a jackhammer. Just as I thought my head would explode, Gloria's head peeked through the door of the waiting room. "Lela?" She caught my eye and smiled, but it was a smile reserved for a troubled child, a mental patient, a cancer sufferer. I stewed in Shame, tasting the bitterness as I swallowed my pride.

Mom and I followed Gloria through a labyrinth of halls to a paneled office. I always thought her office was strange for a psychologist; it was long and skinny. The sofa for patients faced her chair, but the distance between was about thirty feet. Not the intimate attachment I needed to connect with a therapist. Maybe that's why I never liked or trusted her. I certainly didn't trust her after she signed the papers for Stuart's bribe! But today, I needed her.

Mumbling, I introduced Mom and told her why I was there. The psychiatrist seemed shocked. "Why do you think you're an alcoholic, Lela? Your husband mentioned nothing about alcohol, just the Bi-Polar out of control."

"Gloria, Stuart tricked you into signing those papers. And he's probably an alcoholic, too. A mean one. He has screwed me over, kicked me out of the house, tricked me with the Baker Act thing, stolen my money... so much more." Tears flowed as I continued. "But that's beside the point because now I know the truth. Alcohol is my problem. Something else, too. Bi-Polar, surely, but maybe more. Whatever the combination, I'm a looney-tunes and I'm, like, slipping away from reality. I need help."

Gloria made a note without looking at the paper. *Just like Kate, my old therapist, used to do! I still hate that shit!* "Go on," she said. But what more could I say?

"I'm at the end, Gloria. Maybe I can start again at a dual-diagnosis rehab."

She stared at me, shuffling blindly through papers. "I see. Well, yes, you need a referral. But for insurance to pay, you need more than that. You'll need a transfer from another facility. So I'll send you to North Palm and they'll recommend a treatment center. Do you want *inpatient* rehab?"

I nodded, then jerked and fidgeted, speaking in the silence. "Have you ever heard of Recovery Resources? That's the place I've been talking to."

"Excellent choice." The flat, emotionless comment didn't radiate confidence in my decision and anxiety shot through me like a lightning bolt. Suddenly, I was ready to run from her office, tuck tail and run. I grabbed the arm on the side chair, trying my best to stay in control and make sense. Mom saw my nervousness and patted my hand. *Thank you, Mom!*

Gloria turned to her desk and made a note as Mom reached out again, this time to pat my leg. The doctor turned toward a rack of stuffed manila-folder envelopes. "So, I'll fax an order to the hospital, and they will take you to Recovery Resources at some point."

Shocked, I looked at Mom's face. It was white and her jaw had dropped to her chest. She said, "Hospital? Which hospital?"

Gloria answered with a flippant attitude I didn't appreciate. "North Palm

Beach Psychiatric Hospital. That's where I'm sending her."

I stiffened. *A psychiatric hospital?* I blurted out, "But I don't want to go to a crazy hospital! Gloria! I'm not *crazy*, just a drunk with a little mood disorder!" By the end of my outburst, I was panting, out of breath and as scared as I'd ever been.

Gloria looked at me with no expression at all. "Alcoholism and Bi-Polar, Lela? I think that qualifies."

"Qualifies for what?" I squeaked.

"But don't call it 'crazy' or you'll make yourself worry. The doctors there will evaluate you and introduce a twelve-step program, set you in the right direction."

"Oh my God! How long do I have to stay there? I don't want to go! Isn't there another way?" I was frantic now.

"Insurance companies have a protocol, Lela. At least two specialists must agree that you need inpatient treatment. Inpatient programs are expensive, and your insurance company will try to fight paying, even with two referrals."

Gloria turned to Mom. "You will probably have to dispute their denial the first go-round, Mrs. Fox. Can you handle that for her?" Mom nodded, still patting my thigh.

As I cried and watched my hands shake, Mom took over the conversation with the psychiatrist. I was to report to the psychiatric hospital early the next morning, Gloria said, then she passed a handful of papers to me. Loose papers and a thick manila envelope. I felt lost in the system already.

The doctor handed a smaller packet to Mom, a list of what I should and shouldn't pack. "The rules are strict," she said, looking over her glasses and into my soul. "Good luck, Lela. Be well."

The entire appointment took less than ten minutes. I felt railroaded even though it had been my idea all along. It just happened too fast, maybe. It was more than my brain could process and my head spun.

Mom led me out of the office as if I was a child, and I let her because I *felt* like a child, lost in a daze. It was coming upon noon, and more than anything, I needed a drink.

The trip back to the Homing Inn was silent, filled only with Mom's cooing and soft assurances. Yet she kept her jaw clenched, seeming as nervous as I was.

Oh my God! What have I done? I looked at the list of what was prohibited. No hairdryer or curling iron... nothing with a cord, they said, due to "choking hazards."

I was livid. "Mom! They think I'm going to hang myself! They think I'm crazy!" *No way... I just want to live sober, not kill myself while working on it.*

"I'm sure they're overly careful, dear. But her notes include a separate list for the 'typical' rehab center. The rules are less strict. So, here, look at these and don't worry."

Even the "less strict" list of contraband items was long. No liquids at all, no food, no medicine, no laptop or cell phone, no cotton balls. *Cotton balls? What's that about?* The worst, I could only bring one pack of cigarettes. *Great. The SOB's are gonna make me quit smoking at the same time? This is hell!*

As I carried things from Room 1 to the Buick, I saw Baby-Daddy at the pool, standing at the fence and staring at me like a smug sonofabitch. I flashed a memory bringing instant anger at myself, but I avoided it by aiming the anger at Baby-Daddy. I shot him a bird. He smiled and waved in response. Asshole.

Snaggle-Tooth and Lap-Dancer came to my room to talk to Daddy about loading the things left at Stuart's house. They would load what Stuart would let them take, if anything at all, and move it to a storage bay on A-1-A. I had no idea what size storage room I needed, so I rented the biggest one, hoping it wouldn't echo empty for the six-month contract.

Bargaining with Snaggle-Tooth, Daddy offered him much more than any of us expected. The scruffy man's eyes widened, and he shook Daddy's hand with exuberance. Then I saw my father wipe his hand on his pants. I teared up. *What kind of people are you introducing to your sweet parents, Lela? Do you think that's fair?*

Then I realized being fair was totally out of my wheelhouse at the moment. I was doing good to be able to stay on the toilet when I sat to pee. I was like a whirling dervish.

But I hoped Snaggle-Tooth's thrill about the upcoming payday was an assurance he and Lap-Dancer would follow through. Who knew? Alcoholics and addicts aren't the most-dependable sort. Who knew that better than I did?

For the rest of the afternoon, I was oblivious to all around me, beginning the throes of detox. Miserable, I had cold sweats and my entire body shook uncontrollably. Mom realized what was happening and called the rehab center for instruction. As I paced, a beer in a brown paper bag suddenly appeared in my hand. *Dammit, Mom, not ONE! Six! Twelve! A hundred!*

I downed the single beer and demanded another.

Mom wrung her hands and cried. Both parents knew the dangers of detox, had heard about the possibility of seizures, and wanted to do the right thing. But I overheard Mom talking to Daddy. The words "heartbreaking" and "pitiful" rung in my ears.

She made another call to Recovery Resources. I heard her explain to Daddy that they should let me drink normally until I could detox with medical supervision. I collapsed with relief when hearing the news. Mom looked scared, maybe angry with me, but drove to the 7-Eleven to buy a six-pack.

Though I was desperate, I felt like a real ass in sending my prim-and-proper Southern Methodist mother on such an errand. She didn't know a soul in Florida, but I imagined she felt embarrassed, like being naked in public or performing a deliberate sin for all to see.

After all the years of resenting the hell out of that woman, I was overcome with gratitude for her on that day.

Mom returned with a six-pack of cans. Coors, unfortunately, but I didn't complain. After the fourth beer, I felt better. With just a bit of a buzz, I sat up to talk, directing Mom in her careful packing of my suitcase. I felt like a two-year-old and let my parents treat me as if I was.

Daddy, also helping me pack, held up a pair of maroon shorts, pulling the waist tight. "Margaret, look at this," he said. I didn't understand what he was showing her.

"What, Daddy? Those are my favorite shorts. What are you saying?"

Mom walked across the room and snatched the shorts from Daddy's hands, looking at the tag. "Size four." She held them to her face and cried.

I had been a size ten when I married Miller, husband number two, and a size twelve when I left him. As my misery grew, I had shrunk. Now my limbs were spindles and my hip bones prominent. Pale, fragile, sickly small.

I sipped the rest of the beer, staying drunk but not sloppy. Mom put me to bed as if I was a child and I felt overflowing gratitude. Ashamed of needing her, maybe, but I needed her badly. Like a child, I needed my Momma and my tears flowed like rain.

Daddy leaned over to kiss my forehead. "Sleep sweet, little Lela, sleep like my beautiful baby girl." With Daddy's kiss, I sobbed hysterically, ashamed of disappointing my hero, my biggest fan. I cried myself to sleep but tossed and turned. Dreams awakened me a half-dozen times.

I dreaded the next few days, knowing the enormous misery I would face. I thought I had imagined the worst, but I was wrong.

It turned out to be much worse than I had imagined.

A SICK GOODBYE
CHAPTER 12

I awoke to a loud banging on my door. Startled, my eyes opened, but I lay still, deciding whether to answer. The thin curtains showed darkness; it was before dawn. *Cops? Baby-Daddy?* It took a few minutes to clear my head and realize it must be Mom.

Realization hit and my blood pressure skyrocketed with fear. *Oh, God, I'm getting sober today. June 30, 1999. I guess I'll remember this date for a long time.* I yelled through the door, "Just a minute, Mom." She said something in response, in a sing-song voice, but I couldn't hear the words.

Fear and doubts mixed with determination. This day, I knew, would the last day of the horrible life I'd been living, but a step away from the life I'd been comfortable with for so long. I was used to hating myself, criticizing myself, and downplaying the pain of living in my self-imposed prison.

I didn't know what to expect in the "new life" I'd chosen. *Or DID I choose it? Was I forced into it? Do I want it bad enough to go through all the shit?* My life had been shitty for so long I didn't know what else was out there, didn't know what the "new life" was all about. *But what choice do you have, Lela?*

I sighed as the full assortment of questions and affirmations passed through my mind. *One thing is for sure; it will be hell getting there. Can't I just go to sleep and wake up sober and sane?*

When I answered the door, Mom's face held a forced smile. I felt instantly remorseful; she was just as scared, just as unsure as I was. I hated to drag my sweet mother through my own hell. Daddy was standing beside her with his typical goofy grin.

So far, Dad had been kind and loving but seemed lost. He followed behind me and hugged me at every opportunity, unable to help but desperate to do so. Actually, his hugs helped more than anything did.

I got dressed as my parents traipsed to the pitiful hotel office. They checked me out of the seedy room that had been my home for too long. I pulled the door to Room 1 closed, saying goodbye to the darkness inside and the darkness that had shrouded me for years.

Thanks, God... or whoever you are. Thanks for today, my first day sober.

☼ ☼ ☼ ☼ ☼

We stopped to eat breakfast. I was sucking coffee, doubling cream and sugar when I normally drank it black, my foot jacking up and down when I crossed my legs.

Dad said, "You look like you're going to fly away, hon. Are you okay?"

"Just hyper. Scared, I guess."

"Rightly so."

"But you guys... I gotta tell you something. Yesterday, when my mind exploded?" They both watched and listened, nodding nervously... perhaps wondering if I would explode again. "It was just like another, uh, remarkable moment in my life... something that changed my direction long ago."

Dad chuckled, "You've changed directions a hundred times, Lela. You'll need to be more specific."

"This is no joke, Daddy. Not this time." Of course Daddy would be silly with me – that was how we communicated since I was six – but he instantly reacted to my scolding, putting his head down.

"Remember when I came home from that terrible apartment... the summer after my senior year?"

Mom piped in, "I remember you brought roaches home."

"Oh. Sorry."

"Never mind... go on."

"Well, when I decided to leave there and go to college in Rockville, I had some kind of epiphany... a smack-me-in-the-face realization that if I stayed where I was, I'd never get out."

"You had a repeat of that epiphany?"

"Exactly. It's crazy. It's exactly the same. I would have died in that crappy motel!"

"No, no, Lela. Don't go down that road. Just like when you were young, this smack in the face will change the direction of your life. We're here... you're going to rehab. All so you can get you better, come home, and start over."

I wanted to believe her; I wanted the "start over" she described.

Just before the burn of tears came to my eyes, the waitress arrived. I shook off the tearfulness and dug in. "You're gonna be sorry, my baby girl." Daddy warned.

"But I'm starving!" I ignored Daddy's advice to eat light, gobbling eggs, pancakes, and a double order of extra-crisp bacon. My parents sat back to watch me eat. Mom's eyes were like saucers; I guess my table manners weren't up to par.

On the way out, I collapsed on the IHOP bench seat, toppling an elderly man. After two dry heaves, I threw up in the corner of the orange bench. Daddy ran to get napkins as Mom rubbed my back. I croaked, "Water!" and watched a few people leave with their hands over their mouths, but I was too sick to be embarrassed. The thought struck me: *I'm bad for business. It* pounded my head repeatedly.

Mom pushed a glass of water into my hand and I drank greedily. When I looked up, a fat guy in an IHOP apron stood in front of me with a mop, glaring at me and my puddle of vomit. With a straight face, as pale as it was, I said, "I'm getting sober today." I didn't care if he understood or not.

We decided Daddy would drive the van and take me inside when we got to the hospital, and Mom would follow us. It was time... I said a poignant goodbye to Mom in the IHOP parking lot. Tears streamed down my face and dripped off my chin; I didn't bother to wipe them. I let my Momma coddle and cuddle me as I leaned hard on her shoulder. She clucked like the mother hen she'd always been. We gathered in a three-way family hug before I followed them further north.

I talked to myself during the drive... words of encouragement, daring myself to answer with doubt or fear. Halfway there, I wondered again why I had to go all the way to North Palm Beach, but that's what Gloria said to do. *Gloria, the therapist who doesn't give a shit. How the hell did I end up with her? Maybe she's part of my problem.* Catching myself finger-pointing, the little voice in my head screamed. *No, Lela, stop blaming others! This is on YOU. Own it. Blaming others is what got you here in the first place.* Maybe for the first time in my life, I listened to my conscious without smacking the crap out of it.

Daddy and I walked to the hospital's side door as Gloria had directed, passing a dozen or so haunted patients gathered in the smoking area. Their dark, sunken eyes followed our every move as we entered the door with a broken "Entrance" sign.

Inside, an instant echo startled me, as did an overpowering smell. *Urine? Bleach? Burned bread?* Again, I almost collapsed. Daddy dropped my suitcase to stop me from falling, catching me under the arms. "Are you okay, sweetie? Do you need to sit down?" Daddy, ever the protector.

I eased into a cheap, warped, molded-plastic chair and Daddy sat beside me. Identical chairs. He rubbed my back as I put my head between my knees, trying to get rid of the dizziness and stop the sharp pains in my belly. In my peripheral vision, I saw white shoes on the floor. A man's voice: "Ms. Fox?" With a startled jerk, I looked up, and he continued. "Hi there. I'm Joe, your intake nurse."

With a bobbling head, I looked at him. Correction: I *tried* to look at him, but there were three or four choices in my blurry, multi-colored vision. "Uh, I don't feel so good," I said. Then I puked again, inches from Daddy's shoes.

The nurse spoke to Daddy. "Nerves, most likely." Gently, Joe the nurse took my arm and sat me upright. A wet-wipe appeared out of nowhere as he cleaned my mouth. "Ms. Fox, you're in a safe place. You need to say goodbye to your guardian now."

I looked at Daddy and my now-faded eyes instantly overflowed with tears. A veil of desperation fell over me as my can-do attitude cracked like a broken mirror. I pleaded, "Don't go, Daddy! I don't want to be here. Please! Tell them I'm fine. I can't do this! Stay with me!" I saw his eyes tear up as he looked at me with pity, but the Shame I felt didn't stop my begging. "No, I can't! I can't stay here!"

Daddy stood, putting his warm, muscular arms around my shoulders. I mumbled into his shirt, "Take me home, Daddy! Please, I want to go to the farm! Don't let them take me!" I cried on his shoulder for what seemed like a month.

As we hugged, he rubbed my back and patted my hair. Daddy whispered, "Shhh, shhh, baby girl. You're gonna be just fine. These people will help you. You want to get better, right?" Still sobbing, I nodded against his chest.

Daddy bent his knees and peeked up at my face as I looked at the floor, chin on my chest. Then he smiled the silly smile that made me giggle as a kid. "Go get 'em, tiger!" he said. Despite the fear and disgust I felt for myself, I smiled, closing my eyes to blink out the tears.

When I opened my eyes, Daddy was still there, inches from my face. "Ready?" I nodded but couldn't speak.

The nurse touched my arm, and I turned toward him. At a snail's pace, Joe led me toward a room that looked like a doctor's exam room. About fifteen yards into the trip, I turned to say goodbye to my father... my biggest fan, come hell or high water. Daddy gave me a thumbs-up sign and waved.

He thought I had looked away, I suppose, but I saw him drop his head into his hands. My Daddy cried. I leaned against Joe and did the same.

I couldn't take my eyes off him. *Goodbye, Daddy. I'll see you sober.*

EIGHT DAYS IN HELL
CHAPTER 13

It was an ordinary exam room. Joe left and a female nurse appeared, holding a blue paper gown. "Open in the back, please." My tears dotted the gown as I sat on the edge of the table awaiting my fate. Nauseous, anxious... I needed a drink. No, I needed *twenty* drinks.

The thought of never having another drop of alcohol in my life seemed monumental and impossible; I couldn't wrap my head around such a concept. *Nobody can do that. No way. Why am I here? This is all bogus. Pure bullshit.*

Just as I stood to go, a doctor whizzed into the room, flapped his white coattails, sat on the wheeled stool, and snatched a pen from his pocket. There was no greeting or small talk, just a forced smile. The nurse took my blood pressure and stated the reading out loud. The nameless doctor asked, "Do you typically have high blood pressure?

Though I tried to be a badass, the persona that had served me well for so many years, I found myself meek, almost apologetic. "No, it's usually low. Or it used to be. I haven't been to a doctor-doctor for a long time." He looked at me with a stoic expression.

He grabbed my right arm, a little rougher than needed, in my opinion. There was a metered pause as he looked at his watch. "Your heart rate is also high. Are you nervous, Ms. Fox?"

"Terrified."

I expected him to chuckle and commiserate with me, and then lovingly assure me all was well. But no; he was expressionless and silent... as if his personality had been surgically removed. Looking through his reading glasses, he made notes in a folder.

"What are you writing?" I asked, "Why won't you talk to me?" Panic rose, as did my volume. Still, the doctor was silent and expressionless. I could taste the tension in the room and took his white-coat-professionalism as a personal affront. *Nobody treats Lela Fox like that! Who does he think he is? Asshole!*

I was mad as hell but so desperate for help and so sick that I couldn't defend myself against the bastards. *You're a spineless amoeba, Lela. No more than that.*

I had no idea what I was up against, didn't know I was fighting the faceless, rubber-stamp-inspired mental health system. Tears began, first just a few, but by the time I told him of my lifelong struggle with Bi-Polar Disorder, I was sobbing. Still, he sat unaffected, along with the stone-faced nurse.

Doctor Heartless told me to lay back and poked around on my belly. When he pushed on the lower right, I winced. "Tender here?" he asked. A nod. He poked around more. "Your liver is enlarged. Enlargement is the first stage of cirrhosis." My eyes widened. *What the hell? Is he just trying to scare me?* Immediately jumping to the worst-case scenario, I envisioned myself on the organ donation waiting list, yellow with sickness, nothing more than skin and bones.

Perhaps he saw my panic and, trying to calm me, said, "By the time you're ten-years sober, it will have returned to normal." *Ten years! Ha! I can't go four hours!* With the same stern face and monotonous tone, he said, "You need to put on ten pounds, but that will come in time. Otherwise, you are healthy." Saying no more, he stood and left the room, leaving me with the quiet nurse.

Suddenly, she smiled... as if released from the doctor's grip, a kind aura surrounded her. My heart rose in gratitude; I had never been so frightened, and I needed a friend. She touched my shoulder and spoke softly, "Time to get dressed, Lela. Do you need help?"

"Help getting *dressed?* Do you think I'm a *child?*" I snapped, like a smartass teen. How quickly my demeanor could change! I continued to berate her. "And don't use that sugary-sweet voice you'd use with a mental patient! I'm NOT one of those!"

No response and no change in her kind smile... maybe it was plastered on. I tapped my foot, waiting for her to leave the room, but she stayed, leaning casually against the counter.

"Sorry, but I need to watch you dress, Lela. House rules." *Oh, yeah. I'm in a crazy hospital. They think I'm crazy.* I ranted, venting my anger at the doctor and the system and the unfairness of life in general.

She listened patiently, waiting for me to take a breath. It took a while. Finally, she said, "We're trying to help you, Lela."

"Bullshit! You don't *know* me! You think I'm *crazy!* You're treating me like a number, like a fucking prisoner! I need help – you're right about that – but not this kind! You keep talking 'house rules' and 'protocol' and bullshit like that! I'm not your typical psycho patient, dammit! You don't know me or why I'm here!"

The nurse didn't move and didn't respond to my tirade. "Are you ready to get dressed now?" she said, with the plastered-on smile. *Forget it. Fuck it. You're stuck here, Lela. Play by their ridiculous rules. You really don't have a choice.*

I let that realization sink in, pausing for a few minutes. Then with a resigned sigh, I dressed as the nurse watched. "Ready?" she asked. I nodded. When she opened the door, she gently pushed me from behind... into a large room where about thirty people roamed aimlessly.

A man in a button-down shirt and khakis yelled "Everybody! Time for group!" One by one, the menagerie of patients sat in a lopsided circle. The people: a 50/50 mix of genders, mostly young and dressed in wrinkled street clothes. The seating: one-piece molded-plastic lawn chairs. A light bulb came on; crazy patients and metal don't mix. Everything in here would be plastic or bolted to the wall. *Seen that before, huh, Lela? You're an old pro at being a mental patient.*

The nurse led me to the clean-cut man who had called the meeting. Kevin said, "Welcome, nice to see you," and blah, blah, blah. I tried to follow his words, but they ran together in my mind. Suddenly, he pointed to a chair and sharply said, "Sit," like a command to a fucking dog. I opened my mouth, ready to tell him to kiss my ass, but closed it quickly.

You have no power here, Lela. You're a prisoner and this guy is the jailer. He can talk to you like a dog or a peon... anything he wants. You have no rights. So shut up. "Sit," like he says.

Kevin led the meeting, reading from a gray book. Too shaky to listen, I studied each patient in detail. Some were silent and shivering. In detox, I guessed. That scared the shit out of me, knowing I'd be there soon.

Some were squirrely and fidgety, reminding me of Stuart. Their fidgeting sent my mind wandering. *Where is Stuart? What's he doing? And has he been thinking about me?* I just couldn't seem to let go of my concern for him, even when I slapped myself to STOP IT!

Others in the circle slept with chins on their chests. One of the bigger guys, in his mid-twenties I guessed, awoke with a start when the group shared a laugh. Watching him jerk made me chuckle, drawing the attention of Kevin and half the circle. *Screw you guys! It was funny!*

Three minutes later, the guy was asleep again; even funnier to me. Slowly, I relaxed. I thought if I could laugh at this point in time, I might be okay in the long run.

A few of the patients looked normal but about ten looked seriously crazy, schizophrenic maybe, with eyes that darted around the room in paranoia. Watching the crazies sent a knot of anxiety to my nauseous belly, and my imagination went into overdrive.

The staff, about fifteen in white scrubs and sensible shoes, eyed the patients one at a time, completing the circle. When a husky bearded man leveled his eyes at me, I panicked. *How can I convince them I'm not like the others? I'm not crazy! Do I simply say, "I'm just here for a ride to rehab!?"* *Would they believe me? Oh Jeezus, please get me out of here!*

I closed my eyes and forced a shift in focus. Alcohol withdrawal drilled down to nicotine withdrawal. I needed a cigarette BADLY, and the need hit me hard... almost as hard as the need for a drink. Fear crawled on the back of my neck like a centipede, wondering how long before I could smoke the one damn pack they let me bring.

At long last, Kevin stood. "Good meeting, guys. Let's take a break before lunch." The patients lined up at the side door, the one that Daddy and I had entered. An orderly, or whatever she was, held a tray of labeled plastic bags, each holding a single cigarette. Patients paraded by, taking a bag on the way out the door. More fear... panic, really. *What if my cigarette isn't ready yet? What if I'm already lost in the system?*

I repeated the what-ifs even after receiving my cigarette, dreading a face-to-face with these crazy people. *Deep breaths, Lela. Just pretend they're children and ignore them... every one of them.*

The courtyard was mostly full when I stepped out, with everybody holding an unlit cig and forming yet-another line to get a light from one of the orderlies perched on a retaining wall.

What the hell? Why the line? Before I could finish asking the question, I realized the easy answer. Crazy people can't be trusted with fire. They want to harm themselves and others... and will go to any length to destroy what they can.

And they think I'm one of those people.

A mouthful of harsh cigarette smoke eased my anxiety a bit, but my hands still shook like a Parkinson's patient. The back of my throat burned with the taste of bile and a painful heaviness built in my stomach.

I spied a concrete bench away from the crowd and settled in to cry, but a woman close to my age strutted toward me with purpose. Despite the heat, she wore a heavy jacket and her greasy, straight hair fell against the grease-stained collar. "You're new," she said bluntly. I nodded.

Then she pulled a plastic chair next to the bench and introduced herself. "I'm Sara, good to meet ya." She extended her arm for a handshake and I felt obligated to accept it. Hers was a dirty hand, a spiderweb of black within the crevices of her palm and a truckload of dirt under her fingernails and cuticles. *Gross!* I let go as soon as I could.

She seemed manic as hell, taking deep sucks on the cigarette and speaking through the plume of exhaled smoke. "Ya doin' okay? Ya gettin' ready to detox? Ya scared?" I didn't have time to answer; she continued her rat-a-tat speech. "Ya don't have'ta be scared. Usually, ya don't have no seizure or try n' swallow your tongue or nothing. I mean, ya won't *die*. I guess not usually. Mostly it's just bad, bad cold sweats. They feed ya tea and give ya medicine, but to tell ya the truth, it's hell. Sick. So dang sick. But in about a week, ya get better. Don't worry, man. I've done it a dozen times."

I squawked. "A *dozen* times? Why? And I thought it just took three days!"

"No man, longer'n three... maybe ya get lucky and it be five. But me... I keep relapsing, see, really b'fore I do much sober stuff." Taking another deep suck on her cigarette, she blew it out of her nose and waved her hand to diffuse the smoke. "I can't stand these damn thangs! And they don't give ya enough time so ya better smoke 'em fast. Oh, forgot t'ask... what's yer name, man?"

I opened my mouth to tell her my name was Tess, as in "Tess Tosterone," my girls-beach-trip name. In the smile that followed this random thought, I wondered if finding the *second* opportunity to laugh in this place might mean I'd make it out.

I was still smiling about my anonymous name when a female orderly raised the alarm. "It's time, guys!" Just as Sara said would happen. With a half-cigarette left to smoke, I panicked.

"See... told ya," the dirty girl said, then disappeared into the crowd of patients lined up to go inside. Defiant, I stayed where I was and smoked with my nose in the air… as if I hadn't heard the call.

But I wasn't alone in this tactic; about fifteen patients smoked like they'd not heard her command. I found it odd that the orderly seemed accepting of this. Then, five minutes later, she called names, one at a time. I was the last. "In the ashtray, Lela," she instructed.

Back in the group room, I wandered around, not knowing what to do. Soon, Joe the intake nurse and the quiet one from the exam room led me down a wide hall to my room. *Your suite at the Psycho Inn, Madame Lunatic.*

My heart sunk when I walked in the room. Bare, sterile, filled with nothing but echoes. A half-wall of wood cabinets, open on both sides, divided the room into two sleeping areas. They pushed me further in the room to my bed… the one farthest from the door. Straight ahead, my suitcase was open on the floor, everything in disarray. Obviously searched.

Outraged, I spit accusations like bullets. "Who in the hell do you think you are?! I followed your stupid rules, dammit! You have no right to ruffle through my things!"

"But yes, we *do* have a right, Ms. Fox. We are obligated to watch over your health and safety while you're here." I closed my eyes. Joe was right, of course. It didn't feel right; downright rude. *But here you're controlled and managed, Lela. You are a nothing, a nobody. Shut up, sit down, shuffle here, shuffle there. What's my name? They may know at the desk…*

Despite the futility of it all, I raised my voice in a holier-than-thou tone, telling them the search was "illegal" and "unfair treatment." They simply ignored me, arranging things as if I didn't exist. Watching them work, I thought how upset my mother would be to find her careful packing job turned into a chaotic mess.

My room, such as it was, was ready. Joe and the quiet nurse left, saying someone would be in soon to "get me started on the treatment plan," whatever the hell that meant.

My bed, pushed against the short wall, sported a cheap navy bedspread. Facing it, a bolted-on desk held three books: one a pamphlet of rules and regulations for the hospital, and two paperbacks. The largest book was light blue. *Twelve Steps and Twelve Traditions*; the other was thick and dark blue with an embossed title you could barely see. *Alcoholics Anonymous.*

That dark blue book was just like the one I had packed from Stuart's bookcase when he moved in with me at the oh-so-green Rockville house. His ex-wife's book, he had said. *What a dumbass you were to believe that.*

Ready to beat myself up more, I laid back on the bed. The crunch of the plastic cover underneath the pillowcase and sheets was deafening. My running thoughts continued, detailing how low I was. *Stuart. Baby-Daddy. Instant addiction to crack. How could you be with people like that? Duh. Maybe because you're an alcoholic, Lela, that's why. You need help. You're in the right place. Suck it up and take it.*

I never knew I had so many tears. They rolled into my ears and reminded me of a country song I sang as a child, a song Daddy sang to me with a purposely silly southern twang. *"I've got tears in my ears from lying on my back... in my bed, while I cry over youuuuuu."* The juvenile song brought a smile to my face. *Maybe there's hope, you big dumbass. Hang in there.*

Over the next half-hour, I blew my nose every few minutes, dealing with the continual flow of tears that screamed of my fear and sadness for a life soon to be gone. My old life, poof. Expired. I'd miss it, I knew. I'd known no other.

Kevin, the group leader guy, entered my room, cracked a weak joke or two, and asked me to come to his office. "I have a carry-out lunch for you on my desk. You can eat with me." I told him I wasn't hungry but he ignored me. "And bring that dark blue book, please." Together we walked through the group room and down a short hall, entering a cramped office. Jimmy Buffett played from somewhere, a hidden speaker, I guessed.

Stacks of papers on his desk could be measured in feet, not inches. Diplomas and certificates on the walls hung in a haphazard arrangement, a humorous amount of "too many." The largest diploma was from Florida State. Smaller ones read the University of Florida and, *what the hell,* The University of Eastern South Dakota.

Another chuckle. *That's three. So it can't be all bad.*

Kevin smiled, a kind smile, rather crooked. "Do you feel okay?" he asked. I said I felt fine though we both knew it was a lie. "In a while, you will feel not-so-good. Detox isn't pleasant. But we're here to protect you and ease the pain as much as we can."

He paused, moving a manila folder from one stack to the next. "We've handled medical detox for many years and hundreds of patients, Lela, but we know *you've* never gone through it. Don't be afraid and don't give up hope. Trust me; you will feel better soon. In the meantime, you can start *real* recovery."

"Uh... *real* recovery? I thought that's what I was already doing."

He huffed a laugh, almost making fun of me, I thought. "The road is long." Kevin pulled a blue book from his bookshelf, the same *Alcoholics Anonymous* book that had been in my room. "I'd like for you to read a chapter in this book, Lela. The first chapter. It's called 'The Doctor's Opinion.'"

I stared at him without understanding, lost in a haze. "Here, give me your book. I'll mark it." The Post-It-Note seemed to glow in the brightest-possible neon yellow. "In this chapter, you'll learn about alcoholism from the medical point of view. And the doctor who wrote the chapter talks about the strengths of a support group, the fellowship of Alcoholics Anonymous."

He returned the book to my open hand, then came around to my side of the desk, leaning his butt against the corner. He stared at me for a minute, smiling. "Lela, I think you're going to be one of the few who make it. I see it in you."

"Bullshit! You say that to everybody," I snapped.

Kevin continued smiling in his kind way; so kind that it was a bit unnerving. *Like the nurse... they must practice the heartless smile at home.* "No, not to everybody... in fact, I rarely say it." The smile remained when he asked serious questions. "Do you think you've hit your lowest point? Or do you want to risk more jail time, more insanity, lose your job, your car, your family?"

My throat closed as tears fell. With a hiccup of a sob, I said, "I've already lost my job. And with no money, I'll soon lose my van. More insanity, you say? I haven't been sane for a long time, Kevin. So, yeah, I'm the lowest I've ever been."

"Do you have children?"

I nodded, staring into space. "A son, Bo. He's seventeen."

"Then you have a lot to live for. And I understand your parents brought you here. Surely they love you and want you to have a good life."

Back to sit behind the desk, Kevin pulled an envelope from an open file, my chart I assumed. "And this is interesting. Your parents have written a letter, for you to read when you leave here... when you're detoxed and on the road to recovery. That's an unusual thing. It's clear they love you very much."

I couldn't speak. Kevin pushed the box of Kleenex closer and I took a few, wiping under my chin where the tears had dripped. My eyes were sore from so much crying; they burned, so I dared not rub them.

Kevin continued, "Here's my guess: for many years, you've surrounded yourself with people who didn't want the best for you."

I blew a sarcastic laugh. "That's for sure! I mean, my husband–"

He interrupted. "It's not just your husband, Lela." Kevin drilled a serious glare into my painful, watery eyes. "It's anybody and everybody who has enabled your drinking, the drinking that was killing you. You *had* to surround yourself with such people to justify it in your own mind."

I put my head down, feeling the sting of his words. He was right; I had rejected anybody who may have had my best interests at heart... including my family, in many ways. In the end, I'd left myself with nobody to trust. *That's why it's the end. But do you even remember what it feels like to trust somebody, or how to accept help?*

As if hearing my self-talk, Kevin said, "I hope you learn there are people who actually want to help you, and that you can trust those people." I stared at him, wondering what it would mean to let go and trust. *Dare I trust Kevin, who believes I'll succeed? I mean, maybe he works here because he wants to help people, even people like me.*

"You're at the crossroads where all alcoholics stand at some point, Lela. Trust me; I know that scary feeling. Been there, done that."

"You're an alcoholic?"

"Sober nineteen years." He smiled with glowing-white teeth as I shook my head with disbelief.

"Nineteen years is impossible!"

"Possible and true." He smiled sincerely then; my heart missed a beat. I felt a rush of what could only be called love coming from Kevin. He continued, "Let's go back to your room and I'll introduce you to the nurses who'll take care of you during the withdrawal process.

He stood by the door and gestured for me to go first. I was in a daze, out of the reality of sitting in a chair in a crazy hospital. Something clicked in my head. The conversation and thoughts I'd had in the last five minutes would determine my entire future and it all came together in a snap. To get sober, I had to trust the people who wanted to help me, the people who knew how to get sober and stay sober.

It was like trusting a plumber to fix a leak. I wouldn't know how to fix it; that's what a specialist is for.

Cold sweats, vomiting every hour, snatching the medicine from the faceless nurses, shaking while sipping the tea they insisted I drink. When I refused to drink their cold water, a burly male nurse inserted an I.V. in my arm. They tried to make me eat and, even though I was hungry, the thought of food nauseated me. I sipped at soup, took the ham off the sandwich for a bite or two. Nothing more. I gagged with every bite.

Throughout the week, I slept off and on, dreaming bizarre, frightful dreams. One was a definite nightmare. Bo was in a deep hole, like a well, and I couldn't reach him. He cried out to me... "Momma, Momma!" and oh-so-slowly morphed into an infant, crying and crying. I woke up with a jerk and a new resolve: I would get sober for Bo, the same as when I walked away from the train because of him. *Lela, you have to make up for some serious lost time.*

Starting on the fourth day, they made me go to the group sessions, twice a day. I tolerated them only because I could have a cigarette afterward. Starting on the fifth day, I had to go to the cafeteria with the group, even if I didn't eat, and I didn't.

On the sixth day, they tried to make me go to an AA meeting held somewhere in the guts of the hospital. I refused and was written up for it. I just wasn't ready to hear people talk about their own struggles when I couldn't bear to think of my own. And I seriously doubted the value of telling other people how much I wanted to get the hell out of there.

Kevin said my refusal to go was a bad sign. "Changing direction requires taking direction," he said, repeating it a gazillion times until I wanted to puke.

On the seventh day, I got out of bed and sat at the desk in my room. Tears flowed when I realized the enormity of what Kevin had said. "Now we start *real* recovery." Just because my brain was clear of alcohol didn't mean I was sober-minded. I knew if I could break out of there, I'd go straight to the liquor store. I wanted a drink as much as I didn't want it.

Kevin said to trust him; that concept pounded in my mind and I recited the word "trust" repeatedly in my mind. After a while, it became a calming mantra.

Untouched, the book with Kevin's neon Post-It-Note lay on my bolted-to-the-wall desk. Focus was difficult, but I scanned the marked page a bit. The chapter was in the form of a letter, written by a doctor to... somebody; I couldn't figure out who. Almost against my will, I began to read.

In formal-as-hell language, this doctor said alcoholism was a disease, an allergy. Then he described *me*, beginning with the hideous, selfish, visceral *need* I felt when I was thirteen years old... drunk on Miller beer in the gravel alley with those albino sisters.

He said alcoholics needed to drink to feel normal, *check*, and they thought everybody drank the way they did: to get drunk on purpose. *Check.* Also, alcoholics didn't have hangovers in the last stages of their drinking because a drink cured what they now considered a hangover. *Check.* And a morning drink meant they would drink all day. *Check.*

The author discussed "the phenomenon of craving." And all alcoholics, he said, lost friends and relationships with family. I thought of my sister Jennifer, my friend Debra, Damon, and Bo's dad, Andy. *Check, check and check.* He described my life, without even knowing me!

This "doctor," using elegant language, detailed my behavior and innermost feelings, and my inevitable downfall. He called it a "bottom." *Yep, that's me. That's what Kevin was asking about, I guess.*

At the end of the chapter, I flipped through other parts of the book, glancing at the titles of upcoming chapters. A few caught my eye: "There is a Solution" and "How it Works." Also written in fancy language, those chapters talked more about alcoholism, and how alcoholics share the same screwed-up ways of thinking. I scanned the pages for a while, stopping abruptly when the author mentioned something about a "spiritual experience."

Wait! Shit! It's talking about GOD. That's not what I thought! I don't WANT God! I don't NEED God! What's this religion bullshit? Am I being railroaded into a church? A cult? Not just no, but HELL NO!

I threw the book at the wall and collapsed, sobbing and growling.

I was clear in my thoughts as I screamed to the empty room. "Trusting *people* is one thing – maybe I can do that – but trusting a bullshit religious *theory* that nobody can prove? A *thing* that punishes people while it speaks of love? I *don't* and *won't* trust in such Almighty-God bullshit!"

Tears bloomed from my eyes; I was crushed that AA wasn't going to help me, desperate now for something that might. "DAMMIT!"

I curled up on the floor and cried for a half-hour, maybe more, then screamed at the ceiling. "What does *God* have to do with not drinking!" More tears, more anger, more hopelessness.

The scream brought the orderlies. Four of them picked me up like I was in a hammock and flung me on the plastic-wrapped bed. I answered, "Leave me alone!" to their barrage of questions; they eventually gave up and left. The burly guy, Harold, yelled over his shoulder as he left, "Five minutes, Ms.

Fox." I had no idea what he meant.

Desperate, I tried to reconsider my anti-religion stance, imagining the one, tiny "good thing" about the God of my childhood. With my eyes closed, I remembered a scene from a Sunday-school book when I was six-or-so. A square stock photo... a beam of sunlight bursting through the clouds. The caption underneath: "God is Everywhere."

That was the only visual that came to me, and though I willed it to change my broader views, it did not. Not one bit.

Everything around me fell flat, and I yelled at the ceiling again, "Spiritual experience, my ass! Go to hell, AA."

Ironically, I still have the copy of the *Alcoholics Anonymous* book I threw at the wall in 1999. The pages are full of markings in pen and pencil, and highlighters in a rainbow of colors, each reminding me of a different time I turned to the book for wisdom.

Over the years, I've used it to learn and to teach, and to see how perfectly my Dude matches AA's definition of "a Higher Power."

But, that shitty, pompous, bossy-as-hell blue book, I complained, talked about GOD specifically, dozens and dozens of times. And I would NOT swallow that bitter pill. Not for a long time.

RAW RECRUIT

CHAPTER 14

The psych-ward cafeteria was behind a set of mint-green steel doors and down a long hall. When the orderly blew his sharp whistle, two long tweets, I lined up with the other patients for the trip to dinner, feeling hungry for the first time in a week.

Two obese serving ladies plopped spoonfuls of turkey and dressing, potatoes, and baked apples onto plastic plates. The food looked good, I thought, but my stomach argued with every bite. I choked down only a few mouthfuls and slid my tray in the compost zone before the orderlies could scold me for wasting food.

Soon Paul blew the whistle again. Three short tweets this time, signaling it was time to parade back to the ward. But he took a left halfway down the hall, leading us to a room I'd never seen before.

There were about fifty chairs facing a desk, like a classroom. A few people sat here and there – normal-looking people, not patients. The moment our group entered, I lunged into a chair at the end of a row, sitting alone. More normals arrived, and I dared to catch a glimpse of them and their sparkling hygiene.

A bit uncomfortable, I realized how awful I must look. Four days without a shower, and I hadn't looked in a mirror since I began to detox. I had on jogging shorts, a wrinkled tank, and no bra – and I felt my curls glued to the left side of my head. But I probably looked like the rest of the crazies, I reasoned, and who would care? I wasn't trying to impress the normals, and the crazies were... well, crazy. Who cared about *them?* Not me.

From behind the desk, a guy asked me to scoot over in the row so more people could sit. I ended up sitting next to one of the normals, a curly-haired, thirty-something woman who smiled at me through round rimless glasses. When I returned the smile, it caused a nervous buzz in my ears, so I dropped the smile as fast as possible. But I'd been caught... or something. The woman continued to smile and cocked her head to the left like she was curious about me. I wished she would just quit smiling and mind her own business.

A man with a smooth black ponytail sat behind the desk, wearing khakis Kevin-style. The man's skin was smooth and sun-bronzed, and he spouted words of welcome with sincerity. "Let's have a meeting."

Oh shit, an AA meeting. My first. Holy shit. I already knew AA wasn't for me, but also knew the orderlies wouldn't let me leave. My sigh was loud enough for all to hear and somebody laughed.

Nervous tics. I stretched my neck; it cracked noisily, and I swallowed hard. Terror filled my veins, and I caught myself scanning for the exits, ready for a kick-ass panic attack to overtake me. Scared of the unknown, I suppose. This was all new, and as I breathed... *slowly, Lela, slowly...* I tried to keep an open mind, even about the God bullshit sure to come. The ponytail man read from a printout, defining AA. A fellowship, he said. Kevin had mentioned that word, too.

A normal person on my row read a list of the twelve steps. The first thing made sense: "We admitted we were powerless over alcohol." I understood that and liked the words. *Powerless. Yep. Because I can't control my drinking. Once I start, I can't stop. And I can't stay stopped because I go crazy.*

Then the man read said something about a power greater than ourselves. I remembered that phrase from the book I had thrown against the wall and immediately stiffened... waiting for the word I hated.

Sure enough, the next sentence: "We turned our lives over to the care of God as we understood Him." My jaw clenched and a low growling sound escaped my lips.

My heart rate had zoomed. *Just skip that part and listen to the rest. You want AA to work, right?* The next few sentences were non-religious, and I decided to hang my hopes on them. "Made a list of those we had harmed" echoed between my ears, imaging how long my list would be.

Then, dammit, it said to admit my wrongs to God. *Like a damn confession! What the hell is this? Now it's a Catholic program? Why do they insist on emphasizing the God stuff? What does God have to do with stopping drinking!?*

I sighed, giving up on the idea that AA could help me. No way to leave out the God, I was now convinced, counting the number of times he was mentioned in their basic twelve steps.

My thoughts reeled. How could I even *pretend* to trust a God I had slapped in the face so many times? Why would he have anything to do with me in the first place? If he exists, and if he loves everybody as they say, Lela Fox would be last on the list. She's just an old cheating drunk, selfish and slutty. *Of course he hates me! And I don't blame him. Bottom line: I can't turn my life over to God like the damn Baptists do. Get saved? Such bullshit!*

The smiling woman beside me put her hand on my arm and leaned to whisper in my ear. "Your Higher Power can be a doorknob or a shoe." I looked at her with shock, my eyebrows in a knot.

After a pause, I huffed a sarcastic laugh. The whole time, I thought she was a normal, not a patient. But then she smiled the normal smile again. Soft, clear eyes, styled gold-highlighted hair, clean and unwrinkled clothes. *A normal who talks crazy? Worship a shoe? She's obviously living in another world.*

As the meeting continued, my mind wandered to thoughts of the time I felt God beside me on the Bahamas beach... walking on the impossibly beautiful shoreline... just the two of us having a conversation, like it was normal or something. *Was that day's God real... and still around? Was he still listening to me like he did that day? If I joined this AA thing, would he talk to me again?*

A buzz began low in my eardrums, some weird sense of... *what the hell? Is this, like, me loving myself? Surely not!* Panicked, I remembered how strong those same feelings were on the beach; so strong I'd run away from them like a frightened toddler.

Suddenly, the group spoke in unison, startling me out of my thoughts. "Thanks for sharing," they said. Then a normal on the other side of the room talked about how he used to be selfish and now he's not. *Yeah, right. Lying alcoholic asshole.* I shut him out and looked around the room, amazed by how quickly I could ping-pong from "maybe God is for me" to "shut the hell up about God."

But the room was interesting, a distraction from my unease. A huge banner listed the twelve steps in black and red. On the other side, an identical banner with twelve traditions, whatever they were.

Framed quotes adorned the walls. "Keep it Simple" was my favorite, but there were a dozen or more. "Easy Does It" and "One Day at a Time" made sense. But there were a few about God and those eluded me. "But for the

Grace of God Go I" confused me the most. *What does that mean?*

A series of normal people shared; I heard one word of ten... totally lost. But I noticed something odd. When the normals talked, they introduced themselves as an alcoholic... duh. *Why else would you be here, idiot?*

Overall, I was bummed... saddened that AA turned out to be a church. *Can't I just be normal and not drink?* The meeting and the whole concept was such a disappointment because I had high hopes for a whole week. I hoped AA would help me, but I knew better now... not with the God stuff in there.

And the normal woman beside me saying crazy things baffled me most of all.

Pray to a doorknob? What a kook. She may look like a normal, but she's a fruitcake. Is that what recovery does... turn you into a fruitcake? Then count me out.

Several things were said in unison, seemingly random things. But eventually, I caught on and joined in the chorus a few times. Somehow, that part felt good, like being included in a group of normal people who didn't drink. That's all I wanted, anyway. The flashes of comfort here and there, no matter how short-lived, felt like freedom on a bright, sunny day.

I wanted to speak, to tell them to stop talking about God... to complain about how they were handling this whole thing. They were doing it wrong. Mostly, I wanted to scream, kick my feet, and cry like a kid throwing a fit. Either that or I wanted to run to my room and be alone. Instead, I let my tears fall and wrap under my jaw.

A pang in my gut made me lean forward in pain and once again, the woman beside me patted my shoulder and smiled. I thought it was creepy as hell, but somehow, I felt comforted. A cylinder of calm undulated through my body, inch by inch... from head to hips.

But the calm was zapped seconds later, when a ditzy-looking brunette said, "God is good." *And that sounds so juvenile! Like a little kid's prayer.*

The meeting lasted a long hour. I had understood little. Mostly I'd been pissed off, clenching my jaw each time I heard the word "God," and it was a frequently said word. At first, I had tried to just swallow my anger, but it seeped out. Then I'd tried to replace "God" with the original phrase, "Higher Power," and, admittedly, that had helped. I could handle the Higher Power concept, I thought, but the meeting confused me more than helped me.

I half-listened for another ten minutes, then everybody stood, formed a circle, and held hands. *What the hell?*

The normal woman grabbed my hand and pushed me toward the circle. Everybody chanted what they called the serenity prayer, "God grant me the serenity to change the things I can," something about courage "and the wisdom to know the difference." I'd never heard it and thought it was a cool prayer; it didn't sound so worship-y, even though it still said God.

Then, still holding hands, the people bounced their hands up and down and said, "Keep coming back" and something about working every day. *What does work have to do with being sober?*

The circle broke but the woman wouldn't let go of my hand. In fact, she reached for my left hand, too. As we stood face-to-face, fear and a weird feeling of fear shrouded me, and my tears returned. "Hi," she said, "I'm Jenny. And you're new?

A squeaky voice answered; I was surprised the voice was mine. "Uh, first meeting ever. But it's not for me."

"I saw you squirm every time somebody talked about God, but don't freak out, man. AA isn't religious."

I blew one sarcastic hoot, much louder than I wanted it to be. "Then what the hell *is* it?" I snapped. She didn't answer... and didn't let go of my hands. Calmly, slowly, and with careful kindness, the woman said, "Don't think of the God you knew as a kid. Your Higher Power doesn't have to be God or Jesus. You can make one up! Like I say, a doorknob, a shoe, the sunshine, a palm tree, a Pop-Tart. Anything that's *not yourself.* Because you can't get sober alone."

I didn't understand. She was talking nonsense, I thought. "But that guy said you have to worship God in AA. I heard it loud and clear! He said you *had to*, so what are you talking about?"

The woman smiled and squeezed my hands. "Girl, you don't *have* to do anything! And it's not *worship* – it's friendship and trust. All you really have to do is quit drinking and quit thinking."

Behind her rimless glasses, those sparkling eyes stared deep into mine with a caring I felt under my skin. Her voice was smooth, comforting. "Let yourself be guided. At a meeting, the group can be your guide. But when you're alone, you need some*one* or some*thing*, because you can't do it by yourself." I found no reply.

"Here. Let's sit for a sec." She let go of my hands. Perched on one of the metal chairs, she dove in her purse to find a pen and scrap of paper. "My phone number," she said, smashing the paper into my left hand. "Jenny Jenkins, okay. I'd love it if you would call me. And if you can keep an open mind, I can explain my Higher Power and how she keeps me sober."

"She?"

"Yep. My Higher Power is a she. Simply put, I assembled her from the leftovers of the fire-and-brimstone bullshit I grew up hating. She's my doorknob, you could say." Jenny smiled, wrinkling her freckled nose.

Despite my desire to *not* like her, I felt drawn into her aura; she seemed to glow with confidence.

She asked my name and, like a good salesperson, used it in the next sentence. "Lela, if you want to stay sober, I'll teach you how." I felt intrigued, but pressured. She was pushing me to listen to her an I wasn't cool with that. She looked like she knew something about me, something only a spy would know. My gut reaction was to blow her off and run.

After an uncomfortable pause, I followed my gut. Without saying goodbye, I turned and ran to catch up with the group of crazies.

Jenny called after me. "You are powerless!"

I shouted back, "You are a fruitcake!"

It turns out Jenny Jenkins wasn't a fruitcake at all, not even a whack-job. She'd been sober for twelve years and went to psych-hospital meetings to help the rawest of newcomers. Counseling fresh-out-of-detox women was what she called her "service privilege." The twelfth of the twelve steps.

She became a relentless challenger to my twisted ways of thinking and taught me how to be humble and keep an open mind… concepts totally foreign to me at the time.

With Jenny's insistence and guidance, I learned how to be honest with myself, and how to trust and love others. These concepts had been foreign to me since age thirteen, since the day I first met the hideous ogre of alcoholism.

In those precarious months with Jenny at my side, I clawed a path to emotional sobriety on a steep and treacherous mountain… three steps forward and two steps back. Without Jenny to catch me, I would have fallen off that mountain. Or worse, I would have swung even farther to the dark side.

I thought she was a super-hero, a Wonder Woman, and I'll never forget her.

THE MOMENT OF TRANSITION
STEPPING INTO LIFETIME NUMBER SIX

Packed and ready, I lay back against the headboard waiting for the Recovery Resources driver to pick me up. Lost in my thoughts, I remembered a chorus from my childhood: my sisters cheering, "Ta-da!" when I successfully turned a cartwheel... their hour-long instruction session had finally paid off. "Yay for Lela!" they screamed.

Then Karen ran inside to get Mom, begging me to show her my new talent. More cheers for Lela.

And because my mother was hell-bent to foster her children's confidence, she rewarded me with a bright-pink candle in my biscuit at dinner. It was a happy memory; I felt proud that day... and overjoyed that I'd made my family proud.

Then Kevin brought the letter to my room. The letter Mom and Daddy had left for me to read when I left this crazy place.

When I opened that letter, I entered Lifetime Number Six, a completely new phase of development in the roller-coaster life of Lela Lynn Fox.

That moment also opened my life to new possibilities, and I was 100 percent convinced I'd succeed. I believed the only thing between me and becoming a sober and productive human being was thirty hard days in rehab. Then my life would be joyous and serene from that point forward. Piece of cake, I thought.

Now I laugh at my naivety, but perhaps it was there for a reason. If I'd known what I would face in this new Lifetime, I would've run the other way. Yep, I would have died drunk.

Even more hilarious now, I thought it would be a simple and natural transition to a "normal life" like all smart, talented forty-year-old women enjoyed. I'd get a good job, meet a nice man, find a cozy apartment, get a dog, and relentlessly work toward the Great American Dream, white picket fence and all. A long-overdue dream for Lela Fox.

Reading the letter... Mom's careful script of encouraging words, brimming with undying love and support, and Daddy's barely legible scribbles and famous "Wedgehead" signature.

What I remember most was his closing line, "Head first, Tiger!" It was a tradition of sorts, a flashback to his words when I was a child. The "Tiger" was me in this phrase, the one who had the world by its tail according to my biggest fan. And "Head first" was a reference to his boxing days... which had evolved to mean "Be brave" and/or "Lead with your best shot." It was something only the two of us had shared; words of encouragement only a Daddy can give.

It sounded like nothing to most people, but to me, it meant the world.

After reading the letter ten times, maybe more, I laid it aside to dry; the weight of my tears had already puckered the paper, and I knew this letter would be one to keep. It represented the beginning of a new Lifetime.

Damn, Lela! You haven't felt proud of yourself since you were eight years old! Now you have a chance. Don't fuck it up.

Deep breath. *Here we go.*

Taking the step from Lifetime Number Five, through the bright glitter and goodness into Lifetime Number Six, would be ethereal, harp music and all. It was within moments of happening.

THE ROAD TO REHAB
CHAPTER 15

"Get in." That's all she said. No pleasantries.

An accident on 95-South slowed our progress as the afternoon sun beat through the windshield. I sat in the front passenger seat of a twelve-passenger van beside an Amazon-sized woman, blonde with a professional over-dye in a bright rainbow of Pride colors. Unusual, but gorgeous.

We were on the way to Recovery Resources in Boca Raton. A mere forty miles away, but with this much traffic... who knew how long it would take?

I tried to joke with the driver, asking, "Are we there yet?" but she either didn't understand my humor or dismissed me altogether. After a few other attempts at conversation, I quit trying. We drove in silence, on the road to rehab.

That morning, Kevin and I had a heart-to-heart discussion. He described the realities of a dual-diagnosis rehab and how I could make the most of it. But there was a problem with Kevin: the man wouldn't shut up!

Despite my pleas that he put a plug in it, he kept blabbing about how I was "one of the few who could fight the fight" or "sure to make it," blah, blah. I felt so much pressure that I hyperventilated in his office. He gave me a paper bag to breathe into; he had a stack of them on his desk as if hyperventilating patients stopped by for fun.

Then, as he rambled about the benefits of feeling pressure to succeed, I lost my breakfast on the floor beside his desk. A little splashed on his swivel chair.

So there, KEVIN!

☼ ☼ ☼ ☼ ☼

The Gay-Pride-hair woman finally talked to me, but her words were measured with care. She introduced herself. "I'm Drinnen, by the way."

"Cool name."

"I'll pass that compliment along to my parents."

"Funny."

"I'm here only for your amusement."

I laughed, almost snorted. "Yeah-yeah. My bet is you're here to kick my ass. Trying to weasel your way into my head and force me to be normal."

"Normal is just a setting on the dryer. Forget that kind of language."

More silence. Drinnen barked this time, "Do you have a sponsor?"

"I don't know. Um, there's a girl I've talked to a few times. Jenny. But she's kinda crazy. She thinks God is a woman."

"That's not so crazy. It's *her* Higher Power, not yours. So it's really none of your business."

"But..." *Oh, Jeez, this girl is crazy like Jenny! I KNEW it! Sober is crazy and here I am... hoping to get smart and stable. I'm screwed... seems like I'll get stupid and crazy instead.*

I started again. "You may not understand, Drinnen, but I don't want to get *crazy*... I want to get *sober*. And so far, I'm batting zero. Is every alcoholic a fruitcake? Some kind of free-spirit deviant?"

Drinnen spoke through a smile. "You've been in the hospital where crazy people gather, girl. Know what I mean?" Then she grinned wide, turning toward me briefly.

Oh, a smile. Maybe she DOES have a personality after all. "But about this Higher Power thing, Drinnen... I'm confused. I mean, for what it's worth, Jenny first told me to worship a shoe, another suggestion was a damn Pop-Tart! The whole 'spiritual awakening' bullshit pisses me off."

"Take what you need and leave the rest."

I guess I was expecting an argument, a plea to believe or attempt to "convert me," or maybe just further explanation of what Jenny had said. I wanted to hear that I could be sober in AA without believing in God. I wanted to hear anything but the non-answer that Drinnen gave, and I didn't know how to respond.

So I changed the subject, asking about the curriculum and other patients at Recovery Resources, probing her with a barrage of questions.

She talked for a while, information-only in a snippy tone, and I learned quite a bit. At my insistence, she explained a typical day at the center, where I'd have one-on-one sessions with either the psychiatrist or my therapist and three group meetings. "Then we all go to an AA meeting somewhere in town. Every night... a different meeting every night."

"So no getting out of AA, huh?"

"No chance in hell."

I asked more about the group meetings and she explained with a quote that stuck. "We're here to re-wire your alcoholic brain."

"I need a new circuit breaker or something?" I laughed, just continuing the metaphor.

"If you try to do it yourself, you'll get burned." The smile again, in profile.

"Oh, how shocking!"

"I'm glad you think this is fun. Because it won't be later. Your thinking is pretty fucked up right now."

"My thinking is fine. And I'm not shaking anymore after a whole week in detox so... I don't really get it."

She snapped her head to look at me, eyes wide with surprise. "You think you're going to be 'cured' from a week without booze?" She cackled, which pissed me off.

"Chill out, Drinnen! Be gentle with a newcomer." Sarcastic, I clucked as a mother chicken would.

"It's just a matter of timing. Are you sick and tired of being sick and tired?"

"I heard that at the last meeting in the damn hospital. But you know what... I'm not sick. I'm just tired of screwing everything up. Tired of making bad decisions, and tired of things passing me by when I don't know what's going on. I used to have an edge, ya know... I was sharp, smart, nothing got by me. Slowly, everything melted, all my abilities disappeared. And I just watched it happen."

"That's a way to phrase 'sick and tired,' Lela. Sick of how you were living and too screwed-up to change it."

"Oh. I thought maybe I was... different. Ya know?"

Another cackle. "Sorry. You're not different." Another chuckle, then two. Then she spoke to the roof of the van... as if to God or something, "*All* drunks think they're unique. Completely different from the others!"

Insistent, I interrupted. "But everybody would have a diff–"

"Nope. Sorry. No buts. You're not special. Just an old drunk who thinks too much. How many years did you drink?"

Doing the math in my head, which wasn't easy with a foggy brain, I answered "Almost 27."

"So... according to *my* sponsor, you'll be *halfway* straightened out in 27 years."

"Bullshit!"

"*Not* bullshit."

"But Kevin said I was one of the ones who could make it... fight the fight, walk the walk... all that shit."

"Then you have something to look forward to, but it won't happen for at least ten years, so don't think you're special. You're just one of us and if you believe otherwise, you won't be walking the walk at all."

Stabbing pain behind my eyeballs began, and I knew I was ready to cry. I had expected a pep talk, not a gruff gay bitch with a bad attitude. *Maybe she's not sober in her head yet. Maybe she's not "destined to make it" like Kevin said about me.*

I huffed a snarky *hmmph* and opened my mouth to speak. She held up her palm to shush me. Yep, Drinnen had more to say. "Nothing personal, Lela, but you're a nobody. A nobody with no power. Until you surrender to a *higher* power, you'll be miserable. And if you want to get sober, you have to believe that. Be humble. Be grateful. Be open-minded. That's how you get sober at Recovery Resources."

Why is she being mean to me? Can't she see how scared I am? The anxiety that had been chewing on my stomach lining all morning came forward with a gush, tasting like bile. Determined to *not* lose my cookies in that nice van, I let the silence wash over me. The buzz between my ears, so familiar by then, began in earnest.

My nausea waned in a few minutes, but I was tense, with a clenched jaw, clenched fists, stiff as a tree. *You're trapped, and you asked for it. How stupid can you be, Lela Fox?*

It took a while to speak again, but I had to find out what I was up against... if this kind of cruel treatment would continue. I croaked a question. "So is this some kind of, like, reform school... or like what they do in the Army? Break you down to build you up?"

"Not exactly, and I didn't mean to scare–" She looked at me and did a double-take. "Oh, no! I *did* scare you." She balled her fist and bonked herself on the forehead, mumbling. "Sorry. There's nothing to be afraid of, really, it's just..."

"Just what?" I demanded. When the silence lasted too long, I repeated my demand.

Calm and cool, she changed her tune and spoke in a kind, melodic voice. "Here's the deal: Recovery Resources... we call it R&R... it's not a military school at all. And it's not like jail or a psych hospital. You're free to leave anytime. All I'm saying is that if you think you're different from the people you're getting ready to meet, you'll be one of the losers, even if you stay. The success rate at R&R is no different from the national norm... which I think is like three of 100 people... don't quote me on that figure but it's close."

I dared not speak; my eyes were brimming with tears and I refused to let a single one fall. But all varieties of emotions jerked me. I was mad as hell that Drinnen-Bitch would be so mean to me... afraid I'd made a very bad choice – not just about Recovery Resources specifically, but rehab in general. Mostly, I doubted any of this AA shit would work in the first place.

All of it came to a boiling point.

When the first tear fell, I turned to look out of the window. Pines and palms and perfectly manicured Zosia grass; South Florida and its happy-green appeal.

"Here we go!" Drinnen spoke to the back of my head and I assumed she was ready to hassle me about something else. But I assumed wrong.

We had finally passed the area of the wreck. I looked at the spot carefully, eager to see the carnage, but there was nothing but a tow truck and glass on the highway, half-swept by a sweaty cop.

I couldn't un-hear what Drinnen had said. Some of it I'd already heard in the two AA meetings I'd attended, but her approach was downright rude! *She laughed at me! Treated me like a child! Then did a 180 and tried to play nice. I can't trust this chick any further than I can throw her.*

Her comments had opened my mind, maybe, but fear enveloped me... it radiated from my skin like a magnet pulling an aura, pumping loudly with fear and dread. In and out and in and out, boom-boom-boom until it filled the space between my ears.

There was nothing but silence for the last five miles on I-95, assuming Drinnen couldn't hear the voices in my head tell me I was a born loser and the rehab thing was like pouring money down the drain. *Stupid, stupid, stupid! Get real, Lela Fox.*

☼ ☼ ☼ ☼ ☼

My hands were shaking when the van pulled to the rear entrance of R&R. And when Drinnen gave the order: "Get out," my legs didn't cooperate.

She'd slipped back into drill sergeant mode it seemed, and I'd never been so scared in my life. *What have you signed up for, Lela? Stopping drinking is one thing, but being treated like a slave day after day? Not cool.* I wasn't going to deal with that for thirty days, no way. *Don't they know I've already spent eight days in hell?!*

The pride-rainbow blonde barked "Leave your suitcase in the van." I assumed the R&R people would search it as the hospital people did, and my fragile pride took a hit. Drinnen led me through the back door of the building to a room with a wall of windows on the left. It was about half the size of a football field, maybe, and lit by an excess of fluorescent lights. I assumed this was the group room, as they called it at the crazy hospital, and a meeting was in progress.

About fifty people sat in a lumpy circle; I felt pulverized by a hundred eyeballs... instant feelings of being in the wrong place, feeling naked in public, feeling small and busted. I looked away from the drill of their stares and at the floor. Fear pounded my heart and the dirty taste of terror filled the back of my throat.

Drinnen whispered, "Go on." I hadn't realized I'd stopped just a few feet from the door. I stepped forward, but obviously I wasn't fast enough for her; she swerved around to lead. "Follow me." Drinnen headed for the stack of chairs at the back of the room, then pushed a chair into a gap in the circle.

I sat as quick as I could. *You sure as hell don't want to stand out in THIS crowd. Stay under the radar, Lela... way under.*

Not comfortable looking the patients in the eye, l looked at my chair. Hard plastic and metal, not flimsy plastic like those in the psych ward. *So these people aren't as prone to throwing things.* I relaxed a notch knowing that.

The walls were washed with the same pale-yellow, a color I knew was supposed to calm nerves, keep things tranquil. Unpolished brownish-creamish-beige commercial tile covered the floor. Straight ahead was a hall of offices, and to the right, a slightly ajar door to what looked a recreation room. I could see the corner of a ping-pong table and the screen of an old video game console.

Mom had done the office stuff while I suffered through detox in the crazy hospital. I was so grateful to have insurance, and I assumed Mom's family's money had trickled down so she could afford to pay the rest. I knew it cost a fortune, and happy I couldn't remember the exact amount.

But with everything done in my absence, I didn't have a booklet or any information to orient me. No, they just plopped me here, unaware and scared.

The silent leader of the group wore horn-rimmed glasses and a tropical-print shirt over a pair of well-worn jeans... the very opposite of what Counselor Kevin had worn at the psych hospital. He sat with his legs spread wide, as most men do, but for some reason, I found it inappropriate.

A woman was speaking, and he watched her every move... a hefty bleach-blonde girl with a large, multi-pastel tattoo on her chest cried at high volume and spoke incoherently. I heard every third word or so, lost in my own fear. Fear, amazement, confusion. No, my feelings were stronger than that; I felt pure terror.

The group was eerily similar to the crazy-hospital group, minus the worst of the psychotics. But I'd never seen such tattoos! It wasn't yet the year to be considered cool, and I was still a purist Tennessean about piercings and tattoos, only venturing as far as a second hole in my right ear. Big whoop.

These addicts, though... they were *covered* with tats! Like *artwork!* One guy sported an arm-full, connected together like a painting, stopping at who-knows-where under his blue shirt. Same with his right leg, extending into the hem of his shorts.

That roused a memory of the man I called "King Cobra" who date-raped me when I was eighteen; a memory I'd managed to squash for years. I shuddered, pushing it away. It wasn't the time for adding additional fears and feelings. One thing a time, please.

Most of the patients were young, but there were three women about forty, like me, and one gentleman in his late fifties or so. I glanced at the women one at a time but looked away when they returned my gaze.

Drinnen had said the patient group was a 60/40 mix of addictions to drugs vs. alcohol. This perplexed me and I wondered why they would group us. Drinnen tried to explain, but my first thought was a drug addict was "lower" than an alcoholic... more hopeless, more homeless, more distasteful.

The thought was stubborn; it wouldn't go away despite her explanation of "the same recovery goal."

I scanned each patient, noting each weird thing – and there were plenty of weird things. Orange streaks through a guy's hair, a girl who looked about twelve wearing a nose ring like I'd never seen. Again, if I caught their eye, I looked away, but I was determined to find out if their drug of choice was injectable, drinkable, smokable, or snortable.

In a heartbeat, the feeling of superiority fell as if it had been ripped from my clutches; I felt my fear building to a crescendo. *Help, here it comes... that deafening buzz between my ears, building... building. Damn! So loud! Even louder than the weight of their stares!*

I gasped for air, reaching for my throat, and I felt myself shrink. *They're all looking at you, Lela. You're not like them, not at all, and you're not supposed to be here! Just go home to the farm, go home to Daddy. You're not ready for this... and look at them judging you. THEY know you're a joke, an imposter, and good-for-nothing loser. Run! How far to the door? Where will you go? Is your suitcase still in that van? Shit! Fuck! Get out while you can!*

A millisecond before I jumped to my feet to run, the group leader said, "And hello, Lela. Welcome to Recovery Resources!" His glasses flashed in a reflection of the window; I couldn't see his eyes, only the upturn of his mouth. *Smiling. He's smiling. But look, the rest of them aren't smiling. Oh, God! Help!* He said, "Relax, Lela, we're all in the same boat." The comment was probably meant to help me relax, but nothing could break the armor of my terror.

Breathe... breathe. In through your nose and out through your mouth. Slow, Lela, slow. I breathed as they taught me in detox. Though I did it three times, my heart still raced and my breathing was much too fast. I added "light-headed" to my list of ailments.

You're in rehab, Lela Fox. Don't screw it up and you'll have a chance at a whole new life. I talked to myself as the group continued, zoning in and out on what they said.

The leader cut a rambling patient off in mid-sentence. A young guy, another bleach blonde picked up where she left off, talking down to the group and acting cocky. Among other snarky comments, he said he didn't need to be there, and they could all go screw themselves. I wondered why he didn't walk out if he felt that way. There were no bars on the windows, right?

I didn't see the similarities of my thinking and his until the group leader thanked him for "sharing." *Odd word, especially because he was just bitching.*

My breathing had returned to normal... something about the snotty attitude of that guy brought me to around. The ping-pong ball in my head came to a rest. *Yes, I want to be sober. Yes, I need to be here. Of course I'm scared, just like being in the psych hospital, but I can do this... I can do this... I can do this!*

Forget Drinnen's nay-sayer predictions! You can do it! And these people... these, uh, misfits... they're the ones who can help you.

I had shocked myself by feeling so close to the "misfits" already. How could that be? I realized I'd absorbed Drinnen's comment about being no better or worse than them, no matter what they looked like. *They're just as powerless as you are, Lela.* I squinted with confusion after that thought because Kevin had also said power was found at R&R.

The rehab's Kevin-equivalent walked to an oversized green chalkboard on wheels, parked in the back of the room. Smeared in places, the board featured a drawing of what looked like an upside-down business-organization chart. The label on the bottom box: SOBRIETY. I wondered why it wasn't at the top.

His back was to us, but he never stopped talking as he wrote words on the left side of the diagram: HONESTY, WILLINGNESS, TRUST, all caps. He dotted the chalk near these three words to emphasize them. *Bonk. Bonk. Bonk.* But I wasn't listening. Instead, I looked dreamily at those three words, wondering if they were the keys to getting sober.

Honesty... yeah, I can do that.

Willingness... well, I would do almost anything to get out of the hole I'm in, to escape the drunken hopelessness of my life. Is that what willingness means?

Then, ouch... oh, hell: trust. I don't trust myself to not drink; I don't know how. And as Jenny told me, I don't trust God, nor any human, for any reason, whatsoever. Kevin seconded that. So am I doomed?

I'd zoned out as that thought churned in my mind. When reality returned, the group leader said, "So God, or your Higher Power, can stand by you as you get and stay sober. You can do it if you're willing to work."

That God bullshit again. Well... Alcoholics Anonymous isn't the end-all and be-all of sobriety, surely. There are other ways.

I didn't hear the words that ended the meeting, but suddenly people were up and walking around in the room. Someone yelled, "Put up your chair," and scooting sounds filled my ears. I stayed in my seat, listening to the beat of my heart and trying to hear through the buzz in my head.

Only two of the older women remained in the circle, talking to each other quietly. Talking about me, I was sure of that. The taller one was about my age, maybe a few years older. Beside her sat another mature-looking woman, early forties, probably. While the other patients slid chairs to the stack near me, the two women turned one at a time to smile at me. Fearing the worst, I faked a smile back.

Oh, hell, what now? Those two are plotting against me already!

EARTH TO LELA
CHAPTER 16

I felt a presence beside me. Automatically, I winced, raised my arms and snapped my head around, expecting a threat. But no, it was a tower of a man with sparkling blue eyes above two scrubbed-pink cheeks. "Hey, hey, hey!" he sang, the voice imitating Fat Albert, a cartoon character from my youth. "I'm Eli Schofield, your assigned counselor here." A goofy smile remained after the words stopped.

Though he'd quickly defined himself as friendly, my heart still beat rat-a-tat. "Hi, Eli." It was all I could squeak out; fear had snapped my vocal chords shut.

"This is your lucky day," he said, beaming with a sneaky smile, "You get to see my messy office!" I guess he saw the confusion on my face and explained further. "Paperwork and stuff, plus we need to get to know each other and get started on a treatment plan." Still in a fog, I couldn't comprehend what he said; my eyes roamed his face, his frizzy blonde hair, his Rolling Stones t-shirt.

I guess the pause was long; Eli chanted, "Earth to Lela," waving his hands in front of my face. I shook my head, trying to find the reality of this place and this man. It seemed Eli understood my muddled thoughts; he said, "To my office, right?" I nodded. "It's just down the hall."

I'm not sure what I expected, but it wasn't his "don't-worry-be-happy" approach. *A counselor in a Rolling Stones t-shirt? Is that cool as hell or inappropriate and unprofessional?* Walking behind him, I noticed Eli's "party in the back," a ponytail almost to his waist. A shiny comma of blonde against the navy of his shirt.

I felt like a Goody-Two-Shoes... judging people as my mother would and expecting those in charge to be pristine in appearance, have a clean driving record, and their ducks in a row. *I mean, aren't they like DOCTORS, even the counselors? Aren't I paying enough for them to afford nice clothes?*

Questioning everything about the place now, I sat my straitlaced ass on the seat. *So maybe I should be a South Florida rebel, too. Pink hair and artistic tattoos, at least. But no, here I sit with a pale Tennessee tan, with no personality showing on my body.* No nose piercings or shredded clothes, not even the clunky shoes everybody there seemed to favor.

Open your mind to the diversity of the youngsters in this place, Lela. Be accepting of the weird... just like Karen has tried to teach you. Thinking of Karen, I gave myself permission to relax but wrote a letter in my mind, describing the oddities within the R&R walls. She would be so interested in how it looked, felt, and smelled.

"Welcome to chaos," Eli said, referring to his office. He had told the truth; it looked like a bomb had exploded in the center of a 10x10 room. Papers everywhere, covering every surface of the mismatched furniture, open drawers on the file cabinets in the corner, and maybe fifteen Dr. Pepper cans dotting the bedlam.

He sat on a swivel chair and, quite cordially, said, "Consider this the official welcome to Recovery Resources, Lela Lynn Fox. Welcome to the first step in sobriety."

The full name, huh? Fuck. All I could do was squeak a greeting from my desert-dry mouth, "Thank you, Eli." I couldn't remember feeling so nervous in my adult life. An overwhelming urge to run and hide, the infantile need for my Mommy beat like a pulse.

Eli cut his eyes at me and reached to the left... into a small fridge, and suddenly a bottle of water appeared. I drank greedily. "Better?" I nodded and Eli continued, "The two of us will meet in therapy sessions three times a week, to monitor your progress, make sure you have what you need, solve any problems. I'm your connection, you could say. My job is to do anything and everything to keep you on the road to recovery."

I nodded, swallowing hard.

"Okay, we start with this questionnaire. Insurance requirements, right?" He rolled his eyes and the point was clear: he despised the paperwork. *Oh, he's trying to be friends with me. Not like a doctor at all... and that's on purpose.* "But it's also an assessment of where you are." He sat forward, elbows on his knees. "Ready to bare your soul?" He must have seen my eyes open wide, and he chuckled. "I always start with that teasing line, Lela. No need to bare your soul just yet. But I can tell a lot about a person just from their reaction to that one question.

I wasn't amused but had to ask, "And what did you learn about me in such a short time?"

"Seems you're going to be a difficult case, Lela." Despite the ominous nature of that answer, he maintained a smile, open and on the verge of delightful laughter. It seemed impossible not to like him.

Within the next few minutes, I noticed my heart rate had returned to normal. I remember watching his lips move but don't remember much of what he said. However, one question from the multitude of stapled pages stood out like the beacon on a lighthouse. Eli asked how much and how often I drank. Thinking quickly, I told him a bald-headed lie, saying I drank only a pint of vodka a day and started around noon.

Eli scribbled on the page, talking as he wrote. "I only ask for curiosity. Like everybody else, you've minimized the amount. So in my notes, I'm doubling it.

"That's not fair!" I objected, but he repeated that "everybody" lied and said he didn't hold it against me.

"Lela, even if you'd been completely honest, I would write twice the amount."

He should have tripled it but I said nothing.

Eli continued, "So... by 'start around noon,' do you mean when you first wake up?" With a sigh, I realized he would write that on the paper, anyway, so I admitted the truth. A few more questions and I realized it would do no good to lie to Eli. The man saw right through me. *Face it, Lela: you're not special here. Just a lousy drunk like the rest of the people... just like Drinnen said.*

Twice I tried to brag about not drinking at work but he ignored the comment both times. It was a lie, but it sounded good. At the third mention, I asked, "Don't you want to write that down?" Eli shook his head and moved onto the next question. *Damn, the one good thing I could lie about and he ignores me! Not fair! I should complain!*

Then I realized there was nobody to complain to, nobody at all. I needed *them*, not the other way around. I had no power in that place. It was a new way to look at things for such an uppity, self-focused drunk like me.

Eli asked about my family and friends, my "support system," he called it.

With a dramatic yelp, I burst into tears with overwhelming gratitude for Mom and Dad, and for my sisters. Eli threw a box of tissues my way. When he mentioned friends, I sadly admitted I had none in Florida except my live-in nanny and had lost touch with those in Tennessee except infrequent cards and calls. It was a stretch, but maybe I could give Lola and Damon the title of "supportive friends."

Lola had been my employee and protector; Damon my long-term guardian and pinky-swear friend. He was the one I called when I was lonely and just needed a body nearby. But I loved his heart; he meant the world to me.

Oh, how I miss my friends! Maybe I can get sober and reunite with them... so many friends I've lost! One by one, I've sent them running; appalled by my too-much-fun, way-too-loud, way-too-free attitude.

And Jennifer! Oh, Jeezus, Jennifer! How great it would be to be friends with my sister again! Do this, Lela! Get sober! The rewards are sitting right in front of you.

Eli waved his hands in front of my face. "Earth to Lela! Hello in there!" I came out of my trance and apologized. He said, "No problem. I hope your thoughts were good ones, about the life you'll have as a sober person."

"How did you know what I was thinking?"

He chuckled, leaned back and put his feet on the corner of his desk. That pose cracked me up; it looked like a cartoon, but his tone was serious. "I knew what you were thinking because I know you already. you're not much different than anybody else who comes in here, though you think you most definitely are. You're at the bottom emotionally and physically, and probably financially. You're hopeful but resistant, doubtful but determined, worried that you'll be boring and dull without the alcohol... wondering if you'll ever meet a partner within your new life... am I right?"

I nodded, feeling like a diaphanous piece of gauze in the wind.

"Just trust... do what we say even if you don't understand it. See, we've been where you are. Every counselor here is a recovered addict or alcoholic – all eight of us. We listened to our rehab counselors and made it, against all odds. I mean, we didn't know each other but we all have the same history. And after getting sober, all eight of us then went to school to study addiction and addiction treatment. *That's* how we can predict how you'll feel and what you'll do."

My eyes widened as instinct caused me to be as small as possible... so he couldn't see me so clearly. My privacy had been violated and my fear was in full view, I was convinced. As if reading my mind, he smiled and said, "Lela, I know you, but you can trust me. And when you learn to do that, I can help you get better. Seriously. Not that I'm superhuman, understand, but I've been in the field for fifteen years... helped hundreds of people just like you, okay?"

I zoned out here and there as he spoke more on this topic, and when I checked back into reality, he said, "One thing is for sure, Lela: I am 100 percent on your side." Eli's smile was sincere and we held a gaze for a long five seconds. Slowly, I smiled. I believed him and was surprised that I believed him; I'd trusted few authority figures in my life and none in the last five years or so.

He swung his feet from the desk and stood up in the same motion. "Ready to see your room?"

"I just hope my roommates aren't crazy people who th–"

Eli interrupted. "Oh wait, this is Friday! Grocery store day. And three o'clock. We're right on time!" He explained the set-up with groceries. Mom had paid for that, ahead of time, too, evidently. Each patient had a $50.00 weekly budget to buy whatever they wanted at Publix, giving the receipt to the R&R counselor at the exit of the store.

"But what if I don't spend the full fifty? Does it carry over? Do I get a refund?" Concerned and kind of pissed off, because I didn't want to waste Mom's money. *She's already paid a fortune... I bet she cashed in a retirement account or something.*

"Aha! We've got a worrier. You can chill, Lela. We're not here to rip you off. But yes, you'd get a refund. Your first grocery trip... you need to know the rules. Spend as much as you want, but we monitor what you buy. We don't allow a bunch of junk food and there are strict limits on personal care products so you can't buy just eyeshadow all the time. Got it?"

I nodded, again frozen in fear. Eli continued, "You'll find yourself hungry as you get farther away from alcohol. So listen to your body... it will tell you what it needs.

"I just don't eat much and I don't cook. Unless you call Mac 'n Cheese from the box cooking. And this is bullshit because you and I won't agree on what's nutritious, I'm sure. Some days I eat all fruit, maybe two days in a row, then somedays the thought of food turns my stomach."

"Your file says you're about ten pounds underweight. Eat! If you don't, we'll start managing your diet and I don't think you want that."

"Manage my diet? No way! Are you the Great and Mighty Oz or

something?"

Eli laughed, grabbing a green booklet from his bookshelf. "Here's the rule book. Study it tonight. You'll probably be quizzed by the overnight staff."

"What the hell? Just when I started to relax, you start throwing bullshit rules at me!"

But Eli had scooted behind me and left the office. I flipped through the green booklet, speaking to the empty room. "Damn! There must be thousands of rules here! This isn't what I signed up for!"

I sat in Eli's office alone for several minutes, reading the ridiculousness in the green rule book. There seemed to be no rhyme or reason to the rules, just limits on damn-near everything. *Who do they think they are? And what forty-year-old woman needs to be watched like a child?!*

I set the green book aside. *What forty-year-old woman needs a babysitter? I know this isn't summer camp, for Hell's sake, but I refuse to be a prisoner with this bullshit discipline. I'm outta here.*

Three steps from Eli's office... three steps toward the exit, I turned back. To myself: "I guess THIS forty-year-old woman needs bullshit discipline to stay sober. Only because I'm desperate enough to endure anything.

Rules. Regulations. OCD procedures. Being monitored, managed, and manipulated. The fact that someone else made decisions for me, about what would be best for me, made me crazy. In fact, I was incensed!

The 50/50 mixture of Resentment for being in a controlled environment and Gratitude for the same... I felt torn apart for thirty days. I knew I was in the right place but the rules were hard to swallow and their taste was bitter.

After ten days or so, I realized most of the rules were, literally, random... not designed to protect us. Instead, they were set to teach us concepts like Humility, Respect for Authority, and Discipline.

I grumbled about the rules, but I followed them. Because something had changed; I had no rebel left in me. I didn't want to be kicked out of rehab and I didn't want to waste Momma's money. What I wanted most was to be sober, to succeed, to let my family stop worrying about me.

I wasn't an angel by any means; when they made a rule specific to me, that I stop telling them how to run the place, I stopped trying to convince them of my superior logic. I didn't want to rock the boat.

Those who did rock the boat weren't actually kicked out... they usually walked before R&R completed the paperwork. They left AMA, Against Medical Advice. I shivered to think I'd be desperate enough to do that and leave myself on the streets.

The rules separated the men from the boys, so to speak... those ready for sobriety and those at rehab only because their parents or the courts made them go.

I realize now, twenty years later: the rule-breakers were doomed long before they broke the rules. They were the people who could not or would not completely give themselves to the simple program of recovery; those constitutionally incapable of being honest with themselves.

By obeying the dumb rules, I came to understand Humility, Honesty, even Trust. But I had no idea how much of these three things were required to maintain sobriety.

Being Lela Fox, I had to learn the hard way.

GROCERIES & GOODNIGHTS
CHAPTER 17

I walked into the group room where four patients roamed. And one patient sitting: the obese twenty-something guy slumped in a chair, asleep and drooling.

Two men in their mid-30s were playing Tic-Tac-Toe on the chalkboard and laughing like banshees. X's and O's covered the board, large ones and small ones. These were adults, acting like children, which confused and amused me at the same time. They were having fun. *Can people have fun while struggling to get sober? Can I do that?*

I postponed a cigarette and roamed around the center to find out what was what. I sauntered into the rec room and found four ping-pong players, smacking high fives with the paddles. A little scared, I stood back, afraid a paddle would fly toward me.

The bleach-blonde who cried in the meeting sat in a yellow beanbag chair, reading the same blue book I read at the psych hospital. *No, not the blue book, the Big Book. That's what Jenny said.*

There was a loud commotion in the corner. One of the older women at the video game screen moaned as the others cheered. The taller of the two women shouted "Lois! World record!" and spun around with her arms out wide. It was funny. Her simple joy made me smile. Then she saw me in the doorway and waved me to join their group. *Relief, fear, the feeling of being judged.*

As I took a step toward the woman, Drinnen stuck her head in the room.

"Mail call!" she sang. Everybody stopped, squealed, and ran toward the door and I quickly stepped aside so I wouldn't be trampled. Then I followed the horde outside to the smoking area.

Drinnen stood on a concrete bench with a container of envelopes. Nine packages were at her feet. Her rainbow hair blowing in the breeze, she called name after name and the recipients were rabid in opening their mail.

With all this excitement, I decided I would ask Mom and Dad, my son, and certainly Karen and Jennifer, to send letters. I could understand why patients would want outside communication; just being out of touch for a week in the hospital, I was already in need of the "real world."

The patients read and re-read their letters as I sized up the patients. There seemed to be a unique camaraderie among them, an underlying layer of respect for each other, and I found oddly heartwarming. Though no one had specifically introduced themselves to me, I was surrounded by happy people having a good time and, somehow, I felt included. *Weird. Misfits having fun with each other. But wait! I'm not a misfit! Why am I smiling, then? Why do I feel like I'm a part of the fun already?*

A scuffle broke out in the far corner of the courtyard; somebody had received a box of cookies in the mail and was fighting off hungry, grabby patients. If the laughter hadn't defined it as a fun game, I would've thought it was a jailhouse riot in the making; it was loud. Evidently, this had happened before and they teased Cookie Man unmercifully. Ten hands reached into the tissue-lined cookie box as he swatted ten hands away. "No cookie for you!" he said – in a damn-good Cookie Monster impression.

The scene left me smiling and became a checkmark in the "pro" column of being here. As much as I wanted to be sober, I had so many doubts about the place... though everything had been positive so far.

Or has it been positive? I zoned out, lighting the second cigarette, and wondered when and how I could call my family. So far, this place seemed more liberal than the hospital, but I was only two hours old and I hadn't finished reading Eli's damn green booklet of rules.

Then I thought of my secret and my blood pressure zoomed. I had contraband. My cell phone. I snuck it from my van when Drinnen and I were in the psych hospital parking lot. So far, they hadn't checked my purse for smuggled goods, but my fear escalated with the smallest thought of the smuggled goods. I'd have to hide it in my room somewhere, I knew, and hoped they didn't do random searches.

The fantasy was calling Stuart. Though it made me quake in my boots, I desperately wanted to talk to him. I wanted to know if that lady in the

Bahamas had really foot-raped him or if he'd been somewhere unsavory by choice.

I wanted to ask him about my passport on that trip. Did I really lose it, or did he sell it? I wanted to know what he knew about me and beg him to leave me alone. And maybe, I thought, he'd come to rescue me from this trauma.

Maybe I knew it was a crazy wish, but I needed something to be the same.

How long can you stay bent out of shape and still be sane? You'll drive yourself crazy here, Lela, even if they don't do it for you!

Three empty vans pulled to the back door. Drinnen shouted "Grocery store!" and without hesitation, everybody jumped in a van. Afraid, I held back, not knowing which van I should get in; maybe there were rules. In an instant, all the vans were full, and I stood there, frozen.

Three drivers watched the influx of passengers and an Asian man, mid-twenties, shouted at me. "New girl! Lela, right?" I nodded. "There's room here!" *New girl. Ha.* With a deep breath, I got in the van, prepared to learn and go with the flow.

It wasn't like me to feel uncomfortable in a crowd. *It's not like me to be a regular person, a follower and not the leader of the pack! I have a lot to learn.*

I scrunched down and climbed through the side door, happy to see the two older women who had played the video game earlier. The tall one waved at me yelled, "Sit here!" and I stumbled to the back row. Introductions complete, I learned the tall, older one was Lois and Stephanie was the younger, bubbly one.

Stephanie's accent gave her away; she was from Minnesota. Lois lived in Miami, she said, "Just down the road." I laughed. Miami was far away in my mind, with its tall buildings and horrible traffic. Too much for a country girl.

"Do you want to shop with us?" Lois asked.

"Sure. But I have no idea how they expect me to spend all that money. No way I can eat that much! I'm not a cook – I eat, maybe a piece of toast for dinner... a pack of crackers. I'm cheap and easy to feed."

Lois interrupted. "Oh, I'm a happy cook! Ran a catering company in Miami before I relapsed. Stephanie and I, and two others..." She craned her neck as if she was looking for somebody. "There's Rhonda, sitting up front... we buy the ingredients of meals and I cook. Here's my weekly meal plan," she said, proudly presenting a piece of paper with neat script. "I wish you were in our apartment, Lela... I could put some meat on your skinny bones." Lois laughed.

INSANITY by Lela Fox

The grocery store was just two blocks away, a Publix. The vans stopped at the entrance and 46 patients piled out, entering the store like scurrying ants. Buggy in-hand, I joined my new friends and cruised the produce department.

The more I shopped, the hungrier I became. By the time we reached the frozen meals, which they bypassed, I had a cartful of food. Adding a frozen chicken pot pie, I laughed. So much for being under the fifty-dollar limit! But I had more than a week's food. *Guess you're planning to stay, huh?*

On the way out, I handed my receipt to Drinnen, who stood at the entrance in her typical silence, hands in the air and receipts trailing below. "Write your name on it," she said, gesturing toward the Sharpie marker on the floor.

I was ready to see my apartment and meet my roommates. More than anything, I was ready to use the phone. I needed and wanted to call my son to tell him where I was.

We drove beyond the treatment center and around an arc to reach the adjacent apartment complex. Everybody piled out. Before we reached the steps, a six-foot-plus black man approached me. "Lela?" I nodded, struggling with heavy grocery bags. He took one bag, and I thanked him; my arms were about to break. "I'm Victor, the meds monitor."

I screwed my brow into a question and asked what that meant. "You'll see... it's hard to explain. The meds room is actually in your apartment. Follow me." Victor bounded up the steps two at a time. I saw him on the third-floor landing as I rounded the corner; he opened a red-painted apartment door, leaving it open.

A new-car smell surrounded me. The carpet was new, the walls featured fun, imaginative artwork, the dining table on the left was ebony-stained wood, with white-painted spindle chairs. Nice.

The living room side of the room was huge, featuring a gray-and-turquoise twill-fabric sofa and matching solid-turquoise chair. Live plants cheered the place, one at every opportunity. A sliding glass door to a small concrete deck. A damn nice living room; something I would put together myself.

I set my groceries on the kitchen counter and began the process of putting my food away, pleased that the refrigerator was bigger than any I'd ever owned, a side-by-side with ice and water dispensers on the front.

Victor passed by, saying Abby, my roommate, would be up soon. As I filled the crisper drawer, a young woman huffed in, struggling with four grocery bags and a batik-fabric tote.

"Hi! I'm Abby. You're Lela, and my roommate!" she chirped. An upbeat, late-twenties woman wearing a white tank that showed the color and texture of her nipples, and a 3-D tattoo of a barbed-wire fence around her left bicep. Abby had pulled her hair back in a messy ponytail and its tendrils surrounded a tanned and smiling face.

She heaved her bags onto the island and reached out to shake my hand. "Nice to meet you." I thought she must be from New Jersey or somewhere up there, with a nasal and clipped accent, but she seemed nice. A badass, for sure, but nice. "Well, chick, I guess you're freaked out, being new," she said.

"I have no idea what's going on. And honestly, I want a drink so bad!" Her response was a tinkle of a laugh, like a set of wind chimes. We shared the kitchen as I finished my task, opening and closing cabinet doors until I found the proper places.

Both working in such a small space, we bumped into each other a few times, laughing about it, but I saw her freeze up with being touched. *She's a tough one, alright. Watch your step. Just because you're a hugger doesn't mean everybody is.*

As she emptied the last of her bags, she spoke more directly. "Actually, as long as you don't snore, we'll get along just fine. I've become a light sleeper since I've been here. This place has screwed me up. Or maybe it's just getting clean that's done it. I feel *so* out of it." She put her hands on her hips and looked me up and down, twice. "Heroin, clean and sober 57 days. You?"

"Alcoholic, sober eight days."

"Bless your heart. Hang in there. It gets better, I promise."

"I hope so. I thought by now I would be over the shakes and fucked-up thoughts, but I'm having these awful cravings and I don't know how to handle them."

Victor stuck his head in the kitchen. "Let's go, Lela. I'll give you the tour." I followed him to a bedroom, or maybe I should say a two-sided room, as if a line of tape divided the two sides.

On the window side, every surface was covered... a boom box, hair bands, books, and papers, an explosion of... stuff. A backpack leaned against the wall beside a knee-high pile of laundry. The weird thing: among the chaos, the bed was neatly made, like a Marine's bed.

Victor chuckled. "Obviously that's Abby's side. This one is yours." My side was clean and austere, empty and depressing compared to the personality strewn on Abby's half.

The white duvets and tufted headboards matched, as did the artwork above each bed, funky abstract landscapes. Across from the beds, a massive white dresser filled the wall, one side clean and one side covered with clutter. I chuckled; the array of potions, brushes, and powders was so exaggerated, and the dividing line so obvious, the scene was like a cartoon drawing.

"Abby's not much for organization, but you see her bed is made. That's a requirement here. Do it first thing or get a demerit. Three demerits and you stay in the center all day, not released to come back for lunch."

He was talking fast and saw the panic on my face, I assumed. His eyes softened. "It's okay, Lela. No worries; you'll be fine here. But we do have rules. Surely you understand that." I nodded silently but made a point to sigh loud enough for Victor to hear.

Then he stepped backward into the square-ish hall, pointing to the left. "The bathroom. You can see which sink is yours. Don't leave your shampoo, or anything at all, inside the shower. Put it out here. That includes soap."

Suddenly, the emptiness of the bath counter deemed "my side," coupled with the vacancy of "my side" of the bedroom brought a rash of unwanted tears. It all seemed so temporary, so cookie-cutter, so impersonal.

I screamed for personal attention, had done so for the eight days in the crazy hospital, and I'd not received one bit of special care. Suddenly, I was a child, a baby, and I needed my Momma! Victor caught a glimpse of my tears and seemed shocked. Then he winked. "Still scared? Girrrl! I promise you'll chill out soon. We try to make it easy."

I knew he was a lying sack of shit, but I didn't tell him how nervous I was... how doubtful and ridiculous I felt. I faked a smile and said, "It's just... a lot to take in." The man nodded his understanding. I remembered to ask my key question. "Where is a phone I can use? I want to call my son."

He took a deep breath. "More rules. Phone calls are between seven and nine o'clock. You're lucky because you only have to share with Abby." Then he led me to the other bedroom, on the other side of the kitchen. Lining the far wall, two tall bookcases and a beaten-up metal cabinet with a massive padlock... two desks stretched from the other wall, extending into the middle of the room. No artwork at all in there, I noticed. "This is the meds room," Victor said, "Everybody comes through, three times a day for some, to get their medication. And don't think you can sneak by without taking your meds. We check."

I paused, confused. "Why would a person try to avoid taking their medicine?"

"You'd be surprised," Victor eyed me carefully. "Lela, you're going to be fine. You seem like one of the good ones, somebody who really *wants* to get clean and sober."

"I do. I mean... I *am* one of those good ones." And I meant what I said. "But how would you know that already and why does everybody keep telling me that? Is it some kind of motivation theory bullshit or something?"

"Eli told me you were ready. Plus, yours was a clean admission, no court papers or bullshit." I wondered what bullshit there had been with other people... and how that would define their level of willingness.

Willingness. I'd just learned that word from Jenny and saw it again on the green chalkboard in group. *That word... that concept is key around here it seems. Willing to change, willing to listen, willing to accept the things I can't change... all that.*

"Can I eat now? Somehow I'm hungry."

"Go for it. Just let me know when you want to use the phone. It's got a lock on it."

When the digital clock on the stove turned to 7:01 PM, I stuck my head in the "med room" and caught his eye. Without a word, he stood and reached to his belt for a jangle of keys, nodding to the other man in the room. "Lela, meet Les, another one of the med monitors. We stay here all night, by the way." I bounded forward to shake Les' hand as Victor passed by with the keys.

"See ya, Les," I mumbled.

"Yes, you will," he said.

"Bo, it's Mom." The seventeen-year-old said, simply, "Hey." Speaking carefully as was my plan, I told him where I was, that I'd been sober for eight days and would stay in rehab for thirty more. For the first time, I told him I was an alcoholic. He didn't reply to that statement.

My mission, I said, was learning how to have a sober life, going to AA meetings, and learning about the disease. Bo didn't interrupt my intro, didn't even grunt sounds of understanding. "Are you there, son?"

"Mom is it... like... a hospital?"

I didn't want to tell him about the psych hospital or the hell of detox. "No, baby. I live in a regular apartment and go to a separate building during the day. We have group meetings, like school, I guess you'd call it. I'm free to leave if I want to, but I don't want to. Sweetheart, I want to get sober."

The tears came, finally, in a flood. My throat closed as I squeaked out the rest of the words. "Oh, Bo, I am *so* sorry. I've been a terrible mother, the worst, and for *so long*. But I'm gonna get better and we can have a good time together. I can be a *good* mom to you. Oh, kiddo, I feel so terrible... about everything! I know I've embarrassed you, disappointed you, and probably scarred you for life. Please don't hate me."

"I don't *hate* you, mom! Don't even *say* that." His voice took a turn. It was obvious he was crying, too.

"Bo, will you write me letters?"

"Sure."

"Write down this address." The address and emergency phone numbers were on a label attached to the phone. I read the details out loud, repeating it several times.

Then I went for the cheerful-mom act: "What do you think? Are you happy that I'm gonna get sober? Clean and sober, a brand-new mom? And, by the way, I've left Stuart. For good. He's an evil man, and it seems everybody knew it but me. He didn't do anything to screw you up, did he?

"Yeah, kinda. I just can't believe you married him, Mom. You're right-on that he's evil. Why couldn't *you* see it, too?"

I sighed, wiped my face with a tissue, but more tears fell. *Dammit! Don't cry! Pretend you're strong, pretend you're okay. Don't give him a reason to worry.* "Oh son, I'm so sorry. One day you'll forgive me, but I'll understand if you don't or won't. I'll work extra-hard to regain your trust. Do you understand all of that?" I was babbling.

"Maybe. It would be nice to feel like you were a real person." *A real person? Oh my God, my own son doesn't think I'm a real person! How low have I gone?*

"Bo, I won't let you down. For sure, I'll be a real person again. I fell off a cliff a little, maybe a lot, but I'll be back! Better than ever, I promise. I'll do it for *you*." The flood began. Tears flowed like rain.

I didn't want to be making sobbing sounds on the phone, so I said, "I gotta go, son. Can I call you tomorrow?" Though I felt a little hesitation, he said yes.

"I have a soccer game tomorrow." I didn't even know he was playing soccer for the summer.

"Kick it hard, big guy! Score a goal, okay?"

"Goodbye... Mom. Have a good time!"

I laughed. "Oh no, it's not a good time. It's work."

"Then work hard. And... congratulations, I guess."

I made kissy noises and placed the phone back in its cradle, then I collapsed, face down on the floor, crying as I'd never cried before, not even in jail. I had screwed up so bad, I *had* to get better, do better, and act like a normal human being.

Between sobs, I vowed that I *would* stay sober. "From this day forward. No matter what" I said aloud.

The plan was to call everybody in the family that night, but I found myself emotionally exhausted. As my tears abated, I moved to the living room, sat on the cushy plaid sofa, and flipped on the TV. Sit-coms, the news, a kid show. Nothing. I let my head fall forward to stretch my neck, and it creaked and crunched in all directions. *Welcome to rehab, Lela, where the deer and the antelope play.*

I moved to the bedroom as my mind reeled, laid on the bed and daydreamed about what was next in my world. The plan was to live in a halfway house, a sober house, for the sixty days of outpatient and I tried to envision what that would be like.

I wondered if I could ever work as a writer again. Somehow, I dozed off and only awoke when I heard Abby on the phone in the living room, laughing out loud. With a start, I ran to check the clock in the kitchen. It was 8:45 PM, just barely time to call my parents. I willed Abby to hurry.

When she hung up, I grabbed the phone and punched the buttons with fervor. Though I had decided not to cry on this call, I couldn't keep that promise. Mom cried, and it hurt my heart.

Daddy, as expected, was upbeat and saying his dumb phrases... "Hang tough, Tiger," and "Hooray for our side!" and always, "You're my favorite youngest daughter." These things meant nothing, but tonight, they meant everything.

I relayed the address and phone number, begging them to write. "Packages, too! Cookies and stuff. That would make me so happy," I said, "And could you send a tote bag to carry my books when I walk to the center."

"Whatever your heart desires," Daddy said, repeating an old family joke about Daddy's love letter to Mom when they were dating.

"Better watch it! My heart may have big desires. I need a shit-load of love."

"Coming your way, sweetie."

I asked Dad to give the address to Karen and Jennifer and send my love.

The call was heart-wrenching, and I didn't just cry; I kept crying hard for another half-hour.

I pulled the scrap of paper with Jenny's phone number from my purse and looked at it. *Tomorrow. Jenny, Jenny, Jenny! You have helped me so much already and they say that means you're my sponsor.* I wasn't sure exactly what it meant, but I knew I felt close to her. At that moment, she was like the main artery of my heart.

I decided I'd do whatever Jenny said to do. *Learn to trust, Lela. Be willing, be honest, be sober.*

THINK ABOUT CLOUDS
CHAPTER 18

Les beat on the door – hard. Ten times. "Get up, girls! Time for breakfast!" He knocked again, the same ten times. Instantly awake, I rolled over to look at Abby. A crooked arm covered her eyes, blocking the sun.

A moose-like moan came from under her arm. "Too early! God, I hate them!" Abby half-mumbled and half-yelled in a sleepy voice. "I was having such a cool dream... me and Joe, Hope, Maggie... shooting up, at the lake but some other lake, trees and flowers...like, in the countryside or something. Such a good rush, a perfect high." She rolled over to face me. "Then Les beats on the damn door like a maniac! Why does he *do* that?" With a jerk, she flopped back on the bed and closed her eyes. "I'm not taking a shower. Going to lay here a while. Don't talk to me."

"I haven't said anything," I pointed out.

"Quiet! Don't talk to me!" I smiled, wondering if she was even awake at all. Otherwise, I didn't know what to do... having no clue what was in store for me in the morning routine. My first day. *Do I get coffee? Take a shower? What do I wear? What do I eat?* I chuckled, remembering Dad's summary of the ultimate confusion: "I don't know whether to take a crap or wind my watch." He wouldn't let Mom hear him say that one.

I lay flat for a minute or two, reeling with thoughts of what might happen. *Wow, I haven't had a drink in nine days.* A miracle already. Today I would learn how to not drink tomorrow, and the next day. It would be the first day of the rest of my life, I thought. Then I snickered. *How corny is that?*

Dressed, I walked into the meds room to see Les' smile; it seemed fake and forced. My instant thought was that he didn't like me; I'd done something wrong already. But I said nothing. He pushed his rolling chair toward the locked cabinet and used not just one, but TWO keys, to open it.

Prescription bottles filled six shelves... more medicine than I'd ever seen. It was somewhere between funny as hell and scary. *So much instability in the patients here... and you're one of the unstable ones, too, Ms. Fox.* I felt pigeon-holed, pre-defined as a hopeless Bi-Polar, probably never able to lead a normal, calm life.

But I said none of this to Les; I let his fake smile face remain fake.

Unlike the night before, I was the only patient in the med room and Les found my cup easily. "Here you go, Lela Fox. Tell me your birthdate."

"Happiest day of my momma's life." He smiled but didn't take his eyes off me until I told him the date. Pushing two paper cups in my hand, one small one filled with pills and a larger one with water, he demanded, "Take them all and drink all the water."

"Chill, Les. I know how to take medicine! Jeezus! Who do you think I am!" I was pissed; the attitude was unneeded, at least with me.

"Seriously, drink *all* the water... must stay hydrated around here."

"What's this? Another random rule?" My smartass was showing.

"Not random. Medically necessary."

"Bullshit. Then your fake smile is medically necessary, too?"

"Don't bite the hand that feeds you, ma'am." His smile never waned. "Have a grand day!" he shouted after me. *Right, weirdo. You're too mean to work with crazy patients. You need an attitude adjustment, mister...*

As I walked past the hall, I realized... "Oh, shit, I didn't make up my bed!" I rushed into the room to see that Abby had done it for me. "Wow! Thank you, Abby! That was so nice!"

"Somehow I like doing it now. Starts the day with a little order. As you can see, I'm not one for keeping things all neat in color-coded bins." She blew a sarcastic laugh, and I joined her.

My grin broadened; I said, "Still, Abby... thank you. I'll remember tomorrow. Are you ready to go?"

"Yep. Get ready for a day of hell. Rules and more rules. In group sessions... talking, mostly babbling, from the crazy-ass folks here. But we start with yoga and meditation today with a cool lady named Brynn. If you can do it, I mean *really* meditate, it helps so much."

"I've never tried. Always been too drunk and fell asleep."

Abby laughed. "Now you may be too nervous to breathe and let everything go, at I couldn't at first. Still, try it. I'll take a mat next to you, okay?"

Gratitude spread to my toes. I wondered how I could feel such a strong bond with Abby after knowing her for less than 24 hours. *Curious... I seem to know her completely, and she knows every bit of ME, too.*

Abby danced going down the steps, in time to a hummed tune. I could only hope to feel that happy at the end of the day. A group from behind joined us and, like a pack of wolves, we walked single file down two flights of wooden stairs and into the courtyard. The fountain spewed. Then we walked along a worn path through the grass, arriving at the center's rear parking lot, thirty yards from the back door. A dozen-or-so patients were there, smoking cigarettes and laughing.

They trusted me with fire here; I could carry my own cigarettes and lighter. *Ha, ha! No more crazy hospital, Lela!* The comparison of the psych hospital struck me hard. I realized that despite their rules, I was the one in charge of me... the one who woke up and got dressed, walked to this place to face something I feared.

I had made those choices today, and each day brought another choice of whether to do it again. In another Lifetime I would have been proud of myself, but that day, it filled me with self-doubt. I worried if I was doing it right and dreaded what would happen if I did it wrong.

Abby dashed inside the center, saying she'd be back "in a scoot." The moment she left, my heart sunk and I instantly felt like an outsider, the girl nobody liked. Throbbing against my temples was a palpable need for a drink; I knew how quickly a vodka-tonic would take those feelings away. But I couldn't pick up my crutch anymore, that beautiful bottle of vodka... the cure, the substance that made all my discomfort go away.

In my "former life," vodka fixed everything. So how does a person live without alcohol? One thing's for sure: I'll never be the life of the party again... cuz' I'll never even GO to a party! All my friends will have tattoos and we'll sing "Kumbaya" around the campfire somewhere deep in the woods where the misfits live. My life is over. Meet the ex-Lela Fox.

I stood to the side, smoking my cigarette without mixing with the other patients. They all seemed so comfortable with each other; there was a lot of laughter. Jokes about drugs, about making amends, about working steps and calling sponsors. To be honest, I didn't understand much of it, but after a time, it didn't scare me... didn't disgust me... in fact, it intrigued me.

In the midst of my ping-pong thoughts, feelings of hope again stirred in my soul and I smiled to myself. That's when my friends showed up.

Lois and Stephanie appeared at the end of the path, stepping up the stones to the blacktop behind the center. They both waved at the same time. Stephanie shouted, "Hey, Lela!" I was thrilled she greeted me like a normal person. *Maybe she can be a friend, somebody to lean on. And maybe Lois will invite me to dinner.*

So that'd be three friends here: Abby, Stephanie, and Lois. Can I get sober with three friends? Can they help me find my way?

☼ ☼ ☼ ☼ ☼

I was still fighting with my back-and-forth thoughts when we lay down on the circle of red yoga mats. The room was dark with the blinds drawn and all the lights off. Low, eerie echoes, whale sounds, filled the space, coming from a tape in the boom box of our meditation leader, Brynn.

My nerves jangled, and I knew I'd never relax enough to get into what she called an "absorbed state." Despite my doubts, I was determined to try.

Relaxing was key to learning, Brynn had said, and I knew my anxiety would be my focus if I didn't get rid of it. No matter how much fear I felt, I wanted to learn; I wanted to open my mind. *Anything it takes, Lela. Learn how to live... learn what you missed in those 27 years in the bottle.*

Brynn danced gracefully across the room and sat cross-legged next to me. As I looked at her, she placed a quarter on my forehead. "Concentrate on nothing but the quarter," she said, "And think of a calm place, a happy place, filled with slow waves of peace."

Brynn's hypnotic voice hummed throughout the room; she spoke for a long time but the words disappeared and I could only feel the cadence... my breathing slowed. The "peaceful place" I conjured was a memory from long ago, when I cooed softly to Bo when he was a two-year-old having trouble falling asleep. "Think about clouds, sweetheart," I would say, lying next to him in the yellow big-boy bed. "Clouds, flowers, and a soft summer breeze..."

As if it was entirely natural, my body floated upwards, sliding within the clouds. Utter peace, gentleness, balance, and harmony. Then the sky filled with my cousin Lewis Balyum's face. Lewis the hippie poet, the hitchhiker.

This made no sense, but I continued to feel the peace and stay in the serene place. Lewis, the Dude cousin. I hardly knew him but felt his presence

100 percent. I remembered our easy connection the time he came to visit when I was a teen. There was an overpowering sense of bonding with him then, like a spiritual connection, but I knew nothing about such things at the time.

I tried not to question this vision as tears rolled into my ears. Without a word, I whispered to Lewis, thanking him over and over, a hundred times. I didn't know what I was thanking him for but the feeling was powerful.

Just as the feelings of gratitude engulfed me, Brynn said, "Okay, guys, come back to today, to the here and the now. Come back slowly, slowly, slowly." *No... please... not yet. I'm happy here.*

Abby slapped my mat. "Don't fall asleep, Fox!" She startled the hell out of me, and I rolled my head toward her.

"Bitch... I was into it."

"Are you fucking *crying?*"

"Yeah... I'm a Tear-Bucket Jim... I cry all the time."

"Then you're a wimp. You can't get clean and sober if you're going to *cry* all the time!"

I didn't see who came to my defense; the voice spewed from behind my head. "Give her a break, Abby. Maybe she's just a tender soul. Not everybody's a badass like you." I rolled over to see my defender: Stephanie.

Ignoring them both, I shared my news, my success. "I really did it, y'all! I meditated... like, imagined a whole new world and went there."

"And cried about it! You're fucked-up, Fox." But Abby was teasing, and looking into her eyes, I realized she'd been teasing me all along.

"But how am I going to handle all this emotional crap if I cry at the first strum of heartstrings? My tears drive my Dad crazy, but... I can't help it. And all last week, I cried 24/7."

Stephanie landed gracefully with crossed legs, inches from me. "It's your old friends, here to haunt you."

"Friends who?"

"Let's see..." She counted on her fingers. "Guilt, Shame, Remorse, Self-Hate, Self-Doubt, Denial, all your demons."

"But you don't understand! I saw my cousin!"

Abby's eyes widened. "What the hell? Your *cousin* made you cry?"

"Because it was a happy thing. Not shame and all that. I think it was, like... love. No kidding, guys."

"Drama, drama, drama," Stephanie flipped her wrist forward as if shooing me away.

"Don't give me any grief about this! It was powerful! I've never meditated before, remember? And, I swear... my cousin talked to me without words."

Abby said, "Weird."

I nodded. "Especially because he's dead."

Both girls laughed, with Abby leading the chorus in guffaws. "Get up, Fox! A cigarette awaits. But you might have to share it with your cousin!"

"Ha, ha, Abby. Never mind... I was trying to be honest. Doesn't it say in that book that it's a program of honesty?"

"Yeah, honesty with *yourself!*" Abby grabbed my hand and dragged me toward the door, laughing all the way. I was embarrassed to have made such a fuss, maybe, but appreciative that my friends' bitching about it was in jest.

You're just a highly emotional person, Lela. Too much, but you can't change that! Remember when your therapist said you are an "empath?" That's the problem, but maybe not a bad thing to be. It's not like your husbands have said. You're not "high-maintenance." You're "sensitive and soulful."

I let the others talk; my thoughts stayed in the confines of my head. I wanted to be self-focused... to keep feeling what I'd felt during the meditation. I wanted to open my mind to things like kindness and gratitude.

Do whatever you can to keep the gratitude all day long.

Why I tried to ruin it a few hours later is still a mystery to me.

☼ ☼ ☼ ☼ ☼

I'd finished one cigarette and was in the process of lighting another. Drinnen's head, not hard to miss with the rainbow 'do, appeared behind the door. I watched her scan the crowd, obviously looking for somebody and I hoped it wasn't me.

I dreaded her presence and felt myself trying to become invisible. But my heart beat rat-a-tat. I was scared of Drinnen. *Scared of her reality, maybe.*

Though I could have easily heard her, she screamed. "Lela Fox!"

Daring to speak boldly, I screamed back, "Don't give me any shit, Drinnen!"

The other patients reacted with whoops and catcalls... as if I'd dissed her. But that wasn't my motive. I just wanted to cover my ass, and I had a feeling something was getting ready to expose it.

A 15-MINUTE CHARGE
CHAPTER 19

As a new patient, I spent most of the first morning in the office with Dr. Paul Mallory, the center's resident psychiatrist. Eli led me there; into the fanciest doctor's office I'd ever seen. Upscale in every way. The desk was custom-made, had to be. The massive top looked like a ritzy bar top: at least three inches thick with a bullnose edge and triple-thick lacquer. It was oval, and on the wall behind it were three matching half-oval floating shelves.

This place must be mega-expensive. Poor Momma wrote a big, fat check. All I can do for repayment is stay sober, so there's another reason if you need one. Lela, you have a big job ahead, a lifelong job. The more I talked to myself, the more pressure I felt to succeed and the more daunting the task became. I was sweating with fear when Dr. Mallory waltzed into the office.

With a smile, he flipped open a manila folder with a color-coded tab. A big, red "F," I thought... as I'd thought before when seeing my doctor's records: *F= FAIL. You're a loser, Ms. Fox.* I got lost in shaming myself for a while but snapped back to reality when the doc snapped the folder closed.

"So... tell me about yourself." Such an open-ended question. I hadn't been able to put two sentences together for nine days and he's saying, "Tell me everything?" I sat dumbfounded and silent; he finally noticed and changed his tactic.

"Tell me how you feel right now." This was the second of many questions that stumped me. The entire interview was a struggle, but I found words to answer his simpler questions. He said I wasn't alone in feeling overwhelmed and depressed at the beginning of rehab, "the beginning of the rest of your life," he called it. *Sounds even more stupid coming from him.*

Instead of *me telling him* how I felt, *he told me* what was happening within my mood and my head. At the end of the meeting, I felt extremely grateful for that.

When I first moved to Florida, I didn't take psych drugs because I postponed finding a doctor for months and months. When I left Stuart, running back to Rockville, I never called my former doc to re-start my meds, either. Then back in Florida, another few months passed with no medicine… until I found Gloria. Not much in the way of guidance, but at least she provided the prescriptions. I told all that to Dr. Mallory and admitted that until being admitted to the psych hospital, I hadn't been exactly dependable in taking the meds on time, if at all.

So he suggested starting from scratch, ignoring what I'd been on in the past and creating a new cocktail. "No! *Hell* no! I can't go through all that change when I'm in this place!" Experience had taught me that Bi-Polar Disorder drugs are hit-or-miss, and a change is traumatic, even if it's a change for the better. "Sir, I can't do that! I won't *let* you do that!"

In a nice voice with a sincere smile, he asked if I was a doctor. I shut my mouth.

Dr. Mallory laid out his plan. He kept me on one drug I'd been taking for years, added a low dose of two new mood stabilizers, and added something to help me sleep. I was frantic about changing things, but he carefully explained what early sobriety does to a Bi-Polar person's mood and insisted the new mix might have been what I'd needed all along.

At last, I admitted the fear of diving into a depression was bigger than the fear of a change in medicine. "Actually, Dr. Mallory, a *manic* episode would be the worst because that's when I drank the most. I'd go insane in this place and manic."

"Let's keep you on that nice level line. That's always the goal, of course."

When I left Dr. Mallory's office, I found the other patients outside on the smoking porch. Ready for a cigarette myself, I felt nervous and twitchy, and thoughts ping-ponged in my head. But just as I stubbed out my smoke, Eli called us in for the second session of the morning.

Still in never-never land, I sat through that group session without a clue of its happenings. I remember it was a Big Book study and I read random parts. At the beginning of the meeting, Eli said if we only read the text in italics, we would understand the book.

The AA Big Book is written with a flourish, so to speak. Big words, old-fashioned language, and a formal tone. As a writer, I admired the prose, but as a newbie sober person, I felt lost.

Why haven't they rewritten this damn book? I could do that! That's what I'll do... I mean, I'm a writer, right? I can sell it to the AA managers or whoever they are. Why wouldn't they want a new book, even coming from a newcomer like me? Hell yeah!

I wonder how much they'll pay me. How long will it take? Just think how much power I could add to AA's future! I'll take out some of the "God's" and insert more "Higher Powers," for sure... simplify the damn flowery language... and I'll definitely change the cover. I mean, you can't even read the title on this one!

When we wrapped, everybody rushed the door for a cigarette. Abby, Stephanie, Lois and I trudged back to the apartment in Florida's oppressive afternoon heat. We had an hour to eat and get back. Lois had something in the crockpot; I thought I'd zap a frozen fettucine.

Abby fixed a stir-fry and flipped on the TV. We watched *"The Price is Right,"* laughing about how incorrect we were, guessing every single price wrong by half or more. I was clueless about the prices and I realized I hadn't shopped in a long time. Too busy drinking, I guessed, and with a live-in nanny for a while, I'd steered clear of the grocery store. That thought left a bad taste in my mouth; I pushed it away quickly and reveled in the hilarity we shared. It felt great to giggle, and it had been too long since I'd done so.

Abby left with a girl from down the hall to finish a ping-pong tourney they'd started the day before. As soon as she left, I knew my next move.

Sneak.

I ran to the bedroom closet and dove under my short rack of hanging clothes. Yep, there it was in the dark; my suitcase. Empty but for two things: a cell phone and a charger. Contraband.

I flipped the phone open and pushed the power button. *Dammit!* Dead. In a panic, I searched for an outlet, hoping to find one in the closet. No such luck. My heart knocked at twice the normal rate... boom-boom, boom-boom. I wasn't a good sneak, and I knew if I got caught with the phone, they would kick me out of the center. *Then what will you do, Lela?* My mind reeled with that disastrous possibility, but the other side of my brain screamed louder. *But I have to hear his voice!*

In a rush, I plugged the charger into the outlet behind my bedside table and slid the phone underneath the bed. Finished, I ran back to the sofa, plopping down and assuming the same pose I had held when I left. I tried to act casual, but I was a nervous wreck.

The sound of a key in the lock startled me. Les crossed the threshold, and I felt the color of Guilt rise to my neck, slowly increasing the pressure at the top of my head; I couldn't speak. Les took three steps into the apartment before he looked my way. Then he stopped in his tracks and I froze in place. "Lela! What the hell is *wrong* with you?"

"What? Nothing. Why?"

"You're so pale! Like a ghost, girl! Are you feeling okay?"

My heart pumped so hard I thought surely it was visible through my shirt. "I'm... fine, Les. Kinda freaked out, maybe. My first day, ya know." I flashed a fake smile, but it didn't faze him.

"Okay, well... did you eat? Maybe you're weak, being new and everything." Les seemed honest in his concern.

"Yep, I ate. I'm fine." I looked down and cleared my throat. "Just waiting for the time to go back. Abby's already gone." I felt myself ready to blab, running my mouth, which was my tendency when nervous. I purposely snapped my jaw shut. Les stood in the same place, keys in hand, staring at me.

Then came the true indicator of stress. My palms started itching... burning with tingles and stabs. *Calm down, Lela. You're overreacting and making yourself look guilty.*

"Well, as long as you're okay. But you still don't *look* okay. Whatever. Just came in to get my phone. Can't leave that loose around you guys! Too much temptation, I imagine."

I stammered. "Yeah, probably." In twenty seconds, he disappeared. Only then did I blow out the breath I'd been holding.

Fifteen minutes would be enough time to get a decent charge, I thought. *Just need a minute, anyway.* I tiptoed to the bedroom, closed the door, and locked it. My heart beat loudly in my head, creating a throbbing headache. I crawled under the bed to retrieve my phone, pulling it off the charger. I realized, again, that I was holding my breath. But the power button brought up the logo screen this time. I had 22 percent battery but only one bar of signal strength.

Frantic, I crawled closer to the window, and the signal increased to two bars. *Maybe that will be enough.* I had Stuart's work number in my contacts. I pressed "send."

The phone rang on the other end, four times. With each ring, my heart palpitations increased, reaching a crescendo on the fifth ring when a snappy voice answered.

"Ace Transmissions. Stuart speaking." After a long pause, just after Stuart repeated the greeting, I squeaked a weak "Hi."

"Lela? Where are you?"

"I'm in treatment, rehab."

"Where?"

"I'm not telling you that."

"You should be in jail, bitch." Surprised by his rejection, I pressed "end" with shaking hands.

Why did you even call, dumbass? He called you a bitch! He doesn't want to save you! My heart sunk to my feet and tears burned the back of my eye sockets. *So are you convinced now? He's not on your side and will never be, sober or not.*

The problem wasn't just in my head, but also in my heart. Stuart was my soulmate, my forever-partner; I'd convinced myself of that years ago. *How can I go on without him? Why has he turned his back on me? How could I have let it come to this awful level? It's all my fault*

Heavy with Shame and Guilt, confused by such conflicted feelings, I collapsed against the window frame and cried like a baby.

THE FOURTH DIMENSION
CHAPTER 20

My panic about the phone call to Stuart sent me running back to the center at a fast pace. I left everybody behind and race-walked alone, skipped a cigarette, walked straight inside the building, and plopped into a seat. I sat on my hands so no one could see how hard they shook.

I kicked myself in the ass with self-talk for a solid ten minutes, feeling worse about myself than before I'd booted Baby-Daddy from my room. I felt disgustingly weak, as needy as a self-conscious teen.

It was not unusual to feel such hate for myself, but it was multiplied by the knowledge that I couldn't drink away the Shame or run from the Fear. Disgust and anger at myself overflowed.

You've gone backward, Lela. You've let him do it to you again. What's WRONG with you, girl? He's an ass, hoping for your demise! Why would you expect something different just because YOU have changed? HE hasn't changed and he won't!

YOU'RE AN IDIOT. Now there's no way you can go through with this rehab shit. You can't get sober because you're still a child, a pitiful needy child.

I stood three times to walk out... thinking I'd simply run back to my room and pack, take a taxi to the Homing Inn and smoke crack with Baby-Daddy. The voice in my head was in full agreement.

Do it! Drink yourself into oblivion, choke on your own vomit. Get up from this chair and run – NOW! You have enough money for a while. Do it. Kill yourself! Everybody would be–

Lois swirled to land in the seat beside me, smiling her signature sideways grin. "What's up, Lela Lou?" Then she stopped short. "Oh, no! What happened? Tell me! You look like shit." When I didn't reply, she added, "Maybe I can help! Maybe the group can help!"

My eyes widened as I shook my head no.

"No group?"

"Right. I'm ashamed."

"Ah! Shame! Driving us night and day... trust me, I know. So what did you do? What shameful thing makes you sit here looking like the Grim Reaper?"

"I'm not gonna say."

"No? That bad, huh?"

Lois leaned forward, her elbows on her knees but her eyes never left mine. "I know your type. This isn't my first rodeo, Lela. Not at all. It may not be the same Shame you're feeling now, but I've had my share. Let me tell you my story."

I zoned out for most of it, relieved I wouldn't have to tell her what I'd done. The part I heard taught me a lot, though. Maybe Lois knew what she was doing. Turns out, she had relapsed after sixteen years of the Good Life... the loyal wife of a plastic surgeon in Miami, had scads of sober-women friends, played tennis and had tea... shit like that.

But she quit going to meetings when they interfered with her social schedule and became "inconvenient." Three months with no meetings and, lo-and-behold, she got drunk. For no reason and with no forethought, she walked into the country club one day and decided a glass of wine would be perfectly fine. That one drink turned into a month of solid drinking.

"I am the walking-talking story of Bill Wilson," she said. "Bill says a real alcoholic can never drink with impunity, and I believe him."

I thought about this. If I could make it to a year's sobriety, for instance, I was still nowhere near "free of the monster," as Lois called it. This was lifelong. Instant fear spread through my body, to every extremity. *I don't have the strength! I can't do this!* Tears welled in my eyes. "Lois, I'm scared," I whispered. She turned and reached under my arms to pull me toward her for a hug.

Relieved, I collapsed in her arms, my head on her shoulder and easily the most honest hug I've had with someone outside my family.

Lois cooed in my ear, whispering hope and strength, saying words that sounded like things in the Big Book. The thing I remember most is when she said. "Trust me. Lela, find your Higher Power, then staying sober will be easy. I promise."

Though I doubted it would be "easy" or could be a "promise," I smiled at her. Maybe she was clueless or maybe she was doing something right, offering something I could latch onto and thrive.

The first afternoon session was a full house with all the patients. Eli did a formal presentation, using the chalkboard he loved so damn much.

More about God, bringing more sighs from me, but at least I no longer fumed when hearing the word. My mind was opening, maybe. The plan was to substitute the word "Lewis" every time they said "God." It didn't feel right, in fact, I felt stupid saying it, but it sounded better than the word I hated.

At the break, I noticed a few girls walking along the back of the building and ran to catch up with them. One girl turned with a frightened look. She exclaimed, "No! You can't go to the store with us! People have to be here a week before they can go to the store." *Damn.*

Dumb rules, again... rules that were going to stop me from having the friends I wanted. But I'd made a turnaround from the morning's deep doubts and realized I wanted to follow the rules so I could stay and heal. Maybe I could get rid of the ping-pong thoughts in my head. New doubts, then new resolve... back and forth, repeating until I wanted to puke.

"I'll follow that dumb rule," I told them and slumped back to the smoking porch.

For the second afternoon session, we broke into small groups. Five or six people went to PTSD class, and the rest separated into alcoholics vs. druggies for a book study. Twelve of us scooted chairs into a small circle. Lois, Stephanie and I sat together, notebooks ready and the Big Book at the ready.

The group was an interesting mix, yet all of us were in the same boat. I was the newest, and it was easy to see they were ahead of me because their faces weren't sunken like mine. Instead, they had a pinkish color, and their eyes showed a bit of sparkle.

Eli led the group. He caught my eye as we found the page, nodded, and smiled. I smiled back but fear was front-and-center; it seemed he could see straight through me and knew I had called Stuart.

Yep, Lela, you called the first moment you were alone. Are you a lunatic? Stuart has stomped on your soul, so why would you want to talk to him? If you go back, you'll lose everything you have gained.

The last word echoed in my head. *What I've gained.* Hmm, I had gained a surprising amount of things in ten short days! I had my wits, a small scrap of self-respect, and a taste of hope. I had Jenny, and already, I'd met several people in this sobriety thing who could be respected friends

In my wandering mind, I added names to "my team." Eli, Lois, Dr. Mallory, Stephanie, Abby... even the people here I hadn't met yet. Yep, I had people on my team. Yet I still wanted Stuart to be on my team. Sad. Stupid. Ridiculous.

Eli saw my distraction and called on me first. "Lela, start us off. We're reading from page 24 in the chapter *There is a Solution*, last paragraph." The word "God" was within the paragraph and I pronounced it through clenched teeth. Eli noticed and threw me a questioning look.

Per routine, the next person in the circle read the next paragraph. "Name's David," he said. I hadn't met him, but he was a good reader, loud and confident.

His paragraph spoke of recovering alcoholics' willingness to level their pride and confess their shortcomings, the basic tenets of the twelve steps of Alcoholics Anonymous, Eli said.

David continued to read, "We have found much of heaven," and then he paused, adding a smile to his voice. Now animated, he continued in a comic, raised tone, "And we have been rocketed into the fourth dimension of existence which we... had..." David heard my loud and guttural reaction to this phrase and stopped short.

I screamed. "The fourth dimension?!" Aruuuuuuuugha! That's what Stuart said... how much he loved me! That sonofabBITCHHH!"

The primal rumble started deep in my throat... building, spiking in volume and urgency. I growled like a caged animal, then the growl morphed into a howl, then a scream, then a screech.

"The goddamn fourth dimension... God, *damn* him! I thought he was so fucking romantic!" I screamed, jumping to my feet.

In a fit of rage, like a blackout, I picked up my chair with one hand, grabbing the back panel. I spun around – once, twice, as if swiveling to heave a shotput, then let go of the chair on the third spin. It arched high in the air, bounced off the ceiling and crashed against the far wall, rebounding onto a stack of metal chairs, and up-ending a plant in a pottery crock.

My screech trailed low, becoming a moan, then a sob. I collapsed. Every gasp of air escaped from my lungs and I was a limp doll, a dead weight. Tears ejected. I rolled on my back, legs bent at the hips and knees, screaming and spraying spittle.

"Goddamn! I thought he was so wise! He was, he was..." I hiccupped with sobs. I stuttered, "He was qu-qu-quoting the Big Book! He told me, he said... he said it was me!"

I tried to breathe, but a wail escaped and permeated the air in the room. "He told me *I* was the one who rocketed him to the fourth dimension!" A howl. "And I thought it—" The words kept coming, but the rest were unintelligible. I screamed deep in my throat, feeling tears come from within my core.

The room had gone quiet; only the buzz of tension was audible. As I lay sobbing in the fetal position, Eli came to my side and bent down on one knee. I stiffened and, once more, the air left my lungs. I was numb, exhausted. Too exhausted to be angry anymore.

Eli touched my arm softly and spoke with gentle care. "Lela?"

Out of breath, panting, I realized what a spectacle I had caused. "I'm sorry Eli. But Stuart lied to me about everything! Everything!" I felt like I'd blown the top of my head into the next county. Throbbing pain. *Breathe, Lela. In through your nose, out through your mouth.*

Eli watched me. "That's right, Lela, breathe. Slowly. You're okay. It's all good." The quiet of the room was deafening. The cold of the tile floor pressed against my cheek and sent a chill down my spine. I shivered deep into my soul, drawing tighter into a fetal position.

Still trying to breathe, my throat closed while choking back tears. I had to let go, I had to relax. Eli knelt beside me and held a paper bag to my mouth. "Breathe," he said.

My eyes blinked up to meet Eli's. "It's okay, Lela, slow and calm." Two more breaths into the bag. Slowly, I felt my heart settle down and closed my eyes. *Oh, how ridiculous I must look to the others! What are they thinking of me now?*

"Take the bag, Lela. Keep breathing." Eli stood up and the floating stars that sparkled and danced in front of my eyes dissipated. I felt the cold floor through my clothes, deep in my limbs. I was emotionally spent and hurt to the core.

Cocking his head and offering a chuckle that seemed to represent amazement, Eli announced to both groups, "*This*, folks, is a breakthrough. I think she's ready to get sober now."

HEY, DUDE
CHAPTER 21

Excused from the rest of the session, I went outside to smoke. I coughed through six cigarettes in a row, until I felt sick. It was a hot day, but I didn't sweat; in fact, I felt almost chilly until I sat on the blazing concrete bench. That pain felt wonderfully punishing as I cried, realizing it was also painful sobbing.

Then I paced, back and forth across the courtyard a dozen times or more. My brow screwed in a question; I had no idea how to feel or what to do.

A new perspective, Lela. It's what you needed and what you got. Because... why in the hell did you call Stuart in the first place? Why do you still care about him? A liar! A thief! A man out to destroy you! Yet you yearned to hear his voice, have the assurance of a reconciliation.

With a deep breath, I envisioned a life sober and without Stuart... what would I do? Stay in Florida and get a new job? Run home to Daddy, live at the farm and collapse into my depressed self, every day a struggle to stay off the booze?

My future was a series of unknowns. I fretted, wringing my hands and crying without end. Sick. Nauseated. Tired. And definitely overwhelmed.

Stop this shit! I tried to stop crying because my temples pounded, and I could already feel the swelling of my eyes. *You're gonna be hurting later, Lela. Toughen up, young soldier!* A phrase my dad said, so ridiculous, but it made me cry harder.

Stop! Don't be such a baby, a weak rag doll! Be responsible and focus on what's ahead.

With a sigh, I looked at the sky. Brilliant blue, the color of a crayon, a blue only found in the semi-tropics of sunny South Florida. Big, fluffy clouds – like those in a painting – covered the sky left and right, all the way south to the shore. Despite the pounding of my head, I found myself smiling at the sight.

The scene smelled beachy with an undertone of... *what is it, Lela? Something sweet? No, it's a feeling... something like – oh, my God! It smells like hope, same as when I kicked Baby-Daddy out of my room!*

I wondered how something could smell like a feeling, especially 'hope' when I sat there so hopeless. *An illusion, Lela. Wishful thinking.*

I looked at the sky again, ready to scream in silent anger to a God that loathed me.

As if on cue, a stream of sunlight broke through a billow of clouds, orange and violet on the edges, brilliant white in the center. Like a prism of pure sparkle.

I recognized the image instantly. It was a picture from a childhood memory, from my kindergarten Sunday-school book. The caption on that picture: "God is everywhere." I whispered the phrase, not once but twice. The word "God," the one I so despised, didn't phase me either time.

Although the prism of light beamed bright enough to hurt my eyes, I couldn't bear to look away. I stared until my eyes crossed... until the scene melted into another one altogether. A vision appeared, emerging like waves of heat in the desert, like the intro of a movie's dream sequence.

A vision!? What's happening? Are you out of your MIND?

Among the clouds, a picnic table... deeply wood-grained but somehow polished smooth and shiny. And sitting on the bench, a man. Long and scraggly hair, long beard, both auburn red. It was my cousin Lewis Balyum. He smoked a cigarette, wearing a rumpled flannel shirt, and faded jeans with holes in the knees. And he was barefoot.

Why is Lewis sitting at that picnic table? What the hell is going on? Lewis... but it is Lewis? He smiled at me with the most caring look, the most compassionate, and loving smile imaginable.

A sense of complete and total peace washed over me like a wave. In an instant, my body became weightless and my headache disappeared. Poof, gone.

It felt ridiculous to do it, but I reached toward the man on the picnic bench... so far away. When my arm reached its limit, the scene slowly, slowly faded from view, just as magically as it had appeared. The man's delighted smile never left his kind face, even as he gestured in "tipping his hat" to say goodbye, which he did just as the image paled.

I cringed, sad to see him go, but I wasn't upset. In fact, I felt eerily happy, content, and the very essence of peace warmed my body.

What the holy hell just happened!? I've been visited or something! But by what? An angel? A spirit? Was it a mirage? A hallucination? What, then? But it was... my hitchhiking-poet-taxi-driver-hippie-cousin Lewis Balyum! What the hell?

My mind reeled. *Am I dreaming?* I searched all corners of my mind, trying to wish away the weirdness, convince myself I hadn't seen anything at all. *But it wasn't my imagination, I saw it, clear as day. I know I did!*

I told myself it must have happened because I'd been so upset earlier, maybe because my eyes had been so swollen from crying. But I found it impossible to rationalize the whole thing in earthly terms. There was no alarm bell or emotional turmoil. In fact, I smiled from deep inside... from a place I didn't know I had.

Confused, I looked back at the sky, to the same spot. I felt very humbled and small. The vision had been surreal. *No, not surreal – it was REAL! I know it was real! So was it God? But the dude was my cousin, my DEAD cousin if that matters.*

I whispered to the sky, "Come back! I want to talk to you, dude! I have so much to say, so much I need to know!" The begging exaggerated the light within me, stirring a calm peace.

Somehow, I knew I would get those answers. And sooner than imagined.

☼ ☼ ☼ ☼ ☼

Eli called me to the office immediately after the afternoon session ended. "Lela, Lela," he clucked. "What in the holy hell happened?"

I sighed and stared at him for a few seconds, silent. Eli continued. "First, I *should* say I could kick you out for being violent, but something says it was pure emotion, and the violence was just a byproduct. Am I right?"

I chuckled, cocking my head. "It was emotional all right." Calm and collected, I spoke in staccato. "Turns out my husband is even more of an asshole than I thought. He played me from the beginning. Eli."

Tears dropped lazily as I continued. "I thought Stuart was so peace-filled, so eloquent, saying all the ooey-gooey flowery things that sent my heart aflutter. But he... he said *our love* rocketed him to the fourth dimension..."

My bottom lip began to quiver. "But he... Well, he acted like it was his own idea. I even asked him about the phrase! Hell, Eli, he didn't even admit his alcoholism! Never! Quoting a book he denied reading!" I felt myself getting worked up again. *Deep breaths, Lela. Remember what happened earlier... keep that peace.*

"I can see how that would make you mad, but *throwing a chair*? Why was that needed?"

I had no answer except a shrug. "I reacted without thinking. Kinda like a blackout for the Incredible Hulk or something. Otherwise, I would have turned a bottle of vodka straight up into my mouth. Like you guys say, I didn't want to feel what I was feeling."

"Past tense? You don't feel that way anymore?"

I opened my mouth to speak but stopped. *Dare I tell him?* "Eli, uh... something happened outside." I stopped. *Can I say it? Can I tell anybody, ever? He'll think I'm crazy! He'll tell me it wasn't real.* Eli continued to stare at me, waiting for me to speak. "Eli, I'm not sure I can even explain it. Not sure I want to, either. It's the strangest thing that's ever happened to me."

I worried that to share the details would make it less real and more crazy. I mean... only crazy, psychotic people have visions, right?

"Tell me, Lela. I won't judge you." *He must have read my mind.*

I felt so hesitant, afraid to get started on such a weird story. "Okay... but" I stopped; my emotions were so mixed up! I felt a myriad of ways... calm and peaceful, and crazy-anxious. And I could change on a dime.

Okay, tell him. Find the emotional middle ground and talk. Just the facts, ma'am. "Okay, Eli. Here goes. After what happened, I feel differently about everything. Everything! I can't explain it."

"After WHAT happened?"

"I had a, well, uh... a hallucination or something. It was a dude, but he didn't scare me. In fact, there was total serenity. This... vision or whatever... it took away my fears, every one of them, and a huge scoop of the worst kind of anger. Even my headache – all of it – poof! Gone. Something phenomenal happened out there."

In the telling, I cried, but not from emotion but from gratitude. Eli leaned forward in his chair, his eyes filled with compassion. "What did you see? Or hear? What happened?"

"Oh, I may be crazy, but I saw... I think I saw... an angel. Or something." I hiccupped a sob. "But it was my cousin Lewis. I used to call him Dude. He could light a cigarette with his toes."

Eli didn't move but a slight upturn of his mouth, the suggestion of a smile, assured me I had done right in telling the truth. Somehow, I even felt *proud* of sharing it, then doubts took over: *He's making fun of me! Why did I phrase it that way? Stupid, Lela.*

At last, he spoke. "A dramatic thing?"

I nodded and blew a sarcastic snort. *Stand by your story. It happened. Get that peace back. Keep the feeling.* "Ridiculously dramatic, Eli. I almost feel like I'm making it up or something, but *it was real!*" His expression didn't comfort me; it looked like he didn't believe me.

After a long pause, Eli spoke through a genuine smile. "I don't doubt you, and I don't doubt it was real, Lela. It's not always so dramatic, but I know you and..." he stopped to chuckle. "Yep, yours would be dramatic."

"Mine what? And don't laugh at me."

"I laugh with love. What I think is that you had one helluva lightning-bolt spiritual experience. Do you suddenly feel more... willing? More humble? Did it change your perspective about getting sober?"

Hesitantly, I answered, "I guess you can say all that."

"Have you read enough of the book to understand what a spiritual experience is? And why they say it's required for people like us?"

"Yeah, but it wasn't *God!* It was a *man*. Totally different. So stop with that bullshit again. Trust me, a spiritual experience isn't going to happen for me, Eli! God has given up because I've screwed up *everything* he's given me, at every turn. This... dude... out there, I felt there was love surrounding him, but God? No. Not God. God hates me."

"*My* God hates no one, Lela." It was a slow, calm voice as if from a daydream. "And *my* God looks different every time I see him. I feel his peace in so many things, sometimes in a patient, my fat cat, and this morning I think God smiled at me through my hairbrush."

I dared not laugh, looking at Eli in a new light. He'd often talked about himself and his journey to sobriety, but this was *way* more personal. His "hairbrush vision" sounded as crazy as the one I'd just had.

Eli's Higher Power is a hairbrush? So maybe it's like Jenny says: your Higher Power can be a Pop-Tart or anything you want... is that what's going on here?

Busting through my thoughts, Eli said softly, "Why do you think God is supposed to look a certain way? And why do you think that whoever or whatever you saw *wasn't* God?"

Silence except for the buzz between my ears and a thunderous heartbeat.

Ba-BOOM, ba-BOOM, ba-BOOM.

No, it couldn't have been God! What I saw was irreverent, like an anti-God. "Eli, get real! It's ridiculous to think that God is a hippie with torn jeans! Barefoot and smoking? Seriously!" I rolled my eyes, but my hands were shaking with fear and overwhelming emotion. "No damn 'spiritual experience' involves tipping of straw hats and flannel shirts. It's ridiculous!"

"There are no rules, Lela. Maybe your Higher Power sent a vision of your cousin so you wouldn't run away. He'd know that a Jesus-type in a robe would piss you off instead of give you peace."

His comment gave me pause. *That makes sense.* And perhaps the "sense" is why I went off the chart in denying the vision's significance.

I snarled, "And that's the point! Visions! Like some Bible-thumping zealot. Maybe I saw the burning bush! That would make as much stupid sense! The *whole thing* is stupid, Eli. I'm sorry I even brought it up." I turned, gathered my things, preparing to leave.

Eli leaned back in his chair, his arms like wings as he put his palms on the back of his head. He seemed to be studying something inside his head, lost in thought. "Put your stuff down, girl. You're killing me."

I have no idea why I did what he said; maybe the snarky Lela had left the building... or maybe not. My emotions were still on edge. After a few minutes of silence, I huffed. "*What*, Eli? Let me *go!* I need a cigarette!"

Then he laughed... a hee-haw of a laugh like a donkey. I held my lips thin and reached to pick up my book bag again. As I stood to leave, he said, "Ya know, everybody has a different idea, but I've never heard of a 1960s hippie, and I've never heard him called Dude! That's a new one! Good job!"

How did this get all casual and funny? Why is Eli joking with me? Is he saying the Dude I saw IS my God... my Higher Power? I paused long enough for him to continue the... joke. *Is that what this is? Or some kind of intervention?* He sounded far away. "Lela, you might as well sit down again. I know you're mad and I know why. And I know what you really want to know."

"*Here it comes again.* Why do you think you know so much about me?! I'm not—"

"You were going to ask WHY it happened, right? *Why* and what does it *mean*, right?"

I froze in my steps, then walked back to the chair. "Do you know those answers?"

"No, but *you* do."

"No, I *don't*." Another long silence, unnervingly long. "Okay, dammit. Tell me your theory."

"I don't have a theory. The 'WHY' of it is for you to decide. And when you figure that out, you'll know what it means." He leaned forward in his chair. "Your sponsor... Jenny, right?"

"Oh, hell! Jenny will think I'm crazy! She never told me she had a damn *vision* like some 'saved by the Lord' Pentecostal Baptist, speaking in tongues and shit!"

"It happens differently for everyone. You're not crazy and certainly not a crazy Pentecostal Baptist.

"So you don't think I'm crazy?"

"Not at all."

I sighed. I don't think I'm crazy, either. I know what I saw... and I saw him tip his hat! "What I want to know is if it will happen again." Eli nodded, urging me to continue, and I threw up my hands. The smartass in me disappeared, evidently, as I inhaled a deep sigh. "All I know is I'll never be the same again. Crazy, huh?"

"Not one bit crazy. Remember it says 'a Higher Power *as we understand him.*'" His eyes were drilled into mine.

"Well I don't *understand*, but I want to know more. I want to feel more of this... whatever it is. So peaceful, Eli. So perfect!"

The phone on Eli's desk rang and my heart sunk. I wanted to continue this conversation forever. Torn, he looked at the phone and back at me. "I've got to take this. It's my Higher Power calling." Eli stood.

I laughed, loud. "You're the crazy one."

"Love and peace, Lela, love and peace..." Eli's version of goodbye.

Looking back on that day and those in the months that followed, I understand why I was embarrassed to tell people of my bizarre vision and the relief it brought.

I couldn't yet separate spirituality from religion; I feared people would think I was a Born-Again Christian, a right-wing, close-minded hypocrite like the Baptists I grew up with. I abhorred those people.

I thought if I believed in God, I'd have no friends; no one would understand or trust me.

What I didn't understand was that if people simply looked at me and my down-to-earth messiness, heard my non-accusing voice (not to mention my bad language, they'd see my open mind. And if they didn't, fuck 'em.

But as I've grown to be more open in sobriety, my feelings about Christians have broadened, too. Turns out, some are liberal, all-inclusive people who simply worship their Higher Power in a building called a church. Potluck dinners work for them and that's cool.

I'm grateful I've found other ways and other words for my spirituality because Eli was right: God gave me a hippie in torn jeans because I would have rejected anything in a robe with a Photo-Shopped face.

I wish I could say the rest of the story was all butterflies and ice cream, but that's not how it came down. There were hundreds of challenges yet to come for Lela Fox.

But that's getting ahead of the story.

THE WHORE & THE HERD
CHAPTER 22

The van overflowed with ten squirrely women, including a pensive me. We were on our way to the biggest AA club on our schedule, POWERLESS, the one I liked the most. With 23 days of sobriety under my belt, a level head had returned on most days, and my eyes had opened to a bit of truth about myself and my disease.

Stephanie and I sat quietly in the back while the other women made a ruckus. "I am Bobo Golden!" Andrea squealed, crafting her stripper name; a combination of her first pet's name and the street where she grew up. With that formula, my stripper name would be Sammy Flanders. Ho-hum. I didn't bother to share it.

Strippers. Bleck.

I'd heard a few of the women at R&R talk about the jobs they'd taken to earn money for drugs. "I'd do anything," they had said. Though the term "crack whore" hadn't been used verbatim, the concept was discussed often. I felt bad for those girls; my story was only half as bad and it was eating my lunch.

The scene at The Snatch, when Stuart bought me a lap dance that left me humiliated and dirty, still made my stomach flip and dip. It represented everything that was dirty in my old life.

The humiliation... still raw. Somehow that night felt dirtier than my "interview" to be a day-dancer at the place.

Drunk as a cow, I had gone to The Snatch when Stuart and I had a fight.

Why would I choose The Snatch? I have no idea. Undaunted once I arrived, I dashed backstage to hang with "the girls" and cried about wanting to leave my husband. They encouraged me to do it, but when I said I couldn't afford it, the prettiest girl suggested I get a job as her "junior dancer," whatever that meant.

She talked to her boss, and within a few minutes, I was dancing in a dark room with four men watching, wearing a thong I'd borrowed from one of the girls. I closed my eyes in remembering the Shame of that night, tasting bile. The man on the end had rubbed his crotch watching me, and I thought it confirmed that I was doing a good job. Hot, hot, hot Lela.

Now I thought yuck, yuck, yuck Lela. *How COULD YOU?! How could YOUR MOTHER'S DAUGHTER do such a thing? Margaret Fox, the prude of the Southland, would sink into oblivion if she knew.*

No surprise I wanted to be a drunk stripper, though; I'd been accused of being an exhibitionist many times, starting in the seventh grade when I streaked around a hotel. And since then, I'd made a point of using my body and sex appeal to get my way. I had no Shame; it had been said... boy-oh-boy; I have plenty now!

In my drinking days, I thought sex was all I had... the only thing I could bring to the table. And because I wouldn't, or couldn't, say *no* to anything, I got into some bizarre, somewhat-deviant sexual behavior. Things that brought so much Guilt and Remorse I became buried under it.

A shiver went down my spine. My sexual past was disgusting to me now; it tasted like vomit. When I shuddered, Stephanie flashed a look my way, knotting her brow. I didn't want to talk about it, so I smiled back at her, sending the "I'm okay" signal.

The girls up front continued their yelling and laughing; I continued my solitary thinking. *But... isn't it odd that I think I'm a bi-sexual and find that perfectly normal, not "yucky" at all. Through the years, my lesbian relationships have been the only honest ones. I think maybe that's who and what I am.*

What bothered me was the myriad of *men* I'd slept with... the thought of it sunk my heart. My old friend Shame glowed like a 100-watt bulb, blinding me and separating me from any chance of ever having a normal life. I was sure of that.

I marveled at how desperate I'd been in my drunkenness. And the bitch of it was... I knew I was doing wrong *while I was doing it*; I knew at the whole time! The Guilt choked me then, and it was still kicking my ass.

The "whole sex thing" would be something I'd have to face head-on to keep my recovery going; I knew that. But I feared I'd never be ready to face it. Jenny would be cool and help me through it... if I could even talk about the worst parts.

Her lectures played in my head repeatedly; she was right: I must let go of Shame or I'd drink again. "Forgive yourself or fail," she'd said a hundred times.

I'd have to forgive myself for having more partners than any *man* I'd ever known. For things I'd never told, for being a slut, an easy mark, a manipulative hustler who used sex as currency, playing the vixen to get her way... or to punish my prey, make a point to my husband, sometimes to get a party started.

So much dirtiness wrapped around my psyche... enough to mummify me. Enough to stifle me.

Stephanie touched my shoulder, breaking my concentration. "Are you okay, Lela? You're so quiet...."

I looked at her with a flat, emotionless face. The van had stopped at the red light in front of the POWERLESS club... the red light also adjacent to a strip club much larger than The Snatch.

No shit. The AA club was tucked in a building behind a strip club in West Palm Beach, even in a decent part of town.

The neon sign, in all its glory, flashed red day and night. "Hot All Over! Girls! Girls! Girls!" Each week at POWERLESS, I'd swallowed my Shame as we passed and never told a soul of my connection to a club just like it. But there it was... bitter Shame on my face.

Through a fog, I saw words on a page... a page we read in group yesterday. Something like. "Our troubles, we thought, had been of my own making."

I opened my mouth to tell Stephanie what was on my mind... all about the night at The Snatch, all about spreading my legs so wide.

But I said the opposite. Calm. Cool. Quiet. I said, "Stephanie. I'm not like that anymore... and I don't have to be. Ever again."

"Uhhhh... okaaay." Her dumbfounded face looked comical but, being oh-so-compassionate Stephanie, it was a concerned look. "Am I supposed to know what that means?"

I ignored her question, staring at a spot over her head. "I have more to offer now. I don't need the attention. I can be free."

"I still don't know what–"

"And I don't have to cry about it anymore, either."

Suddenly, Stephanie "popped" with understanding; she realized her role: the supportive friend who agreed with everything no matter what. And she played the part beautifully.

My friend squeezed my hands. "Right! You don't have to cry about that shit because you've *outgrown* it!"

"Because now I'm sober."

"Yes! You're sober and smart!" She huffed a fake-evil laugh that brought a smile to my face.

"I don't have to act that way anymore. Never again!"

Her exaggerated frenzy rose turned to hilarity. "No way! Nada. Never!"

"Exactly! I hate that part of me."

"But you don't have that part anymore."

"It's like vodka made my clothes fly off."

"Without vodka, you're fashionably dressed.

"I hate the leftover dirtiness... the Shame."

"Then *get rid* of it! Abracadabra... *poof!* It's gone!"

"Like magic, I'm sober and sane."

"And clean!"

"*Hell* yeah!"

"You're awesome!"

"You're fantastic!"

"Alcohol stinks."

"Like a rotten rat!"

Our voices had built to a crescendo that put the other girls in silence. I saw eight pairs of eyes staring flatly at us and cracked up... Stephanie was laughing just as hard. Then the two of us fell together in a hug of hysteria. I laughed through tears, relieved and scared at the same time.

Only a woman can understand this combination of silliness and seriousness, I thought... only a woman who'd suffered through the pain of a broken heart and the joy of a sober mind yearning for the other side.

☼ ☼ ☼ ☼ ☼

Wednesday night meetings at the POWERLESS Club were always rousing; different from the ones at other clubs we frequented. That night, I figured out why.

The three R&R vans were the only "druggie buggies" in the parking lot.

Old-timers filled the room – the kind of people who weren't fighting a drink but living a life of sobriety... only fighting against an alcoholic personality who faced everyday problems.

We were never told we couldn't share at the outside meetings we attended, and many (including me) rambled at other clubs. But at POWERLESS, we listened.

Because if you listened, you could learn. And that night, I learned a lot.

After the meeting, I called shotgun because I wanted to talk to Lin, our driver. With excitement in my voice and my head, I said, "That meeting was awesome! I freaked out at first, but they were talking about normal life, Lin! A fun life without drugs and alcohol! Daily inventory of their shortcomings, like they got rid of their sober insanity at some point *beforehand*. Tell me more about this!"

Lin was a soft-spoken Asian man, a counselor like Eli; Stephanie's counselor as a matter of fact. He began a soliloquy that lasted most of the ride back to the center. "Once you've passed the time of daily cravings, Lela, you find *yourself*. You appear, a whole new you with a new head on your shoulders and a shit-load of hope. It's a beautiful thing. Suddenly you like and respect yourself. In fact, you can look in the mirror and say 'I love you,' and you'll truly mean it."

My heart sunk. It would take decades before I could say "I love you" to the face that had ruined my life. "But Lin, I don't mean what may happen when I'm old, I just mean a little bit later... like in a month. Anything further blows my mind."

"One day at a time, Lela, you know that. But sobriety means you begin to grow into the person you were meant to be, at the age you are now, in the prime of your life."

I let him talk, absorbing every word, but he soon turned the tables.

"But that 'new you' is still an alcoholic, with all the screwed-up feelings and thought patterns we have."

"Wait!" I said, "The same thought patterns even *after* I'm sober? That's not fair! And for how long?" It was a whiny question in a tone I hated as soon as I said it. Lin paused and I think I saw his eyes roll... as much as somebody can do when they're driving. I said, "Sorry... I'm acting like–"

"Like a newcomer," He glanced over at me and flashed a smile.

"Har, har, mister. But keep going. I want to know how to deal with... life after I get out of here."

"Let's just start over. Do you have a Higher Power, Lela? A power other than yourself?"

Wow. What a shift in the subject! But listen, Lela... listen to what he says. Your life may depend on it. A mumbled "yes" was all I could muster, but underneath, I wanted to share the whole Dude vision and get his take. I was still shy about it and worried people would call me delusional. Or maybe all those years of drinking *made* me delusional.

Lin kept talking. "See, you and your Higher Power will become friends. Friends... the same as when you're friends with *people*. Of course, you're not on a level playing field or anything... he/she/it is much more powerful, but you become *so* in tune with this power, and it feeds you confidence and joy in everyday things. Suddenly, you'll find gratitude in stupid, simple things like... I don't know... clean sheets and Chapstick. You'll find that talking to people, even customers or bosses or those with... quote, more power than you... communication becomes easy and honest."

"I want that, Lin. I want confidence and joy like you say. A life without chaos and where I can help others. I'm not sober enough to do it now but–"

"Not true, Lela. I've seen you help the new girls, like when you listened and hugged Anita when she cried about her husband. And when you picked up the slack for Abby that day when she was sick. I've seen you do many kind and loving things. Inside, you are a kind person and it's obvious. Maybe it was just hidden by alcohol."

Lin glanced at me and smiled. "I can't wait to see you in *real* twelfth step work. Lela Fox will be awesome! Just stay sober, girl. You're rockin' it!"

I had never felt so supported and encouraged in my life. Gratitude spewed from me like a fountain, a foreign feeling but one so powerful I thought I'd burst. No one had ever said they thought I was kind-hearted or loving, either, and now Lin was another to assume I'd stay sober. I felt pride swell in my chest.

Then Lin said something strange.

Though his eyes focused on the road, it somehow felt like he was speaking loudly and just inches from my face. "But you must still say moo."

My confusion was immediate. "Say what?"

"You can't stay sober unless you're humble... you're just one of the herd. Say moo."

"Uh... Lin... are you just being weird."

"It's not weird, it's a thing. See, you're not special... just one of the cows.

One member of the herd. Do you understand what I mean?"

"Yeah... I'm just a run-of-the-mill old drunk, nothing special. You guys have taught me that, but cows?"

Lin grinned. "Your Higher Power is the bull. Without the bull, you can't produce. So say moo."

The moo thing rang true, as weird as it sounded, and it made me see how important I thought I was.

I went back and forth, but underneath, it was hard to accept that I just a regular alcoholic person. I'd always thought I scored above average; I'd always been a little prettier, smarter, more refined, more talented. All evidence to the contrary was ignored, even when I hated myself for screwing up.

To be told I'd have to step down from my high horse was a shock; I had to swallow hard.

An egomaniac with an inferiority complex is the perfect description.

"Just say moo" became my mantra for twenty years, AA-speak to spark humility when I need a double-dose.

Sometimes, at my home group meetings, the whole room would "moo" when I walked in. It was flattering as hell, and thus, dangerous.

I may bring something *new* to the rooms; I may even be inspirational, but I'm not "all that." Nope, I'm just one of the herd, singing "moo" in a chorus.

And I still sing out of tune.

MAIL CALL
CHAPTER 23

"Don't sugar-coat this shit, Karen! This is *real* stuff, not a fairy tale! It's brutal, and raw, and hard as steel. I'm baring my soul every day, breaking through all the bullshit I used to believe about myself! So quit talking to me like I'm a child... or a mental patient. Here I am fighting for my life and there's nothing 'sweet' about it, dammit!" My hands were slick with sweat as I gripped the phone's handset.

Though trying her best to be supportive, Karen couldn't get out of big-sister mode. Not that I expected her to understand the depths of my emotions and anxiety, but she was placating me, adding sweet syrup about how beautiful life would be sober, blah, blah, blah. I heard so much butterflies-out-the-butt stuff I thought I would barf.

She meant well, but I felt it was a wasted phone call and I hung up in a huff. A disappointment for several reasons; one was that I hadn't gotten to the subject I wanted to share with her. I'd decided to tell her about my vision, the details of Dude. I wanted someone to know that the same illusion was "talking to me" somewhere inside my head. Not only that, when I talked to him, I could somehow feel him listening.

The connection was so strong; I burst into tears with just one thought of him. I think I was trying to pray but never got that far. Still, somehow, he heard me.

Jenny knew the basics of my Higher Power concoction, but not near all of it and not about my cousin Lewis the Dude. I still couldn't trust people to think it was as real as I knew it was.

What if they put me back in the crazy hospital?

But I knew Karen would understand, or at least not consider me koo-koo. After I hung up, I thought it might be easier to write about it, anyway. A letter, but not official mail... more like a journal entry stuffed in an envelope. Karen wouldn't mind the free-form prose, I decided.

Stomping back to my room, I saw Abby was drawing in her sketchbook, headphones on. I waved sheepishly when I sat on the bed and planted my feet to use my thighs as a desk. The magical notebook I'd created was on my bedside table. It brimmed with calligraphy scribbles and circled phrases, color-coordinated with the set of color pencils I bought at Publix.

Okay, write.

My red pen, reserved for important moments of clarity, was poised at a blank page, unmoving. *Hmm... how does a person explain a spiritual experience to a non-alcoholic? Never mind, here goes.*

The letter started with a headline, per my advertising background. "I saw God." No, maybe Dude *is* God, but I still don't like the word.

I started a new sheet: "I saw Dude." With careful wording, I told Karen how the ethereal feelings had stayed with me, the feelings of peace and well-being had stayed, too. Also, I told her about my fears, writing until to the point of emotional exhaustion. For the first time, I closed my eyes and prayed. Instantly overtaken by gratitude, tears rolled down my cheeks and into my ears as I lay on my bed.

I suddenly understood what Lin had said about becoming "friends" with my Higher Power... because my prayer was in the most casual tone I'd ever used... with anybody. As if I was talking to a good buddy. Maybe I hadn't prayed because I didn't know what to say; suddenly I knew exactly how to communicate with the elusive power that had been guiding me.

In silence, with my eyes closed, I "said" to the man in the clouds as he smoked... *Dude, I need some help down here. You confuse the hell out of me. Can you explain yourself? Is it okay to ask that? I'm pretty sure you are my Higher Power... but are you God? Maybe Jesus? Ouch! No, that word scares me. Should it? Did I really see you? Is my strange idea of you offensive? A slap in the face?*

I jerked my eyes open and stopped there, afraid that I had, indeed, insulted God. Jenny said any version of God pleased God... that he/she/it wasn't picky. As long as there is honor in prayer, she had said, your Higher Power would listen.

But my sponsor would be generous with the "whatever you think" concept; she was as creative and open-minded as I was – no, even more. And she'd support me no matter what because she knew my resistance to a Higher Power and hatred of religion. She hammered me with the "God of your own understanding" concept. *Is that attitude allowed in Heaven? Dude, are you God? Are you my doorknob?*

I must have dozed but woke up abruptly.

Knock! Knock! Knock! Ten o'clock PM. Victor said, "Lela, Abby! Time for your nighttime medicine!" *Right, wake up and take your sleeping pill!* The letter to Karen, now snuggled under the covers with me, covered four pages. I remembered my prayer and stared at my shaking hands. *Damn, Lela, you prayed. So why are you now so afraid?*

☼ ☼ ☼ ☼ ☼

My night medication included other important parts of the anti-depressant cocktail Dr. Mallory prescribed, and the regiment seemed to be working. There was no depression, despite the intense self-searching in group and individual therapy, and I wasn't manic. I was sleeping like a normal person, the ideal eight hours and no naps until tonight's random shut-eye.

Before writing the letter, Karen had upset me. *No, I LET her upset me. It was my fault; I take responsibility.* My sweet sister was trying to be nice, but I believed I couldn't let up, that I must be driving, pounding, stretching, hammering... pushing myself into perfect sobriety.

As my jaw clenched, I wondered where the anger came from. I'd prayed; I'd connected to my Higher Power, been able to explain it to Karen in a positive way, and I suspected her mind would be open to my not-so-typical ideas.

So why are you mad, Lela? What's on your mind?

☼ ☼ ☼ ☼ ☼

In our next therapy session, I told Eli, "I want to hurry this up, get started on a sober life. Get a job and a dog. Do I have to stay the full thirty days?"

While he agreed I was flourishing, bravely facing issues that had kept me drinking for decades, he said I wasn't ready. "The meat thermometer isn't at 165 degrees yet," he said. "Not only that, you're in a pink cloud."

"First, I'm not cooking a chicken. And what's a pink cloud?"

"Pink cloud: you're ultra-happy to be sober, ultra-confident that you'll stay that way. It happens to newly sober people all the time. But it's not real and goes away the first time you face a *real* problem or temptation. This confidence is coming too soon, kiddo. You're only *truly* sober when the pink cloud goes away. That's why outpatient sessions are so important. You're in an insulated reality right now. Problems mount when you're on your own."

I brought up the meat thermometer comment at the next meeting with Jenny. Every Thursday, the two of us sat in my turquoise-and-gray living room, spreading papers and tears on the coffee table. Jenny always brought some kind of worksheet and made me admit things that made me cry. *How can a person hurt me so bad and make me feel so good?*

Per her instruction, I called her almost every night. During those phone calls, I sometimes listened to the depths of her wisdom and sometimes I blubbered about my unsurmountable, oh-my-God-horrible problems. She always stopped my blubbering with some damn happy shit I was supposed to think about, or some assignment meant to change my perspective.

When I tried to blame others, Jenny stopped me in mid-sentence, saying "that's beside the point, Lela." But I couldn't quite get the concept of bearing *all* the blame, thinking their part should live alongside my part of the issue. Jenny's repetitive line: "Focus on what *you* did, Lela."

"But–"

"No buts."

She refused to buy into my bullshit or let me make excuses for bad behavior. But when I struggled, her hugs were soft and sincere, and she oozed with understanding. At times, I felt she was my one and only lifeline among my life's most turbulent waters.

She said she was taking it slow with me, but I felt I was growing in leaps and bounds. Our "step work" began with a word-by-word study of the Big Book, starting on the title page. Literally – the title page and how the subtitle says the past-tense of recover. "RecoverED, Lela!" After three intense weeks, Jenny announced that I'd successfully worked the "newcomer version" of the first three steps.

"There are other versions?" I asked.

"In your 'career' as a sober person, you'll do multiple fourth steps, I hope."

"But–"

She knew what my objection would be, I supposed. "Things change, Lela. You grow, you expand your life. And later, you'll understand more about yourself, suddenly be able to understand your twisted motivations. I mean, you have the tenth step for daily issues, but a thorough housecleaning every few years is preferred... or at least that's what my sponsor says. And so far, she's been right."

"So... what? Some sponsors do things differently?"

Jenny laughed. "Always different, Lela. There is no set curriculum because everybody has their own path. Each person has a different story to share, a different idea of how to stay sober. You'll be happy about that one day... when you get another sponsor."

"No! I want *you* to *always* be my sponsor!" Panic set in.

Jenny looked at me with a smile in her eyes. "If you're smart – and you are – you'll have many sponsors."

I didn't understand, rushing to change her mind. I complained that it would be like changing therapists and having to tell my whole background again. Her reply was even more confusing. "Lela, your story gets shorter each time you tell it."

She saw my flat-out confused face and chuckled. "You'll learn so much when you become a sponsor yourself. You'll just have to trust me." My mouth was still open in awe of what I'd just heard. *Me? A sponsor?*

"Let's move on... you asked for my thoughts on your 'pink cloud?'"

Shaking myself back to reality, I cleared my throat. "Yes. Please." I was laser-focused on how fast I could move forward... how to pop the pink cloud and do my fourth step.

Jenny said my pink cloud would be hard to pop. When I asked why, her answer was so spot-on it scared me. Because I was a creative writer, she said, I'd probably created a storybook picture of sobriety, solid as a rock and starring Rebecca of Sunnybrook Farm. I'd "forgotten" to consider how to face life when it gave me lemons, forgotten to allow for realities like financial issues, employment problems, and how to handle my divorce from Stuart.

Sigh. She's right. But how do I imagine the worst-case scenario? How do I know what life will be like when I'm sober and sober-minded?

"That's the whole point, Lela. You're not 'sober-minded' because you're still in rehab, still insulated from all but the most severe realities-to-come." Hearing that truth upset the shit out of me; I was beyond disappointed.

"If it's going to take that long, then fuck it, Jenny!"

"See?"

"See what?"

"See how you still think like an alcoholic?" She puffed up her hair, spiraling curls into it to mock me. "You say 'It's too hard so I'm not doing it!'

So see why I think you're a tough case?"

I sat back on the sofa and sighed. "But, Jenny... you also say I'm 'progressing beautifully!' So which is it?"

She just laughed that tinkling wind chime of a laugh and told me I was cute and inspiring and the exact challenge she needed; she never answered the question.

I hungered to "graduate" the program quickly, so I did everything she and Eli suggested. I kept a journal, shared in group sessions, and listened to every word in meetings outside the center.

Then, with Jenny's help, I started a list of the people I had harmed in my drinking years. The list was long, and the task seemed daunting.

Despite the odds against me, *I* would be the one who beat alcoholism; I believed it with all my heart, felt it in my bones.

But remember, you're just a cow, Lela. I thought of the moo-cow thing often and had always imagined a herd of beef cows going off to slaughter. But as time passed, I felt like a dairy cow, going to the barn for milking, to *give*. I laughed at how ridiculous it was to think that way but I knew the change in thinking was significant. Jenny, a city girl, didn't even know there were different types of cows, which cracked me up but ruined my point. She didn't see this as "making progress" as I did.

All these thoughts were swirling in my overloaded head as I smoked on the back patio on the center; I'd been alone with my thoughts despite being surrounded by twenty or thirty other newly sober alcoholics. Suddenly, Drinnen appeared with a wire cart, stood tall on the concrete bench, and sang, "Mail call!" Again, everybody rushed to surround her and those who'd been inside rushed out. There was nothing better than mail call!

Communication from outside the walls of R&R meant the world to me and my peeps had come through, keeping in touch even when I didn't write back. Mom and Dad wrote sweet letters about their dull and everyday life. They shared news about their garden, how Aunt Val was doing, sent well wishes from my uncles and Granny Liz... and talked on and on about how much the calves had brought at auction. I loved it! A helpful distraction and a reminder that there *is* something beyond rehab.

Jennifer sent letters often, too, and I received a few from my friend Lola, and on occasion, Bo. Karen went out of her way, sending something every single day... cookies and treats, but mostly her packages contained silly stuff. One gift I remember specifically was a set of personalized pencils with the name "Howie Brewer." (Say what? It was so random, it cracked me up.) Also, every Karen package contained thoughtful scribbles of support and encouragement and the same from her husband John.

That day, I received four letters and a package. Lucky day! Bo wrote; I opened that first. Good news, he said: His "A" on an English paper was possible only because of me and the communication skills he'd inherited from me.

Instead of thinking it was good news, it set off an alarm. *What if Bo also inherited alcoholism and Bi-Polar Disorder from me?* That had been a passing worry when I'd been drinking but the fear came screaming forward with that one innocent comment. The tears started. *Here you go again, Tear Bucket Jim.*

I also got a card from Mom and Dad that day, with Mom's careful and neat script, followed by Daddy's unreadable scratching. Jennifer sent a funny card about how "getting well" meant getting older. Lola sent another letter, heartfelt as usual, and signed by my other ex-employee, Caroline. *Wow - Lola must have driven across town just to get Caroline's signature. How nice is that!*

I smiled opening the card from Damon. Even though it was a 59-cent card and stupid, he wrote four paragraphs on the inside. Sweet Damon, always on my side.

The best piece of mail that day came from Karen. A card, blank inside. I realized immediately it was done after I'd fussed at her for "sugar-coating" my situation and treating me like a fragile child.

On one side of the card, she wrote the syrupy-sweet bullshit she knew I hated, then sprayed an adhesive and sprinkled it with sugar. Real sugar. The other side, uncoated, said, "Lela, you ignorant slut." I laughed so hard I cried.

To this day, my underwear drawer is lined with the cards and letters I received in rehab. And to this day, they make me laugh as much as they make me cry.

Especially haunting is seeing my father's writing, reading his encouragement to "march forward like a soldier," and "show 'em how it's done."

It's like Daddy is talking to me from the grave, urging me to push through the crippling grief I have clung to for so long. Daddy's passing changed my life once again and changed my relationship with Dude.

Sorry… that's getting ahead of the story, the story of another Lifetime or two.

TRAUMA EFFECTS
CHAPTER 24

The next week with Dr. Mallory, I held out my hand to show the tremor I'd been noticing. "I'm shaky. You can see the physical part, but I'm also emotionally unsteady a little. I was yearning for more help, but his response was what I expected from a shrink: "The side effects subside over time. I think you're on the right mix, Lela. Hang in there. Let's give it another week."

Sigh. "I know... I know the drill. Just don't jerk me around on mood medicine, please. I go crazy with changes."

His cowlick blew in the air conditioner's breeze. "I know what you mean, and I promise to be gentle." That comment changed my attitude about the stoic Dr. Mallory. His care seemed genuine, so unlike other shrinks I'd seen.

Shaky or not, I was ready to get the hell out of there... go to a halfway house, get an apartment and a job and a life and a plant and a dog. More than anything, I wanted to see my son, and I wanted my cell phone back. After all these days, I'd had it with the stupid rules around there.

Just like an alcoholic, I thought my way was the better way.

"Eli, I *know* I'm ready because I'm just a simple alcoholic... not a gutter rat on heroin." I lowered my voice to mimic a comedian popular at the time. "Lela Fox, high-bottom drunk with a dent in the Mercedes!" The joke was lost on Eli, evidently. "But because of that, I can jump the hump easier than the other, uh, more low-bottom people, right?"

"The high-bottom/low-bottom definitions you're using are, basically, bullshit. No matter how far down the scale you've gone, you need the same discipline and re-wiring of your brain. And some people, 'high-bottom' according to your definition, are the hardest to crack. So you have no advantage."

"But—"

"And no DISadvantage, either. You're just one of the cows."

"That again!" I huffed.

"That *always*, Lela. If you think you're less than or better than any other person in the world, it's a red-siren danger for an alcoholic mind. You just *are*. You're the same as everybody else. And I bet your Dude thinks so, too."

I wouldn't let go of the get-out-quick argument. "Then why have some people been here a long, long time? Aren't they low-bottom people?"

"Again, your terminology isn't—"

"Aw, come *on*, Eli! You know what I'm talking about."

"I know that only petty, newly sober people worry about it or believe it makes a difference."

"So you're calling me 'petty?'"

"Yes. And flat-out wrong... think about it, Lela. You've been in jail, been jerked around emotionally by your husband, tried smoking crack, and you weighed next to nothing when you got here! You aren't such a 'high-bottom drunk' after all."

Stumped, I widened my eyes and looked at Eli with a flat expression.

"Just go on back to your apartment. Talk to Abby about it..."

"No, Abby is a low-bottom and she'll think I'm being overly stupid about my problems."

"No, Lela. You don't get it. It's not a competition! And it's not a race to get better, either."

"Well, I'm not talking to Abby. And Jenny agrees with YOU. NOBODY is hearing what I'm saying!" I stood to pace his office, my bottom lip quivering as tears threatened to fall.

"Have you stopped to think about *why* nobody agrees with you? Because... duh. Maybe, just maybe, could it be because you're wrong? Knowing sobriety for a few weeks, you think you know more than your sponsor, or me?"

"Yes, and Lin, too."

Eli sighed. "You're strong but you're stubborn as hell. I mean that as somewhat of a compliment."

"Somewhat?"

Another sigh. "Let's just talk about it again tomorrow. Maybe journal about it. You work a lot of things out of paper, right?"

"I do."

"Then go... do it! Your color-coordinated journal would love to argue with you about it."

"Don't make fun of my journal, either!"

Eli chuckled and stood over his desk, stashing files in his well-worn leather satchel. "Okay, Lela, I'm going home. It's late. I'll talk to you tomorrow."

I was being kicked out of my own counselor's office, which pissed me off to the Nth degree. But there was nothing to say that would change his mind or make him listen to me. I stomped out and walked straight to my apartment, not even stopping to talk to the low-bottom people who hung out on the smoking patio.

Another morning, the same as the nineteen before it... ten knocks on the door, Victor's yell, ten more knocks. I was quick to wake up that day, feeling like I'd just closed my eyes. *Up and at 'em!* I reached over to mark a big X on the color-coordinated calendar I kept beside my bed.

Twenty-six days without a drink. Almost a whole month. It seems impossible. You're gonna do it, Lela, you're going all the way.

In actuality, the whole thing still terrified me. *"Terrified with a capital T," as Daddy would say. What if this isn't real? What if I get sober and can't find a job, can't function outside of this place?* A buzz started behind my eardrums, throbbing in time with my heartbeat, which was at twice the normal rate.

Stop it, dumbass! You and your magic magnifying mind. It's okay... Dude says so. Your Higher Power says you're gonna do it.

Yesterday, two people had left AMA, Against Medical Advice. They just walked out and didn't come back. They were not the first two to leave, and several had been kicked out for breaking the rules.

Trula, Abby's friend, with full privileges to go to the store, bought a beer there and drank it in the group room, daring them to kick her out. "A cry for help," they called it. Trula's parents were coming from Michigan to take her home. In the meantime, she was in quarantine.

The relapses happening around me were scary, underlining the power of

INSANITY by Lela Fox

addiction and the power required to beat the disease. My gratitude blossomed.

Halfway down the path to the center that day, I realized I'd forgotten to make my bed. I ran back, half-frantic and half-pissed. I was sweating when I entered my room and rushed through the task, doing it half-ass at best; the result was far from perfect. As if on cue, Victor stuck his head in the room, looked at the bed, then back at me with a stern face. "Re-do it."

"Damn, Victor! What's the deal with making the bed, anyway?"

His response was simple: "Discipline. Not ours, *yours*."

Hmmm. MY discipline. Discipling MYSELF. Damn if he isn't right! That's what I need to do... nobody's doing it for me, not even Dude. He comes and goes at MY discretion. Same as my willingness to listen to Jenny, even willingness to read the damn Big Book.

Back at the center and smoking outside, as usual, I tried to tell Abby of this new epiphany when Lin called us inside for the morning sessions. He pulled me aside. "Lela, you're going to a small group today."

"What small group?"

"We call it Trauma Effects."

"What the hell, Lin!? You think I have PTSD?"

"It's not just for people with Post-Traumatic Stress Disorder, Lela." With a scolding tone, he might as well have been shaking his finger at me. "Keep an open mind... you may learn something."

I'd seen the people who attended that group in the weeks I'd been in rehab. There were usually about seven folks and they happened to be the people I knew the least. Outside of that small group, the girls, especially, acted completely uninterested in learning and stayed to themselves. Almost snotty-like. I'd avoided them and they'd avoided me.

In fact, I'd only talked to one of them, one time. A hefty blonde named Angel. She said she'd been at R&R for seven months. *Seven months?! Why?* I knew her drug of choice was heroin and she inferred she'd gone pretty low down the scale. Same with her friend the tall Scottish girl; Angel told me she had also been on the brink of death and had been in rehab for a long time.

So my reaction to Lin's insistence that I go to that group seemed wrong to me. "But those are low-bottom people! What the hell can I learn from *them?*"

"Uh... finish that sentence, Lela?"

My brow wrinkled, wondering what the hell he meant. Finally, I got it. "And what can *they* learn from *me?*"

182

"Right. It always goes both ways."

"But Lin, I don't want to go! I don't *need* to go."

Lin sighed. "I'm sorry you feel that way." I thought I'd convinced him, but he had merely paused. "But you're going, no matter what you say."

He thinks I have PTSD? From Stuart's cruel treatment of me? From a few nights in jail? Could I really have this disorder? Then I chuckled to myself, thinking yet-another ailment would be the icing on my mental health cake... as if I needed *that!*

Five women and two men attended. I thought they must be seriously psychotic with PTSD, or maybe just "unwilling," as Jenny would say. "Incapable of being honest with themselves." Another thought was that their families just wanted them out of the way. *Aha! Or maybe they're hiding here so they don't have to go to jail.*

Wait! I'm assuming they're all low-bottom people anyway. I only know Angel and the Scottish girl. And I don't know their story. Maybe Lin is right... maybe we share something I don't know yet. I made the decision to open my mind.

Lin led the group and winked at me before opening the floor.

Angel started by telling her story. I listened with rapt attention. She was on the lake with a bunch of friends, she said, and injected a guy with a normal, everyday dose of heroin... and he overdosed on the spot. They were on a boat and couldn't get medical help before he died. On top of that, everybody got arrested and taken to jail. The story got worse: Angel was charged with murder. *Murder!*

She kept talking and my jaw dropped another ten inches toward the floor. While she was waiting for trial... it happened again! Same exact thing! *No wonder she's crazy!*

An incredible feeling of gratitude overcame me. *She's earned her mental illness, and all that happened to whiny little Lela Fox and your high-bottom ass was getting hassled by a crazy husband and spending a few nights in jail... big fucking deal. This woman will carry a living hell for the rest of her life!*

My thoughts swirled. *Maybe all that trauma means she'll NEVER get sober. Is that why she's staying so long? Her red-headed Scottish friend, too... does the amount of time in rehab increase the chance of success? Just for them or for everybody?*

A man named Paul spoke and interrupted my thoughts. I hadn't known his name but had seen that he walked with a limp, keeping his head down.

Now I assumed his disability had something to do with his PTSD. I guessed right when he started to talk.

Paul said his gambling bookie threw him out of the car while driving on I-75 at seventy MPH. "If I hadn't been drunk," he said, "It would have killed me." He cried when telling the story, saying he was struggling as much with his gambling addiction as he was with alcohol cravings.

The story touched my heart, and I wanted to give him a hug, but that wasn't allowed in group sessions.

Again, I felt so lucky to have the simple, easy story I had. I was, indeed, just one of the cows. Lin caught my eye, and I shook my head hard as if to say, "Do not call on me!" But Angel stared me down with an evil eye. "What's your story, Curly... what's your name?"

My heart went nuts with fear... ba-BOOM, ba-BOOM. But I answered the woman, hesitantly. "I'm Lela... and my story is nothing. Nothing like you guys. I have no clue why Lin told me to come here."

"Ooh! Denial for Lela!" Angel sang. Grunts of confirmation in the background.

The redhead Scot girl echoed Angel's sentiments. "Trust me – they'll make you talk eventually. Like they did me."

"No, it's, uh, not that at all. It's this special group. I just think..." Seven pairs of eyes drilled into me, but I glanced to the side to see Lin smiling at me. *That sonofabitch tricked me... trying to teach me a lesson.* "See y'all, it was all because of Lin. He thought–"

"No, not what LIN thought! Say what YOU think, what YOU feel."

"Jeezus! Back down, you guys!" Their eyes remained intense, challenging me with looks I remember from the redneck girls in high school. "Okay, okay... here's what I think. I think Lin thought I needed to hear that other people had it worse than me. I've been whiny and bitching about being, uh, mistreated by somebody else. But that's small potatoes! I mean... I've never been accused of murder! Or thrown out of a car!"

"So you got shit on... by life in general and a few assholes in specific," Angel said.

My throat shrunk in diameter; I was so afraid to answer and felt like I would choke. *Lela, you are sooooo out of place here. Shut your mouth because you have no answer, anyway.*

But I didn't have to answer; Angel had merely paused. "You're no different from me, girl. I got shit on with bad luck and bad choices – the choices *I* made because I was high. Because *I* was a long-term fuck-up and out of control. It all boils down to me being the same kind of stupid as you."

My eyes flew wide, wondering how this poor woman could commiserate with someone as "high bottom" as me. "Life sucks, girl. Most people suck, too."

My anxiety hit a high, my hands shaking in fear of being judged, despite her words that said the opposite. *They don't understand. We're too different to be any kind of "alike." That has to be obvious as hell!*

But Angel kept talking. "And they say getting sober doesn't make other people suck less. It just makes *me* suck less. Same as you."

"You mean, what? Wait! I'm not, uh, haven't been–"

The Scottish girl, Olivia, interrupted. "I don't care where you've been, Curly. That's what they teach us in this damn room. There's no such thing as high-bottom or low-bottom, PTSD or whatever, we're all a fatality of the disease of addiction."

The group talked behind Olivia as she stared at me without blinking. I couldn't speak because I was... *wow. Blown away.* This was a whole new way of looking at things for me. *"No matter how long down the scale we have gone..." seems I've read that somewhere. But I'm nothing like them!*

My thoughts were so loud I thought everybody in the room could hear them. *But, like Angel said, she made those shitty decisions herself... and I did the same. Their decisions were just worse? Is that true?*

As if Lin heard my thoughts, he said to the group. "Decisions driven by the judgement of an addict, no matter the outcome, are bad decisions. Angel, you made some whoppers." The group laughed, to my surprise. "But Lela so did you."

Without knowing a thing about my story, Angel and Olivia shouted, "Hell, yeah!" as if it was an expected chant, and the others mumbled agreement.

I felt used, singled out, and pissed off at Lin. "Dammit Lin, you didn't have to put me on the spot like this!"

"Yes, I think I did. And I did it on purpose."

Angel rolled her eyes. "He does it all the time, but people like you help us so much. You'll never know how much..."

Lin interrupted her. "Don't worry: I only put the people who can hear and understand in this group. So I'll answer the question you asked Eli a hundred times: there's no difference between 'high-bottom' or 'low-bottom.' There's no reason for you to feel like you *need* less help or *deserve* less help. We're all here for the same reason."

Olivia spoke again. "Most addicts, drunks included, can't even judge if they're low or high, anyway. Lin's taught me that I thought some pretty bad things were just... normal when I was using. Now I know they're not."

Lin said, "Lela, do you want to tell your story?"

I answered immediately. "No!" Lin stared at me in the silence that followed. I had no intention of whining about an arrest for domestic violence to compare with their trauma. I shook my head at Lin and his hopeful expression one more time.

"Okay, Lela's a chicken, so does anybody else have something?" Everybody gathered their papers and put shit back in their bags. "Circle up for the prayer."

Oh shit, please-please-please don't be the Lord's Prayer. I hate when it's that! No amount of substituting "Dude" makes the church thing go away.

Lin led the prayer, and I was thrilled! It was the promises of AA, the probably bullshit and certainly exaggerated things a drunk can expect from "working the program." Even better, the long prose was shortened in their prayer. *Probably for people like me who hate prayers.*

I wasn't sure I actually believed these "promises" would happen in my pitiful life, but the sound of them did give me hope.

In unison:

- We are going to know a new freedom and a new happiness.
- We will not regret the past nor wish to shut the door on it.
- We will comprehend the word serenity and we will know peace.
- No matter how far down the scale we have gone *(There it is! I knew I remembered it from somewhere!)*, we will see how our experience can benefit others.
- Feelings of uselessness and self-pity will disappear.
- We will lose interest in selfish things and gain interest in our fellows.
- Self-seeking will slip away.
- Our whole attitude and outlook on life will change.
- Fear of people and economic insecurity will leave us.

- We will intuitively know how to handle situations that used to baffle us.
- We suddenly realize that God is doing for us what we could not do for ourselves.

I left feeling loved and supported... as if I was sure to succeed at staying sober even after leaving the insulated environment of R&R. And the way I felt about "low-bottom" people had completely changed.

After the meeting, smoking outside in the courtyard, Lin joined me and said something profound as hell. "There are no passing or failing grades if you stay sober, whether by AA or any other method."

He smiled so sincerely, I immediately put him on a pedestal, something we'd been warned against. Paul, the compulsive gambler, stopped next to me to light his cigarette as Lin turned to go back inside. His sleeve accidentally touched Paul's arm, and Paul turned on a dime, attacking Lin like a rabid dog. WHAM! BAM! Punches to the face and head; blood flowed from Lin's left eyebrow and lips.

Holy shit! An unstable person... and I was just feet from him! Is that what happens to low-bottom people or is he a psychotic... or what? Abby looked at me and my saucer eyes, and she reached for my free hand. "If I was a hugger, I'd hug you right now, girl. You're safe and I love you."

"Thanks, Abby. But don't leave right now. Stay here until my heartbeat returns to normal."

That afternoon, men in white scrubs came in the back door of Recovery Resources. They lifted Paul onto an extra-tall stretcher and attached restraints to his arms and legs.

As it turned out, Paul had been kicked out of six different rehab centers for violence. My *heart* ached for him... my *head* told me to run away fast. Sigh. Sobriety is hard. Figuring out AA people is even harder.

SERENITY SISTERS
CHAPTER 25

"Oh *man*, you shithead! I can't believe you're such a brown-noser!" Abby half-teased, or at least that's what I *thought* she was doing. But then she paused, opened her mouth to speak, and snapped it shut. Obviously, she was holding something back.

"What, Abby? Spit it out."

"You *must* have cheated the system, Fox. Why am *I* still here, dammit? It's been almost sixty days for me and you're out in thirty, almost to the day!" The two of us started down the stairwell on the way to the center. Abby carried my tote bag while I struggled with the bigger suitcase.

"I got out because I did what they wanted me to do... that doesn't make me a brown-noser, just a smart alcoholic."

Abby groaned. "Bullshit."

"It's a combination of things; one is Jenny. They think having a sponsor means you're serious and have a strong support system. So you need to get one, girl! Not just to get out, but it will seriously *help* you."

"Yeah, yeah, yeah. You sound like *them*."

"What about that chick from the POWERLESS club, the biker meeting woman? What's her name?"

"Blake."

"Right. She's nice as hell. And y'all have talked twice. Maybe ask her to be your sponsor.

"No. I'm like... embarrassed to ask or something. Hell, I don't know what to do about anything!" Abby looked defeated, her lips in a pout. "Eli says my meat thermometer isn't hot enough yet."

I hooted. "He said that to me, too! A standard line, I guess." At the staircase landing, I touched Abby's arm to stop her. I had touched the barbed-wire tattoo and saw her bicep twitch. "Wait, Ab. Listen, it's not just Jenny. I know the main reason I'm being released."

"What is it?" Abby's hip cocked and her hand found the groove. She bounced on the hip like a sassy teenager, awaiting my answer. Her snarkiness made me smile.

I spoke my truth. "I'm pretty sure it's because I've run out of money. Or that's what I *said*, anyway. So you do the same, true or not. I'm not spending any more money here. Well, it's my parent's money, but you know what I mean. Who knows what Mom had to sell to get the money for this place! I won't stay here and ask for more. I'm outta here. But I'm coming back for outpatient – sixty days of that, just like they recommend, all while living in a halfway house, which they *also* recommend."

"Brown-noser on all that, too." She looked at her feet, kicking a cigarette butt on the concrete. She exhaled a deep sigh. "So what about me? They know my parents have deep pockets. How can *I* get out of here sooner? Just demand it? Then they'll mark me AMA and no halfway house will take me!"

"Just tell them the same about the money. When I did, suddenly there was an opening at the halfway house when there hadn't been one before."

In the same cocked-hip pose, Abby stared into space.

I hated to believe what I was getting ready to say, but I felt it must be said. "Abby, they may seem all altruistic, but it all comes down to dollars and cents. Money, money, money. As long as you have more to spend, you're not sober enough to get out. Your meat thermometer gets hot enough when they've sucked the bones dry."

"That sucks," she said, still in deep thought and staring into space. Without looking my way, Abby said, "But I think my parents paid for, like, a year. Mom and Dad don't want me to come home."

"But you can go to a halfway house in West Palm Beach, like mine," I urged.

"Serenity Sisters, right? That's where you're going?"

"Yep. Ask to go there and we'll room together again. Maybe Jenny will be a sponsor for both of us! And in the meantime, I'll be back for outpatient. Every damn day. I can't exactly say I'm pumped for it. One minute I think I'm ready to be in the real world and the next minute I'm scared shitless."

I continued to urge her to talk to them as we started down the path. Struggling with the bags and the afternoon heat, we arrived at the back door just as Drinnen pulled up in the van. Drinnen grinned at me. "Ready for the real world?" she asked.

Ignoring the question, I was simply relieved that she was already there; I didn't want to wait around and cause a big, dramatic goodbye ceremony with everybody. Lois had left last week, and I was heartbroken to see her go; it was disheartening to be left behind. So I didn't want my friends, especially Abby, to feel bad about my "graduation."

I opened the van's sliding door, put my bags inside, and hopped in the passenger seat. *A happy camper headed back to the crazy hospital where I left my van. Thrilled to have her own transportation again... and scared to death.*

I'd planned ahead and asked Drinnen to drop by a 7-Eleven for cigarettes on the trip north. That way, I wouldn't have to stop at such a store by myself and be tempted to buy beer. Drinnen thought my plan was smart, too.

"You just might get this, Lela," she said. To my surprise, she rattled on as we sped on I-95 North. She had just celebrated her two-year sobriety anniversary and had her bronze coin in her shorts pocket. "I carry it everywhere. A reminder of the mantra: one day at a time."

"Just say moo," I said.

"Lin! He's a hoot! Never seen a better attitude on a counselor. They burn out easily, you know..."

"Lin has helped me a lot. And, of course, so has Eli. Hell, *all* the people have helped, including the crazy-as-hell patients. Oh! And definitely Dr. Mallory."

"You've got your 'scripts, right?"

"Yes. Drinnen, I'm ready to go forward." There was cheer in my voice and in my heart. *Sober Lela, reporting for duty.*

"And do you have the directions to the halfway house? You know they call if you don't show up. It's a legal thing."

I chuckled. "You only have to tell me things *once* these days."

Drinnen was silent for the last few minutes of the drive, with no words until we arrived in the parking lot and pulled beside my van. "I'll stay here to make sure it starts. The battery may be dead." Her jaw was clenched, and I wondered if it was worry or... what.

After a long pause, we hugged, and I cried. Drinnen wished me luck and I felt like a baby leaving the womb, like I felt when my big sister left home, like I felt when husband-number-one abandoned me. Scared to the Nth degree, knowing a lot was demanded of me and a lot of people were counting on me.

Deep breath.

No amount of self-talk could make the fear go away. So, for the first time, I prayed outside of a facility. I leaned my head back on the van's headrest and closed my eyes.

Dude, put the right path in front of me and lead my stupid little feet even when there are rocks and ruts on that path. I need you, Dude... now more than ever.

I know there wasn't really an answer from Dude, but I'll be damned if I didn't hear some kind of noise, feel some kind of acknowledgement, see a wave in the air. And it didn't freak me out; I accepted it as perfectly normal though I knew I would never tell anybody that.

The rest of the prayer: *Of course, you know what I need. And of course, I don't know. Just... keep me posted. I love you. Stay with me.*

It was the most heartfelt prayer of my life.

The van started on the first try. I waved goodbye to Drinnen through the window, and she blew a kiss.

"Free! Free as a bird!" I cheered out loud, then immediately reeled myself in. Another prayer: *Dude, save me from myself. I'm scared as shit.*

☼ ☼ ☼ ☼ ☼

The trip south was uneventful until I got to the old-beach part of West Palm, where beige, scrubby grass grew amid the sand and abandoned buildings outnumbered those occupied.

Aloud to myself, "There it is." The parking lot was gravel. And the sign, if you want to call it that, said "Serenity Sisters." The sign spoke volumes about the place; cracked by the weather, it was hand-painted, red on white, but sun-faded to pale pink. Amateur. Half-assed, like the rest of the place.

Four women sat on an adjacent cinderblock wall smoking cigarettes, all wearing slouchy tanks and baggy shorts. The one who wore glasses also had oozing scabs on her face and very few teeth. *Betcha she's a crystal-meth addict. Oh, Dude, what IS this place?* At the corner, just two buildings away, I'd passed a crowd of homeless men. Not so much a *bad* part of town, just the oldest.

The house itself was a rectangular stucco building with peeling white paint, two stories high with a staircase on each end. Red doors lined the sidewalk below and the balcony upstairs.

More women were congregated on the upper balcony, I noticed, dressed for work or something – skirts, blouses, and sensible shoes. One wore *tons* of makeup. As they walked down the steps, I got out of my van. The group focused on me; I felt the burn of their eyes.

One shouted, "Are you the new girl? You look old enough to be her." *Great, very nice to meet you, too.* Second thoughts turned into serious doubts. The interaction with that group of girls was faltering; I was uncomfortable, and it seemed they felt the same.

I left my bags in the van and climbed the steps to room 201, as instructed. There were open doors along the way, rooms with cluttered floors and small beds with 1980s-trend bedspreads. Definitely a step down in the luxury department.

Instantly, I knew I wouldn't be here long, not by choice. An "eeww" rose in my throat; I felt my nose go up in a snoot and my high horse gallop past this place. *Watch it, Lela... you're just one of the herd, here to learn how to live, not for a vacation.* But there's nothing like nasty to speed your recovery! I felt like I was back at the Homing Inn.

The door to 201 was also open. A frazzled, braless, overweight woman in a yellow tank looked up when I crossed the threshold. I said, "Rhonda?" She nodded.

"I'm Lela Fox, the new girl." A warped, molded plastic chair stood off to the side, and I tried to sit without letting it touch my skin. No luck; it was slick from use and I slid back into the cool of the chair.

Rhonda jumped up, held her cigarette between her lips and squinted, then reached out to shake my hand. I took a deep breath, smelling a month of body odor.

"Well, first off..." she scooted back into the chair, behind a table that served as a miniature desk. "It's kinda crazy here now, 'cuz we're fixin' to move. End of the week. New digs. You'll like 'em much better. Has a pool, even." Rhonda's accent sounded like what Tennesseans call "L.A." – lower Alabama.

"Well, a move would be great. This doesn't exactly match the picture on your brochure," I said. The front cover featured a line drawing of the building, not a photo, and now I knew why. Still, Eli had said it was a "nice place." *Well, maybe he said they were "good there" instead.* Either way, I planned to tell him off at the next meeting.

The fan swiveled to Rhonda's face and blew the ashes off her cigarette as she was taking a deep draw. "Dammit!" she said, wiping ashes from the papers on the desk. "No air conditionin' and the phone works maybe ha'f the time, this place is a dump!" I said nothing; there was nothing to say.

She opened a drawer, threw a key at me, and said, "You're in 213, in the back with Charlie." Then she threw her head back and laughed. "Now *she's* a piece 'a work, that Charlie is!" She looked me over once again. "You got a job?"

"Nope, but I hope to get my job back after I'm finished with outpatient. That's another sixty days, ya know, maybe less, they said." Her accent was making mine worse... more lazy, more redneck.

"You got a car?"

"That silver van down there."

"Gonna need the plate number. And a copy of your license." As I fumbled through my wallet, she tossed a booklet with a torn red cover toward me, the same sloppy way she had tossed the key. "Here's the book a' rules." Only half-interested, I fanned its twenty-plus pages.

"And here's a warning, little missy." I looked up to see her angry scowl. "Don't piss me off," she said, her crooked finger pointed at me. "Rule breakers are thrown out, no questions, no exceptions, b'cause I don't give a shit. We're not babysitters here." She stubbed her cigarette out and rushed to blow out the smoke in a plume. *This woman is a dyed-in-the-wool redneck. A bad-ass redneckerson from South Alabama.* I didn't plan to cross her. Chics fight alligators down there and win.

I said, "Well, I guess I'll find my room so–

Rhonda interrupted. "AA meetin' in-house tonight. Speaker meeting. A man, so come dressed. Seven sharp and I mean *do not* be late. And keep your mouth shut durin' the meetin'. It's in the rec room downstairs. The door ain't got no number on it, it's just a green door." I nodded and said I'd be there.

"Hey, how long you been sober, anyway. You look pretty good for a junkie."

"Alcoholic," I said.

"Same damn thing. We're just a herd of cows here."

I laughed. "You know Lin, too?"

A wide smile spread her face. "Oh yeah, got clean at Recovery Resources just like you. Two years, seven months for me."

"Thirty-six days," I answered. "June 30, 1999, a day that will live in infamy."

"What the hell is 'infamy?' Don't be usin' no big words with me, little missy! Get off your damn high horse."

"And I'm out! *Gin!*" The winner, a surely-too-young tattooed woman, giggled just as I walked into Room 213. Three other women groaned and slammed their cards on the bed.

One spewed, "Dammit Elsa, you *always* win! I'm not playing anymore!" She stood from the bed and swung around to leave, nearly crashing into me. "Oh. Hi. Who are you? Are you the new woman?"

"I guess so." I gestured to my suitcase for proof. Her face lit up; a beautiful face, smooth as a baby's ass and high cheekbones that screamed a Native American origin. Older, but younger than me... and she reminded me of my friend Lola.

The woman smiled, eyed me up and down, and said to the others without looking away from me, "Guys, it's the new woman. Be nice and say hello." There was a murmur of hellos from the bed.

She swished her head back and pointed to the card players. "That's Elsa, cheater at cards." The young girl raised her hand and nodded. She looked twelve at best. "And that's Patty." Another hand raised, attached to a morbidly obese arm. "And that's Tina." Tina nodded, looking a lot like Abby. She even had a barbed-wire tattoo, but on her wrist instead of her bicep.

"Nice to meet you guys. I'm Lela."

The beautiful maybe-Indian girl snickered. "Oh, I forgot myself! I'm Charlie, short for Charlotte." I smiled, holding back from saying "You're a beautiful woman, Charlie." Because she *was* beautiful. Perfect skin, perfect figure, perfectly toned and strong.

I looked back at the other women and tried to remember the names I'd just been told. *Damn! Too many people, too many to learn.* Charlie interrupted my thoughts. "Lela, we've been waiting for you, even tried to make your side of the room look neat. The girl that left your side of the room... she left without her stuff. We took it all to the dumpster."

"Well... thank you," I said, wondering why the house manager hadn't been the one to get my room ready. Charlie and I walked to the bedroom in the back. "Which bed is mine?" I asked. Both were tucked up tight, like Marines' beds. *I bet they make you do that here, too, just like at rehab.* Charlie pointed to the one pushed tight against the wall. *Oh Jeez.* An extra-long twin, glowing with a stained tie-dyed comforter.

Charlie's dark hair was tied in a pigtail on top of her head and flopped as she talked. "I know what you're thinking... but with that tie-dye, the stain doesn't show. That's Elsa's Dr. Pepper from last week. She and Jolene – that's the girl who ran away – they got into a fight and Elsa threw a full can of Dr. Pepper at her. Spewed everywhere." Charlie continued to ramble; I found it charming.

I put my suitcase on the bed as Charlie disappeared to play a new game of Gin. With a heavy heart, I walked back down the steps to get the rest of my stuff. "You need any help?" Charlie called after me.

"No, I got it! It's a one-man job, anyway."

I spent the afternoon unpacking and meeting more people who wandered in and out of the room. Charlie plopped on her bed and pulled a basket of nail polish toward her. Finally, I asked, "How many people live here? Seems like a zillion."

She paused for some mental math, or at least that's what I assumed. "About eighty, give or take. Some beds are empty.

"I see. And what do you know about the new place we're moving to? Is it really nice like Rhonda said?"

In the background, Elsa blew a raspberry and rolled her eyes. "Rhonda! Don't believe a word that woman says! She's busted me for the tiniest things, and she *lies!*" Fire rose in her eyes. Info about the new place could come later; I didn't want to see a tiny girl pissed off.

I shared my biggest fear. "Y'all, now that I'm out, I'm afraid my soon-to-be-ex-husband will try to find me. It's still anonymous here, right?" I realized I was wringing my hands and tried to stop.

Charlie stammered. "Well, I guess... never thought about it." Then she went back to painting her nails.

I need to tell Rhonda and get assurance about keeping me anonymous. Please! I don't want him to find me.

I shuddered to remember the call I made to him in rehab... then remembered it was the same day I saw Dude for the first time. *Wonder if that's related... I sure changed my tune about wanting to talk to him after that.*

Scumbag. I didn't trust him one bit; all he wanted was hurt me, throw me in jail again, anything to keep me feeling stupid and under his thumb. *Lela, you are stronger now, stronger than he is.*

Ready to play nice to redneck Rhonda, I scurried down the outdoor balcony hall to talk to her about my would-be stalker. The door to 201 was closed and locked. I ran back to ask Charlie what the deal was; why would they lock the door? "Oh, she's somewhere. She doesn't stay here half the time."

I was dumbfounded, still thinking like a rehab inpatient, I guess. *Hmm. I want to be on my own but... I also want protection from the outside world. Guess I can't have both.* I prayed for the pink cloud to protect me a while longer.

Little did I know how hard I'd have to pray for protection from the outside world. And how soon.

A KNOCK AT THE DOOR
CHAPTER 26

"Move, dammit, I want to sit next to Lela!" Charlie meant business, and a young waif of a girl, even smaller than Elsa, succumbed to her demand. She sat next to me, sharing a loveseat that had seen better days. Cringing, I worried about bedbugs and other creatures, though I had realized the place was just old and decrepit, not truly dirty. *Still, upholstery... who knows how many butts have sat here.*

I had arrived at the downstairs rec room 6:45, early for the meeting, and spent ten minutes watching the resident's interactions. They came from all walks of life, all ages, races, and creeds. Definitely a melting pot, a herd of cows seeking the same serenity I was seeking. Just say moo.

At the stroke of seven, Rhonda took the podium, a table-top version, balanced precariously on a water-damaged table. A tall black man stood on her right and the meeting started as any AA meeting does: the serenity prayer, readings of the steps and traditions, announcements, blah, blah, blah.

Rhonda introduced the speaker, Ty Bradley from Miami, who had gotten sober at a West Palm Beach treatment center, stayed at a halfway house in Boca. "Now," Rhonda said, "He's returned to his law practice after drinking it away.

The speaker had a deep and garbled voice and I squirmed, wondering if I could sit through this bullshit. So new in sobriety, I hadn't yet learned the value of a speaker meeting and ended up focusing on myself. *I wonder what I would say if I was a meeting speaker...*

Ty began, "I grew up in privilege, believe it or not. We lived in the 'burbs. Nice house. Two brothers who were high-achievers like me. At school, I played sports, made good grades, even Student Council President one year. *Wow, cool. Me too! Just substitute sisters for brothers.*

My parents were loving, giving people who went out of their way for us, making sure we had what we needed, and sometimes, things we just wanted. Like I had the latest Michael Jordan sneakers, all the latest music tapes, and even some CDs.

Ty stopped to make a joke about most of the folks being too young to remember when music was on cassette tape and not knowing why they still called them "albums." Charlie and I looked at each other knowingly.

I whispered, "Hell, I had a zillion *eight-tracks* in my teens!" I said, dating myself.

Charlie nodded and grimaced. "Me, too. We're old kids." I liked that phrase: old kids.

"Girl, I'm gonna steal that. 'Old kids.'" Charlie smiled, and then put her finger to her lips, shushing me. I looked to the from and, sure enough, Rhonda glared at us then pointed her crooked finger.

The room was silent except for the speaker; there must be strict rules, I thought, because at the meetings I'd attended, chatter filled the background 100 percent of the time. *Maybe it's one of the random rules here... same bullshit rules like at Recovery Resources. "Train the children."*

I cleared my throat and focused again on the speaker. He explained the ideal childhood, much like mine. His oldest brother left when Ty was in fifth grade, the other left when he was in tenth. *Wow. Again, exactly like me.* He was the spoiled baby of the family, he said, and diagnosed Bi-Polar at age sixteen... same as me. *This is getting eerie.*

"I had my first drink of alcohol in the eighth grade," he said. Again, I nodded, amazed at the similarities in our stories. Ty described the same kind of partying in high school, the same timing of a relationship and the plan to run away. While I was planning to elope and hightail it to California, he had planned to run to Mexico with his girlfriend, the one who had straightened him up a little in his senior year. *He's telling my story!*

"After my senior year, and *way* after the deadline, I surrendered to my parents' demands and went to college. They were damn-determined that I go, and made it easy for me to get there, so I thought... hey, college students drink all the time; that's what they're *supposed* to do. So I thought I'd fit right in.

Just like me, he didn't play the field long and entered a turbulent relationship with a girl, a white girl, he said. The basis of their relationship was getting drunk and getting high, just like mine was with Andy Winston, my son's father. Soon, the baby arrived, he said, a boy. *This is getting spooky! How could I have so much in common with a black lawyer from Miami?*

Ty dropped out of college, enrolled again, dropped out, and went back again, each time drinking more and more. Eventually, his drinking zapped his ambition and ability to function and he worked a menial job. When the baby was two years old, he left his wife and everything "zoomed out of control." *Damn, that's me!*

Ty continued, "Then I had a health scare – a small heart attack. I was scared and not really able to deal with the treatment or do what the doctors were telling me to do, so I just drank. I was neglecting myself, my responsibilities as a father, and being a general ass. Then I met a woman who wanted to take care of me. Being entirely selfish, I let her. Laura was her name. She demanded we get married, and I agreed. But the truth was... I didn't love Laura. I was using her. She took care of my boy every other weekend when we had visitation. She took the lead in everything and I sat like a lump on a log, drinking vodka-tonic after vodka-tonic." This blew me away; he was describing MY life! *He even drank the vodka-tonics I preferred, too!*

"Though I was nothing but a drunk, I started a business. Pressure washing. *And for me the business was Moonlight Jewelry.* Pressure washing was relatively new then, and people thought it was a miracle. I made good money for a while, but eventually, I hired helpers to do the work and pretended to be running the business as my part of the deal. But those helpers... we sat around drinking beer all morning before they went out on their routes. Needless to say, that didn't work out so well. To put it simply, I drank the business into the ground. But from there on out, my story is like any other. *What do you mean 'from there on out?' You're describing my exact history, and alcohol was the main character, so talk! Say more!*

"Alcohol took over. My wife left me when the money ran out. We were living in a fancy house up on the hill, but only because *she* made that happen. I was the baggage. And I had to move when the bank took the house."

Most everything else matched my story hit for hit and I was mesmerized. So when there was a loud banging on the door, I jumped and gasped. The girls laughed; it was funny in a Three Stooges kind of way.

But why are they knocking when they could just open the door and come in? They're going to be in trouble for being late anyway, but why call attention to it? On the second loud knock, Rhonda rushed to open the door and there were a few mumbles from the crowd.

The speaker had stopped talking and watched Rhonda carefully, his eyes suddenly widening with surprise. I didn't have a clear view of the door from where I sat, but Charlie was just far enough to the left so she could see.

"A cop!" she said. I leaned forward; saw a shoulder with a police radio attached. As if on cue, his radio squawked with a static-filled transmission; a voice that sounded urgent.

"What's going on?" I asked, though was it was just a thought expressed out loud. Everybody had turned around to see what was happening at the door. There were whispers of "What's he doing here? What papers are those? Is that Terry's summons?" It hit me: I was in the real world again, the world where cops roamed.

A few times, the cops had tried to serve patients at Recovery Resources, and I knew Drinnen spent a lot of time in court with those patients. Maybe this was the same thing. *Another cow, in trouble. Wreckage of the past.*

Rhonda turned toward the crowd of faces. "Lela? Lela Fox?" In that instant, my entire body froze. *What? From a cop? What the hell?*

I stood. "Over here, Rhonda."

"Come here 'n sign, Lela." She motioned for me to come using exaggerated arm movements. The cop's radio squawked again, slicing the silence of the room.

As I walked to the door, Ty said, "Jails, institutions, or death." I had read that from the Big Book, but I wasn't "wanted" or anything. This must be some kind of mistake, I thought. But as I walked closer to the door, close enough to see the cop's scalp through his buzz haircut, close enough to see how tightly the buttons pulled against his beefy frame, I realized what was happening.

"Sign here, Ms. Fox," the policeman instructed. He passed a thick stack of paper, folded in thirds, without the benefit of an envelope. I signed in exchange for the paper bundle. "Thank you. Have a nice evening, now."

I flipped the packet open to show the first page. Divorce papers. Stuart found me. *That sonofabitch!*

I felt faint and Rhonda reached out to steady me. Over her "Are you okay?" comments, I spit words like bullets, "*Rhonda*, DAMMIT! Did you tell somebody I was here today?"

"Just two people. Your rehab center and–"

Agitated, I growled, "And *who*, dammit? TELL ME!"

"Well, I thought it was another thing about your transfer here. He asked if you were a resident and I said yes."

"Isn't this an anonymous place? How could you *do* this? *Damn, Rhonda.*" I didn't realize I was crying until a teardrop appeared on the printed pages. "Dammit! Shit! Jeezus, Rhonda, *now* what am I going to do?"

She smirked, not liking that I had accused her of wrongdoing. "I guess you'll go to court, huh? I mean, you've got a car, and the courthouse is right downtown."

"Fuck you! I need an attorney first!" As I screamed, dozens of faces stared at me but I didn't care. "Never mind," I said and stared Rhonda in the face. I turned to go back to my seat, with tears falling at every step.

Rhonda was finished with me, focusing on our speaker. "Sorry, Ty. It ain't all fun 'n games, ya know." Her voice was chirpy and fake, pissing me off royally. Back at the podium area, she chirped again, "Please go on, Ty."

I sat in a trance. Charlie elbowed me, speaking barely above a whisper. "What is it? A summons?"

"Divorce papers," I said, loud enough for the girls sitting in the floor in front of us to hear. They gave me a look of sorrow but turned back to the speaker. I read every word of the divorce petition – understanding few, but enough to surmise that he wanted everything left in the house. *I'm not sure what Mom and Dad managed to get. But whatever... either way is fine. To hell with you, Stuart Weinstein!*

There was no mention of Stuart repaying what he had stolen from me. *Not stolen, SWINDLED.* There wasn't exactly a theft, but he tricked me every time he was supposed to pay off my credit cards. No records of "theft" or wrongdoing, so I was screwed. *But Lela, you let that happen.* I was numb with hurt. Not because I wanted him... oh no, I wanted the divorce. But to see it in black and white... it tasted like fresh dog shit.

With my head in the depths of the papers, suddenly everybody clapped. The speaker had finished; I hadn't heard the last half. He'd run over in time and Rhonda called for the closing prayer immediately. I didn't stand for the serenity prayer but chanted it silently in my reeling mind. Then I sat while the others milled around and congregated around the speaker.

My mind was screaming at me, the self-talk in planning mode now.

Call Mom and tell her you've been served. And find a lawyer... but how? Maybe Mom will pay for it, or maybe I'll have to take it out of my retirement account and take the big tax hit. The divorce itself will be a rubber stamp thing; I'm definitely not going to contest it. But I sure wish I could get some money for my trouble, some payback for what he stole. I guess I have to show up in court, so that completes the decision about going back to Tennessee soon. Or... wait... do I have to go to court if it's uncontested? A question for my lawyer, I guess.

Oblivious to everything happening around me, I jumped when Rhonda touched my shoulder. "Lela? You okay? What iz it?"

"Divorce papers" was my knee-jerk comment, then I glared at her. "Dammit, Rhonda, I didn't want him to find me! I'm furious at you for ratting me out. I could probably report you to... somebody." Again, I realized I had no power here. *Just a cow, Lela. Say moo.*

At least she apologized. Rhonda sat on the love seat where Charlie had sat and looked me deep in the eye. "Hey, kid, jus' so you know... I'm on yer side. I kin help you find a lawyer. Hell, they're ever'where. Me, I been to drug court three times, and lots of people here have—"

"It's not drug court, Rhonda."

"Maybe the same." She looked at her chipped toenail polish for a while, or that's where her eyes pointed, and I sat in silence. After thirty seconds or so, she leaned up on the loveseat and patted my thigh, hard. "Well, tell me if I kin help. Ya know where t' find me."

Rhonda waddled away as I noticed the room was empty except for a half-dozen women who lounged on the sofas to chatter. The noise was deafening somehow, echoing in my ears. And my head throbbed. I almost wanted to call Stuart, tell him off, so I began a thrashing in my mind... going backward to "edit" it... which made me laugh when I got about sixty seconds into the rant.

Who proofreads a screaming bitch-out to a sonofabitch? It wouldn't matter what I said because he'd sit there so fucking high and mighty with that condescending smile. An internal scream... *oh how much I hate him!*

The more I thought about it, the higher my blood pressure rose. Finally, the buzz in my head brought a killer headache. My thumbs naturally went to my temples, and I burst into tears.

No, no, no, Lela. Keep your shit together. There are tasks ahead and you are now sober and stable, able to take care of business... able to jump tall buildings in a single bound. Make a list. Use your color-coordinated pencils and write in your journal. Call Jenny, cry into the pillow, do whatever, but DO NOT LOSE YOUR SHIT!

Two hours later, after a long conversation with Mom about the divorce lawyer, I realized I had not lost my shit. *It's a miracle. Is this what recovery will be like... everything falling into place? Am I invincible!*

The next day, an ecstatic Charlie came to me spewing words and giggles. I'd been "home" for five minutes after a trying day as an R&R outpatient but gave her my full attention, anyway. It mattered.

"Lela, you'll love it! New beds, new sheets and bedspreads, pillows, everything's new, everything! A brand-new dining table, and so much more space! There's a kitchen in every apartment! Tiny little appliances... a hot plate and a baby refrigerator, but a microwave, plates and silverware, all we could *possibly* need! It's going to be awesome-awesome-awesome!"

Charlie's high cheekbones were flushed, and her smile spread to her sultry smoky-brown eyes. She'd been to see our new place with a handful of other women. "Let's go see it! I don't have a key of course, but let's drive by... you'll flip out!"

"Something to eat first?" I asked. She nodded her head, still jumping with excitement. I'd never seen her so happy; she was acting like a kid! Charlie's attitude boosted mine, and I needed it. It had been a tough day.

But Charlie wouldn't let me rest. We drove by the new place a few times, then parked in the lot and walked into the heart of the place. I instantly understood why she was excited; it was nice as hell. By design, the place looked like an old apartment complex from the 1970s, a tiny one, but designed with apartments around the perimeter of a central courtyard.

In the center, a tiny pool, surrounded by gently used lounge chairs, chained together with a metal cord. There were Mexican workers there, filling the pool, and they eyed us lustfully. *Some things don't change with age; women are still targets. It doesn't matter that Charlie and I are both old as hell.*

We continued our outdoor tour. There was a sliding glass door to a big room downstairs. It looked like a rec room without the recreation stuff. "I think this is going to be the group room," Charlie said.

"For sure."

"And Rhonda said we're getting new sofas. And guess what?" She squealed. "They match!"

"And at the back, there... do you see all those chairs stacked up? They're brand new. And nice! Yeppers, this is a killer group room."

Adjoining the group room was an office with a proper desk, even a computer, which was lacking at the other house. "Maybe this will help Rhonda actually stay in the office during the day. The bitch is gone more than she's there!"

Charlie jumped in. "No kidding. She's a flake, anyway. Showed her colors today, too. Such a redneck!"

I started to ask what happened, and it hit me... I didn't care. So she barks at people; I'd just been trying to stay out of her way. Truthfully, I was still crazy-pissed at her for telling Stuart I was there. Thinking about it sent a chill up my spine. But with the move, the physical address would differ from the one published, so he couldn't come to find me. *Good, another thing that's good. Keep looking for good things, Lela. Gratitude... an attitude of gratitude.*

☼ ☼ ☼ ☼ ☼

I was the last one to move into the new place because I had R&R group all day. In fact, I had to pack my stuff the night before and keep it in my van until I got to the new-and-improved Serenity Sisters house. Around five o'clock, I lugged my suitcase up the staircase... one of four that led to the second-floor perimeter.

Charlie ran out, barefoot, squealing with joy. "Come see, Lela!" What I saw was astounding. Charlie was right; everything was new. New carpet, too; cheap, but new. The whole place glowed neat and clean.

We high-fived at the doorway to our bedroom, twice as big as our previous one. There was enough room for a seating area, and we discussed how to talk them into getting furniture for us to put in that spot.

Our bedspreads matched: big bold floral prints. Very colorful, happy. The sheets were crisp and white, and they smelled of fabric softener. I bounced onto the mattress and it was joyously firm, but not too firm. "Perfect! So I can see why the rent went up, but this is nice. This is a Serenity Sisters kind of place now," I smiled.

Before I finished my comment, Charlie began taking off her clothes. She opened a drawer in the spacious dresser and pulled out her swimsuit. "Let's go swimming!"

She ran down the steps to join another ten women who sat on the lounge chairs. Four were in the pool, squealing and splashing. From the upstairs vantage point, I could see the street in front of the building and noticed the neighborhood around the place looked *tons* better than the other.

"I hope they burn the old building to the ground," I said out loud.

HUMAN RESOURCES
CHAPTER 27

"Congratulations, kid," Eli said. "Can I hug?"

"Absolutely!" I had mastered the art of the sideways hug: how to hug a man without your boobs touching him at all. Eli was giving me a send-off. I'd completed my final day of outpatient treatment and felt strong and sure of myself, the polar opposite of the woman I was when I rolled in the door just ten weeks before.

For the first time in decades, I had clarity of thought and a clear vision of my future. My plan was to call Human Resources at Smyth Software and get my job back.

Thankfully, I didn't have to move out of the halfway house yet; I needed to stay and save a little money, enough money to pay the movers and deposits at my own apartment. Mom had paid for the divorce lawyer, thank God, but I didn't dare ask for more money from her. So the truth was glaring: I had to get back to work in a hurry.

"Hold on to that 90-day chip, Lela," Lin said, "And remember: we invite patients back to speak at six months' sober. I hope to see you." A sideways hug for Lin sent waves of gratitude down my spine and tears began. Funny, I thought, but I would miss the place. I had left my guts in there, poured out my heart and soul on the floor of that big room. Rehab is not an experience one forgets, ever.

Stephanie hugged me for what seemed like an hour. I wrote my number on a scrap of paper and told her to call anytime, but somehow, I knew she wouldn't. There's something about having your calls restricted that made you restrict them yourself. For a goodbye to Abby, not a toucher or a crier, I fake-punched her in the arm and said, "Chin up, chick." She grinned. "Not coming to Serenity Sisters yet?" I asked.

"Meat thermometer still not hot enough."

"Do you agree with him?"

I saw her wheels turning. "Yeah. I see you and how far you've come, Lela... I'm not where you are. And I just... still feel so lost. So damn depressed."

I hated to hear she was still struggling, and especially with the depression part. "Please talk to Dr. Mallory again. They have magic pills here, ya know." Abby laughed. I snuck a kiss on her cheek.

"Get outta here!" she teased, wiping the spot where I'd left lipstick.

At the halfway house on my first "day off" in over three months, I didn't do a thing except worry. Frozen in fear. Lost in my own head, telling myself I was a piece of chicken shit.

Chicken shit because I wouldn't/couldn't call Smyth Software.

The problem was I was afraid of what I supposed to do, so I didn't do it. Instead, I sat by the pool all day. Around three o'clock, I scribbled in my journal, then edited and re-edited my planned "speech" to Kathy, the HR lady. I was ready to call, but the phone seemed to weigh a thousand pounds.

I didn't go to an AA meeting that night, either. I didn't even call Jenny. Instead, I smoked two packs of cigarettes and took two naps.

Okay, Lela. Tomorrow. First thing. No excuses, no hesitation. You're a big girl now, remember? Sober and brave, Eli said. Open that jewel-encrusted box labeled THE GREAT UNKNOWN and dive in. "Face it" instead of "fuck it," as Jenny says. And "head first," as Daddy would say.

I fell asleep talking to myself and eating big chunks of Shame that tasted like earthworms.

Sunrise... everybody up and running around, laughing in the corridors. I felt myself sinking inward... thinking *"Why can't I be happy like they are?"* but stopped myself halfway through. I *was* happy, stable on new Bi-Polar medicine, thanks to Recovery Resources. *So you're going to make that phone call, right? Right. Yeah, you're going to do it. Today. This morning.*

When Charlie left for work, I sat at our kitchen table staring at my phone.

I'd written out what to say but I couldn't focus, couldn't keep my voice from cracking as I read it out loud.

I found a dozen diversions, creating a long to-do list, color-coordinated, of course. Finally, I popped a frozen sausage biscuit in the microwave. *Well, shit. That took all of five minutes.* I called Mom. We talked for maybe ten minutes before she had to go. I called Karen and had to leave a message. My sister Jennifer was unreachable at work, Bo was in school, and my sponsor couldn't take calls at work, either. I had gone through my speed-dial list, then clicked through the contacts but found nobody who could take a call in the middle of the morning.

Still before ten o'clock. I have plenty of time to call. I took a stroll around the block, stopping, literally, to smell the flowers. Never once did I ask myself *why* I was so afraid to call.

I was too afraid to know why I was afraid.

Around noon, I escaped to the air conditioning of my room. *Kathy of Human Resources will be at lunch now.* I popped a CD in the player and jammed out to old music for an hour. *One o'clock. Dammit, it's time, Lela. No more putting it off.* Slowly I punched in the numbers. Three rings later, a chirpy receptionist's voice answered.

I tried to be just as chirpy, but she ended the call on a dead note. "Kathy is gone for the day. Do you want to leave a message?" I replied in the negative. "Thank you for calling Smyth Software, award-winning software for online retailers," she recited. *Groan.*

I slammed my phone shut and immediately put on my swimsuit. To the pool, again. Rhonda stuck her head out of the office door a little after two. "Ya git yer job back yet?"

"She's out for the day," I shouted.

"Well, ya know the rules. Ya work or ya leave."

"Yeah, yeah, yeah." I thought about the other halfway-house women and the jobs they had taken just to be able to stay and pay the now-increased rent. Several were telemarketers, and at least a dozen were grocery baggers, cashiers... any job would do. Despite my new-found training in humility, I wasn't humble on the job issue. I refused to work a menial job. No, I wanted *my* job back, a job worthy of my resume. "Moo" was not in my vocabulary that week. I felt "too good" and too uppity to be there.

I've worked hard to do what they said, let them re-wire my brain, and – dammit – I'm sober! But nobody's patting Lela on the back, now. They've left me flapping in the breeze. And why? I'm so sober even Stuart has left me alone! I just want somebody besides my Daddy to brag on me a little.

"We can't hire you back after you've been fired, Lela. Seems like you would know that," Kathy said. My heart sunk. I didn't have a Plan B.

After a long silence, she said, "I have an idea, though. Let me check with Dale. They have never replaced you in the position and, if there's still a need, maybe you could be a contract worker, work by the hour, say with a three-month contract?"

I expelled the breath I'd been holding. "Oh, Kathy! That would be so, so great," I said. "Honestly, I'm willing to do anything you need me to do."

"Well, congratulations on a successful rehab. That's no small feat, Lela. In fact, my brother...."

With a roll of my eyes, I tuned her out. It seems everybody has a brother or an uncle or a cousin who is an alcoholic, and I never understood why they wanted to tell me about it. But in this case, it was good Kathy thought I was one of the many who suffered and one of the few who kicked it. "Lela, it says something wonderful about your character," she finished the paragraph I hadn't heard the beginning of.

"Well, thanks for saying that, Kathy. I feel great, sharp as a tack, and ready for the challenge of writing again. See, I never knew how to quit drinking before, but I learned. And I'm not going backward, that's for sure! I believe I can make–"

"Well, let me get with Dale and I'll call you back this afternoon."

"Yippee!" I hooted, out loud. I ran downstairs to tell Rhonda, then halfway down the steps, I thought better. *What if Dale says no? He never liked you, anyway. Well of COURSE he didn't like you! I sucked as an employee! Coming in drunk, spending most of my time smoking at the loading dock, bringing my personal problems to work... what employer would have liked that? Lela Fox, you may have already shot yourself in the foot.*

Kicking at a cigarette butt on the sidewalk, I walked back to the apartment in shame, now despondent. Then I chuckled at how fast I had gone from "Yippee!" to "I'm a loser."

My phone rang at 1:20 PM and my mouth immediately turned into a dry desert. As my blood pressure spiked, I chanted to myself. *Breathe, Lela. In through your nose, out through your mouth.* Still, my hands shook when opening my flip phone. "Hello?"

"Dale says yes! Would you rather do a three-month contract or a six-month?" Kathy didn't pause, stopping me at after a one-syllable croak. "But here's the deal: I think the maximum hourly rate will go up soon, so I'd recommend a three-month."

Thrilled and relieved, I leaped from the kitchen chair. "Okay! Three months, then!"

"There are no benefits, of course, and there's the pay issue. It will not equal your former salary. There's a maximum of twenty dollars an hour and you'll keep a timesheet."

I froze, did a little math in my head. Ouch. "That's... a lot less. Nothing else you can do? For a specialist, I mean? One already trained?" I hoped she would say there were exceptions.

"No, Lela. Sorry. Company policy," Kathy seemed sincerely sorry to report this news.

"Well, I can deal with that for a while. I'm just happy to be getting my job back, however it happens."

"Well, remember you're *not* getting your job back. And *never* say that to a coworker. This is a special circumstance and I've bent a few rules for you, Lela Fox. You're a *contract employee only*. Understand?" A suddenly serious Kathy spoke in precise and clipped words.

"Understood. No problem. When can I start?" *I hope she says tomorrow!*

"Monday, nine o'clock. Dale has to re-arrange desk assignments, he said. Oh, and he sends his congratulations, too. About your sobriety, I mean." I groaned silently; I'd hoped she wouldn't tell him the personal part. As if reading my mind, she said, "I thought it was best to tell him the reason for your departure and... what's the word?"

I suggested, "Reincarnation?"

Kathy laughed. "Wish I would've said that to Dale! See, he wasn't exactly agreeable at first."

"Kathy, I will not disappoint."

"Come to my office before you see Dale. Papers to sign."

"No problem. See you at nine on Monday!" My voice had risen an octave; I was excited.

Though I wasn't the down-on-your-knees praying type, I knew it was a time to pray... with thanks for getting my job back.

A prayer for a purpose made me feel like... a user. It seemed so church-y and selfish, and that left the taste of bile in my mouth.

But something different happened that day.

I closed my eyes and felt an instant jolt of connection with Dude. No need for the specific "vision" of my cousin, no need to say words at all. It felt like a smile from the core of the universe and brought tears to my eyes.

The powerful, all-encompassing Love he represented scared me, in fact, and I jerked my eyes open. Suddenly, our apartment seemed a little brighter, and I knew it *wasn't* a more direct angle of the sun in the window. It was a change in my attitude. A dramatic change.

And again, I felt embarrassed by the comparison of being "saved" like the Baptists. But that day, my worry about being shamed for it disappeared. Poof. *Is it because I shared my worry with Dude the instant it appeared?* As I silently told him of my embarrassment, the vision of my cousin slowly wove into my mind's eye. And he was chuckling... as if he thought my worry was cute and silly, and absolutely unnecessary.

I noticed something else about Dude that day: his cigarette was again precisely halfway smoked... like it had been frozen in the prime-time of taste the whole time. As I'd always been, I was amazed by the humanity of my Higher Power.

Exhausted by the emotional turbulence, I tried to speak out loud to Dude but found I didn't need to. It was like he was bouncing my thoughts back to me. I was reminded of what Jenny said: "God knows the whole of you. You don't need to tell him what you need."

I wondered how Mom would feel about that... I knew she had a list of people, places, and things to pray for... and went down the list one by one each day. *Dude/God knows who needs help and exactly what kind of help they need. Who am I to give him instruction!?*

That was the second time since the original vision that I was "overtaken" by my Higher Power, a feeling *still* so dramatic it's embarrassing to explain.

Over the years of my sobriety, my Dude has changed, or evolved, if you want to call it that. My idea of what he looks like has changed, and sometimes an orange-yellow glow behind him is so bright he's blocked from view. I know he stopped smoking at the same time I did.

Though still not mainstream, my Dude has become a bit more conventional. Stay tuned for details because they, too, are a bit twisted.

Like me.

Because as I sit happily here in Lifetime Number Nine, I'm still not exactly one you'd want to take home to Mom.

BY THE HOUR
CHAPTER 28

Monday, my first day back. I had to park a long way from the entrance, on the right side instead of the left. The bench in front of the railroad tracks paralleled my van and before I opened the driver's door, I stared at the bench for a long time, remembering the afternoon I was ready to jump.

I shivered with the memories of hopeless feelings and disgust with myself. It seemed so long ago that I felt that way... not just another Lifetime, but a different generation... the memories were in black and white.

Everything about me was different now. Hopelessness had been replaced with a taste of serenity, a bit of confidence, and the most surprising of all: a little love for myself.

I thought of Lin saying that one day I could look in the mirror and say, "I love you." That thought had stayed with me but I wondered how many decades it would take for me to do that.

With surprising ease, I waved goodbye to the bench and the long-ago thoughts of suicide. A total flip in my thoughts: *I have a lot to look forward to in this new, sober life.* Reminders of bad feelings now augmented the good ones.

☼ ☼ ☼ ☼ ☼

"Sign here and date it, please," Kathy said. I was in the Human Resources office at Smyth Software, both excited and anxious. Kathy laid another paper on top. "Initial here... and here." Pen in hand, I obeyed her commands.

When I signed, she smiled, showing all her gleaming teeth. "Welcome back, Lela. Everybody's expecting you, but Dale is also expecting that your soon-to-be-ex will try to contact you. For that reason, he's changed your phone extension number and concocted a new email address that doesn't match your name anymore. Make sure your contacts know your new address."

How perfectly nerdy... Dale thinking ahead about security, more paranoid than me! But would Stuart be so stupid as to think I'd work here again? Who would think that? How did I even get the crazy idea? But it worked and I am one lucky dog. I want to do my best... be the good employee I used to be so long ago.

The halls had been updated; new artwork all the way down to the entrance to our section. I stuck my head in Dale's office; he was on the phone but waved me in, then smiled and gave a thumbs-up. I felt my jaw relax without realizing it had been clenched; I'd been crazy with worry about what Dale's reception of me would be like, and I knew it could have gone either way. This looked hopeful.

Trying to be small, I sat in front of his desk and tucked my arms and legs close to my body. I scanned his office, studying the shelves of binders. All matching, a specific shade of dark-royal blue with the Smyth Software logo up the spine. A lot of hard work filled those shelves, I knew.

Dale's phone call was winding down. In fact, I could tell he was trying to get the caller to rush toward goodbye, but through the phone, I heard a gruff voice exclaim, "Oh! And another thing!" Dale sat back in his chair in a huff, said "Uh-huh" a dozen more times, and sighed a dozen more.

"I'll take care of it, Marty. Thank you." A pause. "Okay." Another pause. "Okay then." Dale leaned forward toward the phone cradle as if leading the caller to hang up. I found it hilarious. He looked at me and grinned. "Okay then Marty, I'll take care of it." Another pause. "Goodbye." Finally, Dale hung up the phone. He threw his head back and laughed. "Accck! Some people like to hear themselves talk, right?"

We shared a casual laugh before he stood to shake my hand. "Welcome back, Lela! Okay, I've got you all set up anonymously..." Dale began a soliloquy about technical things I didn't understand nor care to understand. He must have noticed my boredom and changed the subject.

He cleared his throat and sat up straighter. "But the best part... the phone call I just escaped? From Marty?" I nodded. "If I remember, you know Microsoft Word very well... isn't that right?"

"Yes, I do. That's why Word Perfect has been so hard for me."

"Well do I have a job for you! Marty in Marketing has a Word document that needs serious formatting work."

"No problem," I said.

"Great. That gives me a few days to get you set up for the next set of updates to the manual." I thought he had already done that; wasn't it the reason I couldn't come back until Monday?

Dale led me to the group of partitions that defined our department's space. My coworkers burst into a chorus of welcoming greetings, but I felt a certain hesitation among them. The same people were there, but some had dramatically changed.

There was Joe, a fat man who farted all the time on the all-protein Atkins diet, but he was easily my favorite of the weird group. We shared a love of Sheltie dogs, like my sweet Murphy, the one I'd raised from a pup. Joe and his partner had six Shelties on a few acres near Lake Okeechobee. Before I left... just spouting the woes of my personal life, I had shared the sharpest nail Stuart hammered in my heart: the sonofabitch had delivered Murphy to a high-kill shelter; he had to go out of his way to go to that particular one and, of course, he'd left a message to let me know. The evil laugh within that message still sickened me.

Hearing the story, Joe went to the shelter immediately and adopted Murphy. I couldn't imagine who would want an obese, twelve-year-old dog, but Joe's heart was as big as his ass.

Though I should've been happy that Murphy found a good home, I was dripping with Shame... ashamed that Joe's heart was bigger than my insane lifestyle. And I still felt Shame about Joe's rescue of my failure. I was sober but still insane about many things. And this was a biggie.

The practical side of me said, "Just wreckage of the past, Lela. When you were drinking, you couldn't take care of the dog, anyway." But the emotional side of me, always speaking the loudest, said, "You irresponsible piece of shit... couldn't even take care of a defenseless dog!

With no way to repay his kindness, I sat in my Shame my last three weeks on the job, never asking about Murphy or his other dogs... things we used to discuss easily. Our friendship would never be the same. *Your fault, idiot, ALL your fault.*

Another of the Smyth Software writers that made me feel anxious: Robert. I called him Spooky Robert. Shaved bald in the era it was considered weird, tiny round glasses, chubby, and with eyes that burned fire through your skin. Hard to ignore, Spooky Robert had a spooky crush on me despite having an ugly wife and three ugly children.

In what was supposed to be just a light conversation on the smoking dock one day, Robert told me aliens had abducted him as a child. He called himself a "Grey," one of many, he said, telling me of support-group meetings he attended every month. Spooky Robert was a pure weirdo who could turn into Prince Charming with the snap of a finger. It was hard to like him, hard to dislike him, and impossible to trust him.

That Monday when I entered the department, the look Robert threw my way sent a chill down my spine. *Is it possible he's even crazier now?*

Then Joe the Sheltie saver, stepped in to hug me. Shocked, I said, "Ralph! Oh my God! You've lost so much weight!"

"Fifty pounds!" he boasted. Still obese, but his jowls no longer waddled when he talked. There was a long gaze between us, impossible to define, but we both knew it had to do with the dog.

The others hadn't changed a bit; Red still wore the DEFCON lapel button over his nipple, The Razor still looked like a GQ model, Frat Boy still wore polished loafers, Rebecca was still syrupy-sweet and sickening. "Lela, your desk is here now," Dale said, pointing to the back corner in the front section. *I may be happier here if Ralph still farts like a mule.* I could only see a slice of his face on the diagonal... only his pudgy fingers on the keyboard and the front of his tightly shirted belly. The weight loss hadn't made a dent in the size of his gut.

My desk was behind Spooky Robert's; our backs would be to each other. No doubt I would have preferred to be in the back room where I was before, but at least I wasn't side by side with Robert.

Re-introductions done, I found myself in a happy and confident mood. I set up my desk with the knick-knacks and kitchy doo-dads that had always surrounded me, then took a brisk walk to Marketing to pick up the CD of the Microsoft Word document. "It's a mess," Marty said, "Please fix as much as you can. But I don't need it for a while, so take your time." I promised to do my best.

When I tried to load the disc onto my computer, it wouldn't take my password and locked me out of the system. Dale came to poke a few buttons and arrived at a password-reset screen. With a deep breath, I paused. *New life, so why not a new "theme" of passwords.* I typed "AuntVal2."

Had I known how significant her name would become in another Lifetime, I would have used all caps.

DONUTS FOR DINNER
CHAPTER 29

"Your quote was $500, not $600! You're cheating me, you *slime!*" My nostrils flared, eyes popped wide, and I streamed with sweat, upper lips to crotch.

The big boss of the moving team looked down and shrugged. "Look, lady. It just took longer. That storage garage? Had more stuff than you said. What can I say?"

"What can you *say?* To start, you can say you'll HONOR YOUR DAMN ESTIMATE!" I had budgeted the move to my Boynton Beach apartment to the penny and had the exact amount of cash, including a nice trip for each of the burly men. "Well, you assholes better work it out because now there's nothing left for a tip.

It was his turn to glare at me. Then he turned on his heel and yelled to his buddies, "She screwed us! Let's get out of here." I ran after him. My TV was on the back deck of the truck and I saw the blonde guy throw it in the truck and lock the double doors before they drove away

They stole my TV! The only one I have! The one that used to be Stuart's!

I ran back inside the apartment to call Mom, panicked and blabbering. "The men are on the truck! I can't *call* them! What do I do?"

"Call the police," was her simple and sensible reply. "But first, take a deep breath and calm yourself, Lela. What is it you say? In through your nose and out through your mouth?"

"Okay, Mom, I'm calling the police. Call you back later." No time for breathing, I decided, and just as I punched the "9" of "9-1-1," the blonde mover rushed in the open door and set my TV on the floor. He didn't say a word; just turned and ran.

I closed my phone with shaking hands. Feeling my heartbeat in every cell of my head, I found a chair and took Mom's advice. *Breathe, Lela, breathe.* I found a wall plug and the TV turned on. *At least there's that.*

Mom hadn't approved of my early-move plan. I couldn't take the pressure of the halfway house anymore; too much drama, I decided. And the combination of rent for Serenity Sisters and the storage unit was almost as much as a real apartment. *Don't fool yourself, Lela. It's not "almost." Unless you count one-third as "almost."*

So I called my stockbroker again. He seemed concerned about another withdrawal and asked twice if I was okay. "Fine as frog hair," I'd said, grimacing at my way-too-Southern phrase. But I looked down on myself and smiled. There I was, out in the real world, living a real life. I would have smiled and worked to pat myself on the back, but I looked at the mess of the living room and found it impossible to relax. Too much to do.

When the movers unloaded the sofa, I found it didn't fit where I planned and that threw everything else in disarray. The stuff for closet storage was scattered in various nooks and crannies. Boxes with no labels lined the walls, reminding me that Mom and Dad had packed from Stuart's in a hurry. Everything everywhere; the most disorganized move I'd ever had.

I thought of my friend Lola and how beautifully she had organized my move from Tennessee to West Palm Beach. *Back in the day when others had to do my work... when I was 100 percent dysfunctional.*

I paused to let that thought sink in and realized I was still dysfunctional. *Sober but unable to solve simple tasks. Insane sobriety. But remember what Jenny said: sometimes the first year sober is worse than the last year drinking. Surely that won't be me... surely the past few months aren't examples of the months to come. I need Dude to send some CALM my way. Even if I could just meditate... it would help.*

Anxiety ran high and the move had sent me over the top. Another issue: it was time to find a shrink "on the outside," as Dr. Mallory at R&R called them. If nothing else, I needed refills... and I planned to ask he/she about my increased anxiety. But had I investigated new docs? Hell no. *Stubborn Lela, chicken-shit woman.* My latest excuse was I didn't have the money. No insurance, but in those days, it was still affordable to self-pay. Yet I continued to avoid the issue, hoping I could beg Dr. Mallory to bend the rules for me one more time.

So if you can't afford a doctor, how can you afford rent for this apartment? I ignored the common-sense voice in my head and found a way to justify almost all the stupid decisions I had made in the past five months.

I knew two things: the apartment *was* affordable and leaving Serenity Sisters guaranteed Stuart couldn't find me. The location wasn't the best, but it was nice enough. The lack of a security gate concerned me, but that's why I could afford the place. I took every other precaution to stay incognito and make it hard for Stuart to find me. I rented a Post Office box again, changed my cell phone number again, and my home phone was unlisted, with the extra notation of "restricted."

The layout of the apartment was almost identical to one of the many apartments I rented when married to Bo's dad. I insisted on a lower-level apartment, especially because the staircases in the complex were rusty with sparse metal bars; it screamed UNSAFE to me. Not only that, I have a weird fear of sleeping on an upper floor, a fear I've had since childhood.

No foyer, a small dining area on the right, adjoining a living room with a sliding glass door and vertical blinds. The galley kitchen was small but big enough for as little as I cooked. A short hall led to the Master bedroom with two over-sized walk-in storage closets.

Less than ideal was the sliding glass door in the bedroom that paralleled my bed, so close to my mattress that you could reach through it and touch me as I slept. With a shiver, I envisioned a peeping-Tom through the vertical blinds.

Errands. The first was to get wooden dowels to block the sliding-glass doors, a sliding lock with a chain for the front door, and a screwdriver to install it. As I would many times over the next year, I stopped by the Dunkin' Donuts two buildings down, inhaling a duo of glazed before I even made it home.

Then I set my sights on the living room, tugging on furniture to create a proper place for guests and a practical setup for watching TV. The room came together after a few tries. Around ten PM, I made my bed and fell into it, exhausted.

The next day, Sunday, I pushed myself even harder. After finding the coffee pot, I opened boxes and worked throughout the day. By midnight, I had finished, even hanging the pictures.

As always, I thought of my sister Karen while hanging the pictures. In her shop back home, she had framed dozens of cool-as-shit pictures for me. It helped that second-husband Miller McKeown had collected awesome pieces of art and I'd been able to claim them in the war of our divorce.

Monday morning, my muscles screamed at me, sore from all the reaching, tugging, and pushing. *You're too old to work at that pace, Lela. Next time take your time.* A pause in my thoughts corrected the notion. *No, there wouldn't be a next time because I will never move again. It's just too hard.*

Staying in Florida had been a touchy issue with my whole family; they wanted me back in Tennessee and away from Stuart. But I was relieved I wouldn't have to put forth the effort to make such huge changes. I still felt discombobulated as hell, spinning thoughts in a bird-body, like I was flying overhead and searching for a place to perch. I wanted to feel much more grounded before I made a big decision about anything.

For that next week, I wasn't up-to-par at work, not as productive as I should've been. To compensate for my failings, I set ridiculously high expectations for myself. The problem was that I was missing the mark, big time and every time.

When determination didn't work, I tried to write off my inefficiency and blame it on the newness of my sobriety. The past months had been crazy in every way, but I believed I'd get better soon. I *had* to believe that.

My biggest worry was that while my prayers to Dude were constant during the process of moving and settling in, I wasn't feeling so close to him. Without warning, I lost my vision and wasn't hearing the feedback he usually sent to my heart. That scared the hell out of me.

What if I lose my connection altogether? What if I'm doing something wrong and disappearance is his way of showing displeasure? Jenny could answer those questions for me. *And speaking of Jenny, haven't you been neglecting to connect with HER, too? Might the two facts be related?*

☼ ☼ ☼ ☼ ☼

One evening, about a month after I'd moved, I sat at my desk doing my favorite thing: writing for fun, this time fiction. It was a short story about a Peeping Tom named Tom who spied on a single woman named Charlotte the Show Girl. It was a mystery, a comedy, a romance-in-disguise.

My cell phone rang. Only a handful of people knew my new number, so I answered with a silly flourish in a bad-acting tone. "Hellooooo!"

"Hey! How are you?" I froze. It was Stuart. My blood pressure spiraled up, bringing immediate dizziness and a deafening buzz between my ears.

A pause to recover my senses, then I screamed, "DON'T CALL ME! EVER! Understand, you fat asshole? How did you get this number?" I fumed with anger, spitting dots of saliva on the phone.

"Wait, wait, Lela, you haven't answered my divorce complaint, a *legal* document. The papers say you must answer within thirty days. You're late and that's *illegal*."

I lied. "Listen to me, Butthead, I don't have a lawyer and I don't have time for you. Besides, I'm not supposed to talk to you, now or ever. Restraining order, remember, you turd? And you'll probably say I called *you*. Stuart Weinstein, you are an evil man and you can just kiss my ass while I fart – got it? I'll sign your fucking papers when I damn good and ready!"

He had to have the last word. "Such a redneck bitch... can't you just be a decent human being?"

And I took the bait. "Can't you just pay the money you stole from me? You manipulated me and it cost me thousands!" Now my hands were shaking uncontrollably, the angriest I'd been since throwing the chair in rehab.

The earpiece filled with Stuart's maniacal laughter. "Good luck in seeing a *penny* of that money. It's not *my* fault you're stupid."

In an octave twice-higher than my norm, I screamed in frustration, an unrecognizable pair of syllables, then hung up. *How did he get my number? Who did he PAY to get it? Should I change it again? What should I do?*

I went to bed with the same questions on my mind, too proud to call my sponsor, or Charlie, or Karen, or Daddy, or anybody. I didn't want their input, I decided, because I knew what it would be. *Everybody except Jenny thinks I should've moved back home... that I should've put my tail between my legs and run away.*

But I had my own ideas.

I thought I can be a badass and beat him at his own game, by God. *Lela, find your superhero cape... time to put on your big-girl panties and fight back!*

☼ ☼ ☼ ☼ ☼

It was the fourth week of working on the Microsoft Word document for Marty in Marketing, and I'd made little progress. I sauntered down the hall and knocked on Dale's door frame.

"Hey boss, that Marketing project is a real bitch... and I thought you wanted me to start on the manual as soon as possible, so... do you have anything ready for me yet?"

Dale's body froze, his face in a panic. "I've forgotten all about you. Oh! I mean... all about your *work*. I'll get on that this afternoon, Lela. In the meantime, just keep working on the Word project. Are you finished?"

"Dale, it's 312 pages and a total mess. Honestly, it will take months to completely finish. I think it'd be better to start over. Do you want me to do that?"

"No, you've spent enough time on it already. Uh... I'll get back to you, to get you started on some updates." Dale seemed embarrassed; it seemed he had truly forgotten about me. But there was an undertone of... something in his voice and his body remained stiff during the entire conversation. *What the hell is up?*

In those weeks, I managed to stay away from Spooky Robert with a few equally spooky exceptions, but all were brief moments of being uncomfortable. Still, I was deeply afraid of Robert and it seemed his weirdness had turned toward the evil side.

He followed me to the back dock to smoke two times, so I stopped going unless accompanied by someone. Twice a day, I would knock on Laura Johnson's carrel and invite her to go smoke with me. When Spooky Robert figured out what I was doing, he stopped following me.

After a week of this, I relaxed a bit. But the next day, he slipped a note under my mouse while I was at lunch.

> *I HAD A DREAM ABOUT YOU LAST NIGHT*

The note and the concept made me shiver. Baffled and down-right scared, my response was to do and say nothing. Later in the afternoon, he laid another note on my desk while I was out smoking with Laura.

> *YOU NEED TO HEAR ABOUT THE DREAM.*
> *STAY LATE TONIGHT.*

I left early, around 4:30. Technically, I didn't need to ask permission because I was paid by the hour, but I thought it would be proper to let the boss know I was leaving. With my purse on my shoulder, I stopped by his office. Dale cocked his head and squinted at me with a questioning look, obviously curious about my early departure. So I lied; said I had a dentist appointment.

Dale was as practical as he was suspicious, it seemed. "This late? A dentist open after-hours?"

I panicked, realizing I had to tell yet-another lie, act like a drunk would act. "Uh... it's a clinic down in Boynton Beach that stays open 'til seven. Just a cleaning."

I was still shaking when I started the van. The anxiety about the lie combined with the anxiety about Spooky Robert sent me reeling. *What am I going to do? He's harassing me... is that something to report to Human Resources? But he'll know it's me. Everybody else likes Robert and treats him normal... and he acts normal around them. It's just me. Somehow, it's gotta be my fault.*

Jenny's voice spoke in my head. *No, it's not your fault and why haven't you outgrown that self-bashing yet, Lela Fox? You're sober and you're in the right. Now grow up! Stand up! Do something to make him stop.*

Deep in thought, I pondered my options all the way to the intersection where I *could've* turned left to go home. But that night, I succumbed to having donuts for dinner – again. A Boston Market was on the other corner and I rotated between the two offerings: good-for-me dinner, bad-for-me dinner. That day, I ordered three donuts in the drive-thru and savored them with ooh's and aah's from the sofa.

I tried, but my friend Guilt roared in the background... the Guilt about my shitty diet ate at me. So I opened my laptop to type a mantra. "Rule: Donuts for dinner only twice a week." I printed it and posted it on the refrigerator.

Only then did I notice the blink of the answering machine and turned it to "playback" while rustling around in the kitchen.

Beeeeep...

> *Lela, it's Stuart, in case you didn't know. [laugh] I'm out on the porch with Rock-Bob the dog, watching the palm trees sway. Just thinking of you. It's a beautiful night. See, because, I know you still love me... as much as I love you. We had a good thing, you know. [pause] And I think we could've made it work if you hadn't gotten so mad that night. But it's just because you were drunk. So if you're really sober now, things will change. I see you're back at work, so you must be doing okay. Yay for you. If you won't throw any more dishes, I'd like to see you. Like, tonight. If you can. [sigh] What do you think? I love you, baby. Call me.*

There were tears on my cheeks, tears of Anger and Fear, maybe a little Regret. As my heart broke, my thoughts reeled. *No, I don't want to see you at all, you fucker! How could I have EVER thought you were nice, or kind, or in love with me? And how DARE you assume I'd want to see you! What an asshole you are... trying to manipulate me again! Just leave me alone!*

Still staring at the answering machine, my hand reached toward the erase button, then stopped. Instead, I pressed "save." *I might need this message later. Who knows why or how, but I'm saving it. Evidence, maybe.*

I clicked through the call history, noted the phone number, and wrote it in huge numbers with the biggest, blackest Sharpie I could find. Teary-eyed, I posted the devilish DO NOT ANSWER phone number on the fridge, next to the "Donuts for dinner" note.

And now he's found my unlisted home phone number, too! How? HOW? Why won't he just leave me alone? I'm a nervous wreck! It's happening... I'm losing my mind.

This time I pledged to talk to Jenny about it and we'd have the perfect opportunity at our scheduled meeting in two days.

We met at my place now, which made me feel important, worthy of an independent life, and our meetings could be longer and more intense. She had taught me a lot, and now I needed her more than ever.

Jenny, help me! Dude! Help me! I could hear Jenny's coos of assurance in the back of my mind, but no soothing sounds from my Higher Power.

Come back to me, Dude. I need you.

VICTIM'S RIGHTS
CHAPTER 30

"I think you need to call the police, tell them what he's doing to you," Jenny said. "And the dog barking messages... that's spooky-weird. But more than that, Lela, he's *dangerous*. Stalking you! He got not one but BOTH phone numbers, he knew you were back at work... and I bet he knows where you live." She was showing her concern, but mostly her anger.

I agreed that Stuart was dangerous, but my fears weren't of getting jumped in an alley. Rather, I expected him to turn the blame on breaking the no-contact order on me, and soon. "I worry even though I have evidence that says it's HIM."

"Still saving those messages?"

"I even saved the one of Rock-Bob barking."

"But he's leaving messages of love and devotion, never a direct threat, so it only proves he's contacted you. And he has every right to do that. You can't contact him, but nothing in the restraining order says he can't contact you."

It was a carefully plotted campaign, and he'd played his cards well. Even with the evidence of the recorded messages, I couldn't testify that I'd felt threatened. It was all a game of manipulation; he was playing with my head... and my head was in a place that left it increasingly vulnerable.

Every thought I had ping-ponged off the other side of my brain. As my Dad would've said, "I didn't know whether to take a crap or wind my watch."

"Not only that, Jenny, the court date for him to make the temporary restraining order *permanent* is coming up. I bet you a dollar he accuses me of contacting him, says he lives in fear for his life," I said, continuing my ramble. "Then I'm really screwed."

"I'm not going let you be screwed on this. You have a phone book?" We were at my apartment; at the dining table I'd bought at a thrift store. It was cheap, and it was ugly, but it served the purpose. I plopped the book on the table and slid it toward her.

"But Jenny, nobody out there can help me... and I can't afford another lawyer. So... what are you–"

"Hush," she interrupted, "Give me a pen and paper. Here's something: Victim's Rights, a Palm Beach Country domestic abuse resource agency called VPS: Victim's Protective Services." She scribbled on the paper I'd given her. "Call them, or just go there. Tell them you need help and that you're a victim, too."

"Well, I *am* a victim, Jenny, but in the eye of the law, I'm the *accused*. That's an agency *he* would go to." I argued.

"But you've got to go *somewhere*. There must be help for you, sweetie! This can't go on... and on and on and on." She pushed the paper toward me. As I entered the deep space of my paranoid thoughts, she snatched the paper back.

"Here's another one. It like legal help for domestic abuse victims. Legal advice, maybe, and the more people you call, the more likely you'll find some help. I'm writing down all of these."

I remained silent as Jenny continued through the government section of the book. "Man, if you were on the other side to begin with, you'd have all kinds of help. So I'm just going to assume the same agencies can help you now, from the other side of the equation."

The paper that had begun with one phone number now listed a dozen. Maybe action would be better than inaction, but I felt so... young and dumb, so used.

Like he said, "it's not my fault that you're stupid."

☼ ☼ ☼ ☼ ☼

I told Dale I was taking the afternoon off. He flipped his hand in a dismissive "goodbye" without a word. I drove to the courthouse in West Palm and circled the block, finding a parking spot on the street, directly in front of the entrance. *A good omen, maybe?* I put the list of agencies, suite numbers noted, in the front pocket of my pants.

My first destination: VPS, Victim's Protective Services. I brought my case number and the mini-cassette from my answering machine for the... *would it be called a counselor?*

I sat in the waiting area for twenty minutes before being called back to sit at a desk with an overweight black woman with a mass of beautiful braided hair. She smiled with her entire face when she asked how she could help.

"He keeps calling me, harassing me, telling me where I've been and what I've been doing. But there's a restraining order. I'm about to fall apart emotionally..." I couldn't say more. Stating my fears out loud, to a stranger brought the point home. I was terrified of Stuart Weinstein and waiting for the other shoe to drop.

She read the computer screen that detailed the case, talking at the same time. "But... the restraining order was filed against *you*, Ms. Fox. *You* are charged with domestic violence!"

"Right, but that part is all a lie... and from another lifetime. Now, he's stalking me, leaving messages almost every day, scaring the hell out of me. It's fine that I can't contact *him*... I want nothing to do with him! What I *want* is for him to leave me alone. I've tried to file a restraining order twice... and can't because of the existing one."

She looked at me and frowned, one eyebrow up and the other one down. Then she spoke... in a snappy and accusatory voice, emphasizing keywords as if slapping me in the face with them. "You are not the *victim* in this case, ma'am, you are the *perpetrator*, the *accused*. In fact..." she pecked on her keyboard. "You were *charged*, pled *guilty*, then *ignored* the stipulations of the order, resulting in *another* arrest! So how could you *possibly* call yourself a *victim?* Both eyebrows arched as she crossed her arms across her generous torso; her body language shutting me out.

I tried again, explaining my current innocence and his stalking, but no matter how I phrased it, she shook her head no. Finally, she interrupted my blubbering. "Look, ma'am, I have a waiting-room-full of women who are in *danger.* Their husbands or boyfriends are threatening them with *guns!* They had to run away to *shelters!*" She paused, throwing up her hands and rolling her eyes. "And you sit here telling me he left a message of a *dog barking?* Where do you get *off* thinking you need *help?* Especially from *me!* We protect *the victim's* rights!"

I answered her with tears and a nod. I gathered my bag of papers and stood. As I walked away, I heard her voice behind me. "Next victim!"

Another agency on the same floor... the same result.

Third floor, end of the hall... the same. In fact, a similar scene repeated at six other "victim's resource agencies" in the courthouse.

One guy in a fifth-floor victim's agency threatened to re-arrest me, to cite me for misusing county funds simply by showing up in their office. "How *dare* you?" he said.

Yep, I was screwed.

Helplessness. Assured defeat. More of the same anxiety that had driven me to distraction... I couldn't handle it anymore.

I decided to show up in court when he went to make the order permanent, play the tape for the judge, and get a restraining order out of it directly from him.

Even if to just get it on record that he was contacting me... it was better than doing nothing, and a reason for a little hope.

But my smart plan, so well-thought-out, exploded in my face.

OUTRAGEOUS LIES
CHAPTER 31

Stuart's face looked like hell. One eye was black and blue, and the other nearly swollen shut... beet-red around the edges. He had a small bandage on near his ear, with a larger spot shaved free of his wiry gray hair. He looked like he had been in a bar fight.

"Yes, Your Honor, I want the restraining order to be permanent," he said. "This shameless woman continues to threaten me, stalk me. She calls, sometimes a dozen times a day, interrupting my work. My employer is at the other end of the courthouse, filing a complaint against her as we speak. Ms. Fox has broken the temporary version of the no-contact order numerous times, but she's sly. She crosses the line quickly, then retreats before the police can show up. She's practiced, sir, and must have done this before."

Stuart stood behind the mahogany podium and stated this with just enough fumbling to make it seem unpracticed. But it *was* practiced. And it seemed he believed his lies.

"First, I must ask... what has happened to you, sir? Were you in an accident?"

"An accident? No! Her pimp beat me up last night. Jumped me in the parking lot after work. Left me for dead."

The judge glanced at me and frowned. I was unsure of what to do. *Should I refute him now or keep my mouth shut until the judge asks me to speak?* The podium where I stood rocked; I was locking and unlocking my knees, nervous as a cat.

"So when Ms. Fox contacts you—"

"*Harasses* me, actually, Your Honor."

The judged pursed his lips, obviously pissed that he'd been interrupted. "Have you called the police, Mr. Weinstein... when Ms. Fox harasses you?" He removed his half-lens glasses and studied Stuart's face, even closer than before.

Stuart paused. The silence spooked me; I felt I *needed* to say something to break the tension. I tried a few deep breaths, but they did nothing to calm me. The background noises blended together, creating a symphony of panic as the judge stared me down. I attempted a smile, but fear kept my face in a grimace, and surely my eyes looked like saucers. The judge switched his glance back to Stuart.

"Again, have you reported Ms. Fox's behavior and threats?"

"No Your Honor, I have not."

"And why not, sir?"

"As I said, she's quick. Won't let herself be caught. An experienced stalker, I think. And now she's scaring my son!"

Your son? What the hell are you talking about? I stared at Stuart's profile with pure hate, incensed he would tell such outrageous lies so easily. *How can he DO this? Surely the judge will see through this bullshit!*

"I see," said the judge, then picked up a pen. "And the age of your son?"

"Just a child! He's seven and pure innocence! Spends most days looking over his shoulder. He'll need therapy for this without a doubt, and for his whole life! Your Honor, I think this woman should be locked up."

The judge snapped, "I'll be the judge of that, if you will, Mr. Weinstein." I laughed at the pun, accidentally blowing a raspberry. I covered my mouth, but the damage had been done. The judge shot me a look... the evil eye. *Oh no, Lela, you dumbass!*

I wanted to scream at the judge: *When will I get MY turn? When can I tell MY side, tell you what an asshole he is! These are all LIES!*

I shook my head to clear it, reminding myself Stuart had the upper hand. *He is the victim and you have no power; the whole damn courthouse has made that clear. So shut up... maybe he'll dig his own grave.*

The judge was listening to Stuart intently, seemed to be on his side. The result was I looked guilty as hell, and the unfairness of it all ate at my skin... ate into my brain and my face. *Don't do it, Lela. Don't take the bait. You'll get your turn. I think so... maybe.... until then, keep your mouth shut! Sit on your hands.*

After Stuart's next accusation, specifically that I showed up at his shop and "chased customers away," I couldn't stand it any longer. I burst out. Yelling at Stuart, I spewed, "You're lying through your teeth!" Turning to the judge, I said, "Sir, these are all lies! It's *Stuart* who's been stalking and harassing *me!*"

The judge jumped at my outburst but his response was calm and measured. "Ms. Fox! You do not have the floor. You'll have a chance to speak. In the meantime, ma'am, I suggest you withhold your comments. That's not a suggestion but an order. Do you understand?" I nodded. Tears welled in my eyes. Frustration. Fear. Sadness. Anger.

Stuart continued to speak as the judge looked down at what I assumed was the police report. The sonofabitch turned to me, eyes full of venom, drilling them into me as he spoke. He got caught taunting me, though; the judge asked him to "address his comments to the bench."

Stuart's list of my "wrongs" was long, and I stood with my butt cheeks clenched tight and my throat squeezed shut. I felt ready to burst, to run, to scream. When I realized I was holding my breath, I blew out a shaky and loud sigh. The judge noticed.

"Ms. Fox! I told you and I tell you again, Mr. Weinstein has the floor!"

"But..." The word slipped out before I could stop it. Immediately, my shoulders fell, releasing the tension that was enveloping my body. I mumbled, "Sorry, Your Honor."

I can't listen to any more of this or I'll lose my mind. For a minute, I heard Stuart's voice fading in and out; I was no longer able to hear the words, only the poisonous tone. The deep voice of the judge snapped me back to the horror of this day.

"Ms. Fox, you had something to say?"

"Yes, Your Honor." I took a moment to gather my wits and thoughts. "Sir, I have *not* broken the restraining order, nor do I intend to. Trust me, I don't want to see or talk to Mr. Weinstein *at all!* It's *him* who is calling *me*, and I have proof. I don't answer the calls, of course, but Mr. Weinstein leaves long, creepy messages, begging me to meet him somewhere, go to his house... trying to manipulate me. And I have these messages on tape, ready for you to hear." Stuart's face fell, then snapped back with a sneer at me.

The judge said simply, "I will listen."

With relief, I dove below the podium pulling a mini-cassette player from my purse on the floor. When I re-emerged, the bailiff's hand was on my podium, palm out, and it startled me. Of course, I looked stupid when I jumped and squealed, and Stuart blew a snarky laugh.

"Mr. Weinstein?"

"Yes, Your Honor."

"That's enough. If you can't keep a straight face in my courtroom, I will ask you to leave."

"Yes, Your Honor. Sorry, Your Honor."

Their conversation made it even harder for me to focus and I fumbled with the device. "Uh... here's the cassette, and... give me a second to cue up the messages." My hands were shaking, and I pressed the wrong button, so it took a ridiculous amount of time to get to the right screen. The bailiff drummed his fingers on my podium and the judge continued to leer at me.

Stuart was laughing silently behind his hand. "Okay, here, just press this button. Some are hard to hear, Your Honor."

The judge held his gaze, looking deep into my bundle of nerves. "I'll listen in chambers. The parties may be seated."

On the way to the row of chairs behind me, my arms jerked, shaking so hard. *Why didn't you get a lawyer, Lela?* Then I answered myself. *Because I never thought he would tell such lies! Ah... but you should've known! Don't you know to expect only the worst from him?*

In my peripheral vision, I saw Stuart fidget. *The sonofabitch always fidgets. But now I'm the one in the right, the one with proof. After the judge hears that tape, Stuart will be in big trouble, maybe go to jail.* I felt sure of myself, but still an emotional mess.

I dared to look at him as he stared straight ahead. His cuts and bruises were serious. I wondered what the hell happened. *A bar fight? Really?* Purple bruises lined his high cheekbones and his left ear featured a deep, bloody cut. *Whatever happened, he definitely lost.*

While the judge was away, I had time to calm my nerves. I knew I was the only with a legitimate right to complain and wouldn't have if I'd stayed in hiding like everybody wanted me to.

Fifteen minutes after he left, the judge returned with the expected "All rise" order from the bailiff, who also gestured for us to return to our podiums.

The judge looked at me over the top of his glasses. "Ms. Fox, most of the messages I could not hear. And I don't know if you think it was a joke to include a recording of a dog barking, but I did not find it funny in the least."

I interrupted. "It was his dog, Your Honor. The voice in the background was his, uh, Mr. Weinstein's, telling the dog to bark into the phone." Stuart huffed a *phfft* sound.

The judge snapped his head to leer at my soon-to-be-ex, and Stuart's satisfied smile disappeared. Still glaring, the judge said, knowingly, "I see."

My heart raced. *The judge believes me!* "Mr. Weinstein, I have no proof that it's your voice on these messages. Otherwise, I would charge you. Because you can't accuse Ms. Fox of breaking the order while you continue to contact her. She has no defense, see... because, under Florida law, she can't file a no-contact order against you at this time."

A quick, business-like reply, "Yes, Your Honor."

The judge looked at me with somewhat of an empathetic expression. "I see your predicament, Ms. Fox." The judge looked back at Stuart, then at me, then back at Stuart. He sighed and removed his glasses, chewing on the earpiece. "This is a difficult case. I believe you both." *Believes us both? How can he possibly believe Stuart?*

"He's lying, Your Honor, I never–"

"Quiet!" His eyes pierced mine. An apology would be a bad idea, I thought, so I looked away, unable to maintain his gaze.

"This problem cannot be solved with a restraining order, whether temporary or permanent. The two of you need to be separated and perhaps that will stop the harassing." The judge leaned back in his chair and paused for what seemed like hours. Thinking, I supposed. At last leaning forward, he said, "Ms. Fox, unfortunately, because you are the one charged with domestic assault, I have to choose you for separation."

Shaking my head, I said, "Your Honor, I don't underst–"

He spoke to the bailiff. "County jail. Three days." The gavel fell and my heart stopped. "Stay away from each other!" He spoke louder than needed, louder than the echo in my head.

I looked at Stuart in amazement. He tried to hide his taunting, but he pointed a finger at me and laughed silently. *Fuck you. To hell with you.*

Me? Go to jail? I did nothing! I opened my mouth to say these things to the judge, talk to him, beg him to consider another solution, but he was looking at another file, concentrating. Our case was over. I was going to jail.

In an instant, the bailiff took my arm and led me through a side door. Three steps into the hall and my knees felt like spaghetti. I asked the bailiff to stop. "I think I'm going to faint," I said.

Thankfully, he caught me in mid-collapse, before I hit the concrete floor.

It had all happened so fast! The result was such a shock that I didn't realize how royally I'd been screwed for a while; by then I wore an orange uniform with an inmate number stamped on the pocket.

But the time in jail would serve as a turning point for me, an eye-opening discovery after the climb of Kilimanjaro.

In Lifetime Number Seven, I found out why Stuart looked like he'd been beaten that day. My dad spilled the beans to Karen's husband but never told me.

With some South Florida union connections, Daddy had arranged a "meeting" with Stuart in the parking lot of Ace Transmissions. The instruction was to hurt and maim, but not kill.

When I found out, I wasn't amused. In fact, I didn't like it at all. It was so like my Daddy, but so UNlike my Dude.

My, my, my... how things change.

MIXED-UP WITH A MIX-UP
CHAPTER 32

I was in a dream state, it seemed. The bailiff hadn't handcuffed me, not in the courtroom, nor in the small "intake room," or so the sign called it. He looked at me kindly from behind a desk and motioned me to sit on a hard-plastic chair.

I could think of only one explanation for his kindness. I guessed he understood my sentence – *oh-my-God, a sentence!* – was unfair. He loaned me a scrap of paper and let me write phone numbers from my phone's contacts list because he felt sorry for me. What other explanation could there be? Guilty people don't get favors!

The bailiff inventoried my belongings, bagged them, and dangled handcuffs from the end of his finger. With a weak "I'm sorry, ma'am," he clasped my wrists behind my back.

Honestly, I can't remember full details of the rest of that day, only that I kept repeating "Oh my God! Oh my God!" There was nothing else to say, but my mind was on full-throttle. *I'm not supposed to be going to jail! I'm sober! More than three months sober! Sober people don't go to jail!*

I remember when we walked outside, a short path to the bowels of the adjacent jail building, the memory clear only because it was raining, and I couldn't cover my hair with handcuffs on. It was a humiliating walk. Another Walk of Shame for Lela Fox.

Fingerprints, mug shot, a baggy orange jumpsuit... and I cried through the long process. As the third officer in the series led me to a cell, she muttered, "Crazy women crying all the damn time."

Through my flow of tears, I answered, "If you only knew the fuck-up that landed me here, you'd be crying, too."

"No Puffs tissues in your cell, ma'am, so you best stop the snot. No cry-baby ever made it in jail." She shoved me to the left, using a strange kind of key to open a cell. A 20-something white girl was on the bottom bunk, wide-eyed and silent. "You're both going to Belle Glade soon so don't get comfortable," the officer sneered.

Forgetting my jail etiquette, I immediately spoke to my cellmate, "What's Belle Glade?"

There was a shakiness in her voice as she squashed herself farther back on the bunk and shrugged. "They told me it's the long-term facility, inland near Lake Okeechobee."

I was so freaked out I could barely squeak out a response, feeling on the edge of a breakdown. "*Long-term?* I'm just supposed to be here for *three days!* That's not long term! The judge said, and I quote, 'Three days in *county jail.*' Just three days, *here!*

Then I realized saying "just three days" was a scary misnomer. Three days in jail was a lifetime. My longest jail visit so far had been two-and-a-half days, and that was another screw-up back home in Rockville.

I raised my voice as anger joined my fear. "There's been some kind of mistake, a *BIG mistake.* I mean, I shouldn't even be here in the first place! Oh, God! What am I going to do?" More tears streamed down my cheeks as I sat on the edge of the bottom bunk next to the girl.

"Hey, don't get your cooties down here, lady!" The girl was serious.

"Chill, chick. No cooties on me. What are you in for, anyway? You don't look like a hardened criminal."

"It's a long story, a mix-up with my cousin in Orlando. But my dad's an attorney and trying to get it straightened out. And this sucks cheese. I've never been in jail before."

"How long have you been here?"

"Since yesterday."

"I just don't understand why they would take me to... the prison, I guess it is, right?"

"They said 'detention facility' and that sounds better. Don't say 'prison.' Please."

I sighed, put my head in my hands, and a new rack of sobs began. "Well, it's not the county jail, so it's a prison. Prison for people who have no hope of getting out anytime soon. Three *days*, not three *years*! That's not the place for me! Sounds like a total fuck-up."

"Sorry, man. It sucks, all of it sucks."

"Maybe your dad would help me, too? 'Cause I think I'll end up needing a lawyer."

The girl laughed. "I'd say my dad has his hands full." She paused and blew a long sigh. "But I've only talked to him once."

With that, I realized nobody knew where I was, and they hadn't let me make a phone call. I told Dale I'd be in by noon, and it was already past that. Only Jenny knew I was going to court that morning. I hadn't told my parents or anybody in my new circle of AA friends, including my friend and neighbor Ruth. *And why would they think to guess you'd be in jail? You're sober! You're working the steps, making great progress! And you broke no laws, none at all! You have an apartment, a job... you're fulfilling all the responsibilities. Why the hell are you here?*

"I'm going to the top bunk to cry myself to sleep. I'm Lela, by the way."

She reached out her hand. "I'm Griffin. Nice to meet you."

"Griffin? Cool name."

"My mother's maiden name, actually."

"It's not one you would forget."

"I wish the cops would forget it. It's also my male cousin's name. Thus the mix-up."

With a chuckle, I answered. "I hear ya," but I didn't give a shit about her problem... way too focused on mine. "How long 'til they come to get us, ya think?"

"No idea."

"I'm going up, then. God knows... I'm so tired of crying! Maybe a nap will help me figure out a way to get out of this." With great effort, I hoisted myself to the top bunk, a thin mattress covered with a discolored sheet and the crunch of a plastic cover underneath. Same crunch with the pillow. Every time I moved my head, the noise of the plastic cover roused me. It reminded me of the detox week in the crazy hospital where plastic covered everything.

I slept fitfully, in and out for about three hours, dreaming screwed-up scenarios that left me upset and confused.

Trays of movie-prop dinner passed through the slot of the bars, bringing another round of sobs. Inedible, I thought, even the smooshy apple. *It's gonna be a long three days, Lela. Stiff upper lip required. You're sober and Dude knows you're here. Dude knows you need help. You don't even need to ask for it.*

The thought brought more tears, but surprisingly, they were tears of gratitude. *This sobriety shit is crazy. How can you feel grateful in this situation?* As my mind continued to whirl, another round of thoughts came, Jenny's words. "I bitched about having no shoes until I saw a man who had no feet." Yep, it could be worse.

Little did I know how quickly it would become worse; ten times worse than I could have imagined.

SKINNY JACKIE & BIG TERRA
CHAPTER 33

"But I *need* my medicine! Without it, I'm Bi-Polar bat-shit crazy! Why can't you get this arranged, dammit!?" Flames shot from my eyes, inches from the face of the bitch in charge.

She growled, "Stuff it, Fox. Things run on *our* time. You're the one wearing the jumpsuit – got it?" The chunky deputy spoke to me over the counter in the group room as the other prisoners lined up for their medication.

I ran my fingers through three-day-dirty hair. "Look, man, it's dangerous to cold-turkey off one of my psych meds. Like, I could have seizures, swallow my tongue. How d'you like *that?* This is, like, prisoner abuse! I could sue!"

The deputy threw her head back and laughed aloud. "Why would I abuse you when the other inmates are doing a pretty good job on their own? It's easy to see that several of the women... uh... ADMIRE you a lot. Better watch your step. You'll need more than Skinny Jackie to protect your ass."

"How dare you laugh about that! I need your *help*, not your *jokes*." The deputy turned her back, chuckling under her breath.

She was right about all of it: I had no power there, my "fellow inmates" were taunting me, and I'd best watch my step. I upped my efforts to get her help, desperate for a prescription and protection from Big Terra. "You can't DO this, Ms. Deputy! *I need to see somebody in charge!*"

"Tell your troubles to Skinny Jackie. She runs the place on your side."

Skinny Jackie had been my protector since I arrived. As I took the assigned top bunk in the corner of the Section Three room, Jackie sauntered over to welcome me home.

A light-skinned black girl in her mid-30's, I guessed, she was very tall and weighed a hundred pounds soaking wet... painfully thin. Jackie gave me the tour of the ward and explained the set-up. Four sections connected to the group room but there were no cells. About 25 bunk beds lined the walls of our section: a square, cold, cinder-block room... two payphones and a row of open toilets faced a row of sinks with plastic mirrors above.

Deeper in the bathroom area were six open showerheads in a tiled room that reminded me of the bathhouse at Girl Scout camp from fourth grade.

Big, fat, black Terra, short a few teeth, had harassed me for the past two days. The first time was in the bath area as I brushed my teeth in the middle sink. Terra approached me from behind and smashed her obese body against mine, grunting and moaning. My pelvic bone was banging against the sink, then she reached to put her pudgy hands on my breasts and kneaded roughly. I thought I was going to be raped and all the women and deputies would watch and laugh. Terrified.

Just as Terra put her hand over my mouth to stop me from yelling, Skinny Jackie came into the bathroom and tried to pull Terra's hands away. "Leave the old bitch alone! She ain't hurting nobody!"

Fat Terra whipped her hand backward and caught Jackie in the jaw, then turned and said, "I'll beat you 'til you spit teeth, Jackie. Leave us alone! Jackie got up to take a swing at Terra, and they scrambled."

My opportunity to escape... I ran to my bunk and dove under the covers as they fought it out with their smart mouths. I stayed in bed for the rest of the afternoon. Just before dinner, Terra waddled to my corner and said she would "help me take a shower" later. Fear spiked; she was strong and determined, and the deputies weren't so concerned for my safety.

I wanted to return to my bunk, but we were required to stay in the group room during certain hours. Everything happened in that steel-reinforced echo chamber, including meal service.

Dinner... we scattered to sit around a spread of bolted-down tables, each with eight attached circular seats. Ordered to wait until all were served, like trained dogs, then everybody ate like starving pigs.

I used a fork to poke a hole in the top of the orange and squeezed the juice into my mouth as I had done as a child. Jackie nodded to my untouched main course. "You gonna eat that?" she asked.

"Want it?"

"Hell, yeah. But we gotta switch seats. Can't be moving no trays."

I stood and moved to the next table as Jackie scarfed down the Swiss steak and fake mashed potatoes. The next morning, I took the soggy toast for myself and gave her the plastic-looking eggs and bacon, but even Jackie wouldn't eat the oatmeal. Meals broke up the monotony, bringing four sections together to create a ward of about 200 women.

Though I didn't have my carefully formatted, color-coordinated calendar, I still kept count of the days I'd been sober, now 121. I marveled at the number and patted myself on the back because I had fought hard for each hour of each day.

And now I was in jail.

So far, I'd killed time and maintained some sanity by staying in touch with my family and Jenny. Though Jackie said calls from jail costs two dollars a minute, Mom told me to call anytime and all the time. After two days, though, my sponsor said I had to quit calling so much and even then, we could talk for only two minutes at a time. Jenny had money, but, still... I guess I became a pain in the ass for everybody.

Also on my second day in the detention facility, there'd been an AA meeting and I'd been bursting with eagerness to talk about my Higher Power, was even prepared to admit having "visions."

The meeting started with the Serenity Prayer, but the leader didn't even read the preamble, not the steps and traditions, nothing AA-oriented at all. It was nothing more than a social meeting, talking about who got out and how quickly they had come back. These women weren't sober, weren't trying to live sober, just using the "meetings" to bide time. I was pissed.

There was one bonus: the leader gave me a few recovery books to read, donated them to the ward but let me keep them until I left. I read the books carefully, searching the personal stories for one about being in jail while sober. There was no such thing.

Once a day we paraded outside for "physical exercise." The yard in front of the building featured a small basketball court and a broken sidewalk around it. Nothing more. One side of the yard was a 10-foot fence open to the free world, with a view of a dusty construction site. The sound of jackhammers and screaming power saws echoed across the yard, and the shirtless workers whistled and cat-called at us non-stop. *These men are below scum. Hitting on prisoners! Sounds like something Stuart would do. He gets off on people with no power, taking advantage of those he can impress with his wealth and influence.*

I walked sidewalk laps with Griffin, who had ended up in section four. She said her dad had met a dead-end in fighting her case, caught in the red tape and those who based time on the hours between breaks instead of the hours of nine to five.

"Well, Griffin, this is day three for me. I thought they would have come for me already, but I guess the first half-day doesn't count. Maybe later this afternoon, or surely tomorrow morning."

"Don't count on anything around here, Lela. You have no say-so in the timing of anything."

Griffin was wise beyond her years and as straight as an arrow. She'd requested and received a Bible to read and quoted scripture that helped her get through. I took deep breaths to take the Jesus taste out of my mouth when she shared her bullshit with me.

Because turn-about is fair play, I'd told her about Dude, though hesitantly. I was testing how a religious person would judge my beliefs... as odd as they may or may not be. It was obvious she didn't approve, or consider them "real," but she didn't Shame me; that was all I needed to know. Mom was still worried that I'd made God spittin' mad with my sacrilegious ideas.

Thankfully, Griffin changed the subject. "It figures they would bring us out here at two o'clock, the hottest part of the day. I'm sweating like a man."

"I'm sweating like a chicken," I said, borrowing my father's phrase. Griffin laughed and for the next fifteen minutes, we walked and laughed, and I almost forgot where I was and how terrible I felt.

The whistle blew. We paraded inside. Those who had played basketball flashed with red, sweaty faces and their body odor filled the entry vestibule; I could almost taste the smell, but I dared not gag. Had to play a tough prisoner at all times.

☼ ☼ ☼ ☼ ☼

Day four. *Ta-da! I get out today! Back to normal! Back to work!* I stayed prone for several minutes, plotting my day and the rest of my week. Mom had called Dale at my insistence. He told her to call Kathy in Human

Resources, who said I'd still have my job because I was on contract, not "obligated" to work at all, but they'd both seemed plenty pissed, Mom said.

I felt guilty about missing so many days. *I'll go in this afternoon, as soon as I get out, no matter what.*

Mom had also called Jenny to thank her for agreeing to take me to the impound lot for my van. I'd left it parked on the street across from the courthouse, only feeding the meter enough to cover two hours. Jenny had called to verify its whereabouts and knew the procedure for getting it out.

My sweet mother had told me about Jenny's continuing concern over my pink cloud. "I don't understand it much, Lela. I'm thrilled that you've kept a good attitude through this nightmare, but Jenny says it's not real and, therefore, dangerous. Mom quoted her, "Ms. Fox, Lela's not out of the woods yet."

☀ ☀ ☀ ☀ ☀

After lunch on that fourth day, I walked to the counter where the deputies stood. It was like a nurses' station at the edge of the group room and two deputies were always there, armed and vigilant in their overseer duties. The boss, at least for today, was Deputy Maynard, puffy and so short you could barely see her over the high counter. "When will they come to get me today, Maynard?"

"What makes you think you're getting out of this place, Fox?" She poked on the keyboard and checked her computer screen. "I have no release orders for you or anybody else, just permission for a parade to see the Christian singers after dinner."

"Christian singers?" Her expressionless face snapped me into the realization that my hatred of Christian singers was the least of my worries. An octave above my normal voice, I screamed, "So you have no orders for my medicine *or* for my release?"

"Do I have to tell you twice? Fox, you're not going anywhere."

I screamed, "But I was only supposed to be here for three days! Look at my records and see! I get out today, actually should have been out yesterday!"

"Lower your voice. You don't want to know what I could do to you if I get pissed."

The blow of reality hit me in the gut, hard. Tears flowed like a fountain and my emotions spiraled to the moon. Scared, disappointed, pissed, despondent, out of control in all ways. Helplessness was only half of it; the withdrawal from my meds had whacked me out, especially going cold-turkey from Lithium, with its attendant shaky hands, ping-pong thoughts, and nausea.

Overcome, I collapsed on the floor in front of the deputies' counter, curling into a fetal position and sobbing hysterically. Not that I expected her to, but Maynard didn't come around to check on a prisoner in distress.

A few minutes later, Griffin came. My friend kneeled down close to my face and asked what was wrong. I told her as best I could, but my teeth were chattering, and I could hardly catch my breath.

Griffin must have heard the words "medicine" and "get out" because that's what she said to Deputy Maynard. "This woman needs help! She's catatonic!" she screamed, "Do your damn job and get her to the doctor and tell the warden, or whoever, there's a mistake. Look at her! She's having a nervous breakdown!"

Deputy Maynard blew a sarcastic laugh. "Do you think I'm stupid? *All* the inmates throw fits trying to get to the nurse, get named officially crazy so they can get out. Fox is no different, and she doesn't need you, Prince Charming. Step away, *now*."

After another hour of laying on the floor, trembling, crying, and curling tighter in a fetal position, I got up and limped to my bunk. Exhausted. Defeated. Hopeless. My heart rate had returned to normal only because I wished it would slow to zero.

With my head down, I shuffled backward and picked up a payphone. After Mom confirmed she would pay the charges, the sounds of the operator releasing the call clunked through the line. I began babbling as soon as she said "hello."

I couldn't speak intelligently, only able to cry and plead. "Momma, I need you. Thank you for loving me." Blah, blah, blah. More drama. Mom cried, too. Daddy took the phone, not specifically knowing what was wrong, and purred his words of love and support in such wonderfully Daddy ways, ending with "You're tough, tiger. Grab 'em by the tail."

Finally, I was able to speak clearly enough to be understood. "Mom, they're not letting me out today. And I wonder if they ever will. I really think I'm lost in the system somehow. Like I've said, I'm not even supposed to be in this place to begin with!"

"What do you mean?"

"There are no orders to let me out today and, officially, this is four days, not three. There's been some kind of mistake. And *still* no medicine."

I called her again that night, and she dropped a bomb. "Lela, I called the jail and they have no record of you being there at all. There's been a serious mix-up and they're not concerned about it at all. I'm going crazy here! Now, and I mean *now*, you need a lawyer."

"Uh... they don't know I'm here?"

"They told me you were mentally ill and probably making it up."

"Oh, hell. What to do now?"

"This time I don't care what you say, I am hiring a lawyer for you. Tell me the name of your divorce lawyer again because maybe she'll be able to refer me. You'll need a criminal attorney."

"Oh, God! Don't even say 'criminal,' please. This whole thing is a fuck-up."

"Lela! Language! I know you're in a tough place, honey, but pl–"

"Mom. I don't need a lecture, please." A long sigh escaped as I leaned against the wall next to the phone, attached to the earpiece with an extra-short cord. "Okay, Mom. Maybe a lawyer can break through the red tape because they sure as hell aren't listening to me."

"Or me. Do you want me to come to Florida, honey? Maybe I can do something more in person. It's hard to shake people on the phone."

"Shake people? What are you talking about?"

"Baby, I am out of my Tennessee league. If I was there, I could be a lot more insistent."

"Just let the lawyer do it, Mom. No need to drive all this way. As upset as I am, I know God is on my side... and in this instance, I'll call Dude 'God' for your benefit."

"Thank you and you can believe we've been praying non-stop. I even put your name on the prayer list at church... not mentioning why, of course."

That fact made me cry even harder. *My poor parents. I've put them through hell and, even sober, I'm still doing it. Dude forgive me.*

Through tears, I gave the name of my divorce lawyer, though she had done little for me except answer the divorce petition with a plea to delay. I was just too screwed up to face it, and Stuart hadn't budged in agreeing to pay me back the money he had stolen.

As it turned out, there was a criminal attorney in my divorce lawyer's firm who agreed to take the case. His name was Felix Fella, which I found hilarious. I'd never hired an attorney through a third party who worked over the phone which also struck me as funny. Funny, maybe, but I was terrified, putting my life in the hands of an unknown goofball with a dumb name. And the goofball was obviously busy; he couldn't see me until the following week.

Eight horrendous days later, Felix Fella came to the jail to meet with me. He had petitioned for an emergency hearing in family court before the same judge who sentenced me to three days. The request was approved. With a pat on my hand, he assured me a simple appearance would clear the error. "Hang in there, Ms. Fox," he said in a rich, sing-song Haitian accent, "You'll be free very, very soon.

The day of the hearing would be my thirteenth day in jail.

Thirteen days, and each day I'd begged for my Bi-Polar meds. None came. Each day my hunger led me to eat a little more of what they called food, still giving the rest to Skinny Jackie. As I shared less and less food with her, Jackie's friendliness toward me waned. She wasn't so careful in protecting me from Terra, but I was sneaky enough to steer clear of the big woman's threats and advances on my own. I was lucky.

Nausea from sudden Lithium withdrawal became a messy issue. I vomited at the strike of each hour, it seemed, and my anxiety was high enough to emit a high-pitched sound.

By that time, the skin between my toes had blistered from the rubber flip-flops they forced us to wear. Two choices: I could wear the flip-flops and bleed or take them off and walk on the nasty floor. I opted for the nasty floor; thinking about it sent me running to throw up many times over several days.

I washed my feet in the sink every night. Because my hands and legs shook so violently, I splashed water everywhere. Deputy Maynard must have seen me through the wire-reinforced glass wall and suddenly she was screaming at me. "Clean it up! Clean it up!"

Shaking, humiliated, I squeaked the question: "Where's the mop?"

"No mop for you, Cinderella. Clean it up!" The other inmates joined the chorus, even Jackie. *On my hands and knees in a nasty jail bathroom, feeling ashamed in front of a bunch of criminals. A new low, Lela.*

✧ ✧ ✧ ✧ ✧

After eight days without a shower, I had Griffin stand guard in my section bath area as I scrubbed the stink off my thin and fragile body. Before I finished, Griffin got caught in the wrong section and they forced her to leave. The second time I asked for her help, she crouched low and found a hiding place, but the whole thing was a farce... as if little Griffin could stop a determined big, fat, Terra.

The day before my court date, a skaggy blonde with ebony roots approached me in the group room. "Are you Lela?"

"Who wants to know?"

"My name is Roxie and I'm supposed to tell you that Stuart says 'hi.'"

My body stiffened. *What the hell? Stuart knows this prisoner? She looks like a prostitute!* I swallowed hard, determined to keep a flat voice. "How do you know Stuart? And who *are* you?"

"Well, I *was* Jeremy's nanny. Stuart hired me but now I'm in here, so I guess I'm not a nanny anymore." Her tinkling laugh sickened me.

"What happened to Yona the nanny?"

"Hell if I know. I think she didn't approve of Stuart dating what she said was a prostitute... but that's not what I am."

"Right. Sure."

"So don't too far away, Mizz Lela. Stuart wants me to keep tabs on you. I get money for each report."

"Fuck you! And fuck *him!*" I turned to go back to my bunk, upset and shaking, on the verge of getting sick again. *More shit, more Stuart shit. Why can't he just leave me alone, dammit! And how does he know I'm still here? More stalking, more bullshit. Please, Dude, make Stuart stay away from me!*

CLERICAL ERROR
CHAPTER 34

A sweaty deputy came into the ward just as they unloaded the breakfast trays. I could see trickles of perspiration roll down his face as he whispered to Deputy Maynard. Without a pause, Maynard called my name in an irritated voice. "FOX!" Her bark startled me though I was watching and thought I knew what was ready to happen. It was the morning for my hearing at the courthouse.

Sweaty-Deputy handcuffed me to his wrist, and we walked past four or five buildings to a bus at the prison entrance. There were maybe twelve inmates on the bus, a nine of them females, each cuffed wrists-to-waists and shackled. Sweaty pushed me down on a lumpy seat and cuffed me in the same way.

The bus baked in the Florida heat; the smell was ripe. But for the first time in thirteen days, I could see an expanse of land. Grass, green bushes, palm trees, the accouterments of freedom. Sweaty left after a long chat with the driver, and returned many times, each time with a new inmate. The pattern emerged; men sat on the right side... women on the left.

When the bus was almost full, Sweaty brought my seatmate: a double-sized woman with an Afro so wide it tickled my face, and body odor so strong I had to hold back a gag. I dared not speak.

The courthouse was forty-five miles toward the coast and the ride was comically bouncy with worn-out shocks on the bus. Though I was anxious as hell, clueless about what would happen in the courtroom, I enjoyed the ride and the sights I hadn't seen in... a year, it seemed.

When the bus stopped at the underground courthouse entrance, Sweaty lined us in a specific order, then connected our ankles in a chain-gang style. I was third in the line, but my head hung the lowest of all the inmates; I was ashamed and humiliated. *A chain gang, Lela. And you're sober! You let that asshole do this to you so easily. YOU and YOUR stupid decisions! And see where it got you...*

As we passed the Family Court section, they disconnected the first four in the gang, me included. Our smaller shackled group made a parade through a hall and into the courtroom via a side door. As before, we sat together in a box to the judge's right.

People trickled in to sit in the gallery of the courtroom. With nothing else to do, I studied each face and tried to imagine their circumstances, figure out why there were here. My imagination went wild, playing games with stories more horrid than mine.

At last, the bailiff shouted, "All rise!" and the judge sauntered to the bench. He made a long list of announcements unrelated to me and I went back to my game of creating stories for the observers; I'd gone through the first row already.

And then I spotted Stuart in the gallery. Second row, last on the right... closest to me. *Oh. My. God.*

The buzz between my temples nearly deafened me and my hands shook as I brushed away a lock of hair. Stuart stared at me with daggers in his eyes and a smug look on his face, taunting me.

My eyes closed, heart pumping out of control... my blood pressure rose to the apex and dizziness sent my stomach into a lurch. *In through your nose, Lela, out through your mouth. He's an ass but he can't keep you in jail. That's not why he's here.* Then a thought struck: *Why IS he here? And how does he know I'm here in the first place?*

My jumpsuit had never felt so neon orange.

An hour passed as they called case after case, and it was a notable hour for me. Fighting back tears and trying not to glare at Stuart, feeling like a common criminal, smelling my fellow inmate's increasing body odor, feeling like I'd wet my pants, and disgusted by the drip of sweat that fell from my armpits to the side of my boob... it was the moment my mood broke.

I was mad enough to drink, to drink "at him" without even thinking about myself, or Dude, or my family. *Fuck it! Fuck it ALL!*

My mind left the reality of the courtroom and built an elaborate fantasy of how good being drunk would feel, imagining a tall drink by the pool somewhere tropical, the world's coldest beer while floating on the lake with my laughing friends, envisioning a sloppy-drunk, naked Lela surrounded by men craning their necks to watch.

I was in the fantasy full-force when I heard my name and I snapped to attention. A good-looking man in a three-piece suit stepped to the counsel's table and spoke with a deep, rich voice. "Felix Fella, Your Honor, I am the attorney of record for Ms. Fox."

The man looked toward the box where I sat... waiting for me to speak, I assumed, but I froze, not knowing what to do or say. My mouth instantly went dry and my hands shook hard enough to rattle the chain around my waist. The Felix man said, "Ms. Fox, please stand," and gestured toward the prisoner area.

It took great effort to stand unsupported. I felt dizzy and leaned forward to sturdy myself. There was dead silence in the courtroom, lasting through ten beats of my booming heart.

At last, I lifted my head and looked at the bench. When the judge saw my face, there was an obvious flash of recognition and his face reddened. Before my lawyer began the proceedings, the judge said, "Ms. Fox, you're still here?" I nodded. With his face now crimson, I knew, now for sure, I'd been lost in the system. The judge had fucked up... or a string of lazy people down the line hadn't noted an obvious mistake.

After that, I remember little except the announcement that I was to be released that afternoon. *Released!* But the judge ordered that I wear a GPS ankle bracelet for three months. "House arrest," he called it.

With the pound of the gavel, there was a noise from the gallery: Stuart laughing, loud. The judge snapped a look at the audience, ready to call down whoever made the noise. His jaw dropped as he recognized Stuart and more crimson crept up from his jaw. Yep, he had screwed up, and he knew it.

But I was free! Free to go home, smoke a cigarette, eat a doughnut, do anything I wanted. I didn't understand what house arrest all was about, and I didn't really care.

☼ ☼ ☼ ☼ ☼

We waited in the courtroom box for a long time, hours after the other inmates' cases had been completed. Nobody but me had been given the OK for release. Finally, Sweaty himself came through the almost-empty courtroom to retrieve us.

The reverse of the process brought us back to the detention facility. On the bus, I appeared calm on the outside, but inside, I screamed with manic eagerness to get out, out, out, out! Alas, things move turtle-slow on jailers' time. After almost an hour waiting on the bus, they took me back to the ward to wait longer.

I went straight for the payphone and called Jenny to tell her the news. We made a plan for getting my van, going to my place for what she called "decompression therapy." She said she'd been studying treatment people rescued from a cult.

"A cult? Jenny! Jail is not a cult! And somehow, for all these days of bullshit, I've been sober enough and spiritual enough to know I was going to be okay. Dude was here with me, or that's what it felt like." Then I realized I was talking in the past tense and another shiver of gratitude tingled down my spine.

"But Jenny, there *was* something horrible about court today." Tears rose to the edge of my eyes; I willed them to retreat. "Stuart was there, watching. And I, like, zoned out, dreamed I was drinking. Reality came crashing down. I'm afraid I'll drink if he screws with me again."

"We'll talk about that later... practical tasks first, but I'm not leaving you tonight. Don't worry."

"Thank you, my dear friend. What would I do without you?"

"Your life would be a living hell. I am pure sunshine, right? Bringing joy, riches, and chocolate to all people at all times, right?"

I laughed. "Not quite that, Jen. Do you need one of your own lectures?"

"I'm kidding." Of course, I knew she was but she been so serious in our talks over the last two weeks. She'd firmly preached acceptance in a calm and assured manner and her attitude had helped me through what could have been a more horrific situation. Out of the blue, she said, "I love you, Lela, and I'm proud of you."

I cried, touched by Jenny's caring attitude. *She loves me, she teaches me what to do and how to act. I owe my sobriety to the tough, whip-snapping Jenny Jenkins.* But when I expressed those thoughts, she screamed, "No, Lela! *I* don't keep you sober. It's *you*, you and Dude. I'm just a mouthpiece and *my* Higher Power guides me in what to say. Believe me, this is bigger than anything human. Otherwise, neither of us would be sober."

We talked much longer than Jenny's imposed two-minute limit. Tears flowed on both ends, but the call ended with an all-business discussion of how, when, and where to pick me up. Jenny said she would call the jail for details. They certainly kept me in the dark; a regular citizen might pull more weight.

Three hours later, maybe more, a deputy arrived to retrieve me from the ward. Handcuffed to her wrist, we walked a long way, past the exit of the place, to a vinyl-sided trailer-building and into an office-like reception area. The deputy took the cuffs off and left me to wait.

And wait.

And wait.

At last, a woman in street clothes appeared beside the magazine rack and called my name.

"Ms. Fox, I'm going to set you up with the GPS monitoring system and arrange the details of your release." Cool. Only one word echoed in my mind: RELEASE.

"This is your official scheduling form. Write your work hours, which are excused from monitoring. And you're allowed two hours for shopping, once a week, so choose a day and write that down in the second section."

I struggled to remember what normal life was like and panicked at the thought of having my time so restricted. "But what about AA meetings? Please tell me those are allowed! Ma'am, I have to stay sober!" A shiver of pride overcame me as I thought about getting back to my calendar. "In fact, as of today, I've been sober for 132 days."

"Wonderful!" Her face lit up like a candle. "And, yes, twelve-step meetings are allowed, up to one a day, even a weekly meeting with your sponsor, if you have one."

"Oh yes, I have one!"

"Then write the times for meetings and seeing your sponsor in the third section." The woman took the form and pondered it. "Looks like you have a lot of freedom, Ms. Fox. This isn't typical."

"Maybe most people don't have a sober life outside of jail, ma'am." I felt high-and-mighty, "better than," as Jenny would call it. It didn't occur to me that being "better than" a criminal wasn't that much better in the scheme of things.

She attached the waterproof ankle monitor, showed me how to hook up the box, and passed a sheaf of papers to "study with care." They listed the consequences of being out of range, the instant arrest for cutting through the bands, etcetera.

The verbal instructions continued but my mind reeled, blotting out her words. *When do I get to go home? When can I call Jenny? And when is this woman going to shut up? When, when, when?* My thoughts spiraled out of control, manic and downright scary.

Thankfully, I didn't have to go back to the ward and didn't have to wait long until a regular cop entered and put me in the back of his patrol car. A forty-five-minute ride, back to the jail where this mess had started.

I stood in line for a "Release Clerk," signed a bunch of papers and they passed a large Zip-lock bag through the small window. My belongings, emptied from my purse, with inventory tags on each item.

My first thought was a cigarette, but I checked to see if I had enough battery on my phone to call Jenny outside. *Cool! I'd turned the power off... how did I think of that in my state of panic?*

I rushed outside to light up a Virginia Slim. Oh, my God! Nothing had ever tasted better!

Freedom! My nerves were on high alert, but I calmed myself enough to sit on the curb and call Jenny as I lit my second cigarette. Twenty minutes later, we were on our way to the impound lot on 95-North, to arrive just before they closed.

It took standing in six different lines to get my van, even though Jenny had come with cash. The bill was 386 dollars and some change. I found myself angry at the system all over again and began a rage, stopped short by Jenny's acceptance speech. As we walked to my van in the graveyard of vehicles, she announced the impound fee payment was "on her" and I wasn't allowed to pay her back. My entire body relaxed in relief and tears exploded from my already-swollen eyes.

At 6:10 PM, I drove my dusty van through the heavy gates of the impound lot and headed home. Jenny followed as if I was ready to bolt, not letting a single car between us, even when it was dangerous to change lanes along with me.

I must have thrown her for a loop when I pulled into the Dunkin' Donuts drive-thru next to my apartment complex, ordering my dinner of three glazed. Jenny followed me through the line but followed me straight through. Obviously, she hadn't placed an order. I didn't care; all I cared about was being free.

I parked in the assigned spot for 12-A and saw my apartment door wide open, a slice of my empty bookcase, the place ransacked.

Please, Stuart, no! You sonofabitch!

FROM CRAZY TO CALM
CHAPTER 35

Jenny was first in the door; I tripped and fell before crossing the threshold and decided to stay there and sob. I heard Jenny's words from the living room, "*Hooolleeee shit!*" and my stomach shot to my throat. The taste of fatty sausage rose and I willed myself to keep the morning's breakfast down.

"Come on in, Lela. But be prepared. It's bad." I closed my eyes, unable to bear seeing what I knew would break my heart.

It was *meant* to break my heart. *That sonofabitch... or was it really him?* "Tell me it's not that bad, Jenny. Tell me it wasn't him." But I knew it was bad, and I knew it was him.

"Yes, it was him. Come on. You're going to need a hug."

Slowly... slowly... I edged toward the entrance. Once inside, I screamed, "Oh, my God! NO! You mother*FUCKER!*"

The sofa had been spray-painted in neon orange with the words: "LOVE, STUART," and the coffee table was gone. The lamp I had customized myself laid in a crash of white glass with the cute turquoise shade stomped flat.

My dining table was tipped over and all four legs had been broken. The back ladder of a dining chair hung askew from the chandelier, creating a haunted-house shadow. The spray-painted message spread across all three dining room walls: "WELCOME HOME, BITCH."

I tiptoed to the kitchen, fearing the worst. Yep, just as bad as I imagined... every drawer and cabinet was open, and the contents slung throughout the room. He'd dumped the trash on top of the stove, fodder for the hundreds of flies that buzzed the room. Knives, forks, and spoons sweetened the mess.

Only one square on the counter was clear. The dustless place where my cordless phone had been. "Oh shit, Jenny! He's stolen all the electronics, too!" I ran down the hall, anticipating the theft of my computer system. "Please, let my laptop and printer be there!"

But the room was bare of cords. "Dammit, Jenny! No way! He took *everything*... shit! Even my alarm clock!"

Suddenly Jenny was by my side, giving the hug she had offered earlier. I, literally, collapsed into her arms, sobbing and speaking unintelligible syllables. She cooed the appropriate phrases, "You'll be okay, honey," and the assuring bullshit that did nothing but emphasize I'd never be okay again.

I broke away from the hug, still scanning the room for missing items. "I can't afford to replace all this stuff, Jenny! And I have no energy to clean this crap up!"

"I think... Lela, somehow God will provide."

"*Stop* that shit! My God doesn't hand out hundred-dollar-bills just because I need them, you dipshit!"

Oops! I shouldn't have said that.

With a *tsk, tsk, tsk,* Jenny wagged her finger and spoke to me in an out-of-character angry voice. "Restraint of tongue and pen, my dear. I am not your punching bag."

"Sorry, Jenny. You're right, of course."

"Besides, you won't like how I fight back." I snapped a look to see her level of seriousness. Thankfully, she held a shit-eating grin, looking over the rims of her tiny glasses.

"Get a notepad to start your plan, man. You'll probably need a pink notepad for this."

"Ha, ha, smartass! I can't help that I'm extremely organized!" The beginning of a smile upturned my lips. *Maybe I can handle this. Shooooooooooo, Lela. Deep breaths.*

"You do well with big projects, you told me once. Because you learned it making TV commercials and videos, right?"

I gave a nod, agreeing with the thought. "Yeah, I guess I did."

"So use your God-given talent and well-earned experience to get your shit together. You have it in you, Lela. You won't crumble. You'll take charge, see? Even with that," and she pointed to a spot on the carpet. An empty spot.

"What?"

"That's the contents of your pink cloud."

I looked at her begrudgingly and huffed a sigh. "No doubt, this is a real-world problem. But Jenny... even a perfectly sober person would freak out if this happened to them! I think I'm doing–"

"Yes, you're handling it well except there are other things to think about, too."

"How can you think about anything except..." I spread my arms to indicate the room, "Anything but *this!* I'm going to lose my mind trying to–"

"A pink cloud isn't just about drinking, Lela."

"Then wha–"

"Insanity can replace your sobriety in a variety of ways."

Angry now, I raised my voice. "I don't understand and don't have time for your enlightened crap, Jenny!"

She stared at me for a long while, her eyes full of empathy and love. I was frantic to keep searching the apartment, find out more of what was stolen or destroyed, but I couldn't look away from her eyes. At last, she sighed and took my hand. "You remember when Eli said you were going to be a tough case?"

"Yeah, but this is not–"

"Drama, Lela! Endless drama! Your life *swirls* with it. Part because of Stuart, part because you still treat yourself like a turd, part because you go too fast, push yourself to go and do and do it now! Now! Now! Now! You drive *yourself* crazy! You can't do that right now. In fact, now more than ever, you must plot out your recovery... slowly but carefully, starting now."

Tears burned my eyes. "That's so sweet, Jenny. And I think–"

"No! It wasn't meant to be *sweet* and the *last* thing you should do is THINK!" *Don't you get it?*"

Confused... honestly confused. I threw up my hands. "No, I don't get it. I'm just worried about how long it's been since I've backed up my computer and I want to mark the sober days off my calendar and check the–"

"No! Stop! All that can wait!" Jenny turned away from me and growled with frustration. "Here..." she grabbed my hand, dragging me toward the bed. "On your knees."

"What the hell? Are you going to beat me?"

"Maybe."

"What!?"

"Kneel!"

Whoa! Jenny was angry; I'd never seen her angry. "What the hell, Jenny?"

"We must make it official... it's a rite of passage You may not like it but now's the perfect time. And I have it all planned out for you."

I dared to raise my voice again. "What are you *talking* about!? I'm too freaked out to *kneel*, of all things. Are you out of your mind?"

"Come on," she insisted, "Right here beside the bed."

"Uh, the timing is bad here, Jenny. And please don't tell me to pray for my enemies. I can't do it! I can't pray for Stuart. Please don't make me!"

"Give me your hand." Her tone had softened, but her words were clipped. She meant for me to obey, which really pissed me off. *Doesn't she know how much I have to do?!*

I was halfway to my knees when the concept of a dirty bed occurred to me. "First, I've got to get these sheets off! Homeless people may have slept here with the door wide open, or Stuart could've–"

"Later! Just... stop! Stop thinking! Make your mind blank. Completely blank. An empty canvas! A blank slate! You *must* re-wire yourself! Add calm to your vocabulary! C-A-L-M!"

Jenny's words rolled across my brain like oil on plastic; I was already twelve steps ahead. Then my eyes darted toward the closet and I wondered aloud. "He probably took anything he can pawn."

"STOP! No talking! No worrying! No *anything!* Lela, FOCUS!"

"But... my grandmother's rings!"

"Give me your hand. You're making me crazy. You have to *adult* for the next thirty seconds, even if I have to sit on you to do it." She exaggerated a sigh and flashed the "Jenny look," head cocked, eyes toward the ceiling, lips pursed – her look of not-so-patient waiting when I rambled bullshit.

"Don't look at me like that! I have real problems here!"

"And you always will. Right now, you need to take a thirty second break to help you handle the problem in a better way."

She had backed me into a corner; my only defense was tears. I didn't want the reality I'd been dealt. My bottom lip began to quiver... my throat squeezed tight and snot began to flow... all as I reached out to hug my life-saving sponsor. "Jenny, what am I going to doooo?" My voice squeaked up an octave, ending in a whine and a barrage of tears.

"I can help. Just stop crying. Stop talking. Stop thinking. Take a breath

and sit here with me. We have to cross a bridge: the third step prayer."
Jenny's voice changed to a tone much more controlled and serious. I gave in
after a long sigh.

"Okay, dammit. Just make it quick."

Jenny rolled her eyes, again pulling my hand to urge me to kneel beside
the bed. Once I settled, she pulled a folded-up paper from her back pocket.
"I've rewritten it especially for you, Miss Anti-Everything."

"Re-written what?"

"Just listen. It's a prayer and a promise to God or Dude or whatever
Higher Power you end up with." Then she read from the paper, speaking as
casually to her Higher Power as I speak to Dude.

> *"Hey there, Higher Power... it's me. I'm at a turning
> point, big time, and I need your help. So I offer myself to
> you completely, asking you to teach me whatever you
> want me to know, to mold me as you wish. Please take
> away my selfishness so I can do more of what you want
> me to do. Because I know doing all this will erase my
> difficulties, and then I can learn even more from you.
> Please let other people see this miracle in me so they might
> believe it could happen to them, too. Higher Power, I want
> to do what you want me to do, always!"*

The silence lasted a full ten seconds after Jenny finished. "That's a cool
prayer, Jen. I like that."

"It's called the third step prayer, rewritten just for you."

"Why rewritten?"

"It had 'thy' and 'thee' and all the Biblical words you hate. It means the
same this way." I nodded, thanking her for the effort. I really *did* like the
prayer; it was just bad timing. "I'd like you to memorize it. I'm making that
an assignment."

"No assignments today!" I felt sure she was kidding... then her arched
eyebrows said otherwise. "In case you haven't noticed, I've been fucking
robbed, Jenny! You act like this hasn't even happened!" Assignment, my
ass..."

Then my manic mind took off on a tear, reeling with to-do's. "But I *will*
memorize it, then I'll print the prayer and post it on my fridge or get a little
frame to display it on my desk, and get it laminated to say out loud when I

go to bed. And maybe I'll–"

"Arhldrrggg!" she growled with frustration. "Lela! Slow down! Rest!" She gripped my shoulders and pulled me toward her, her eyes locking into mine with vise grips. "And it's not a prayer to *guide* you. It's a *promise* – to God, to Dude. A *promise* to change your outlook, your life. Something you *so desperately* need to do! Lela, do you understand me?"

I nodded, feeling stronger. I'd never expected Jenny to go so spiritual in my time of crisis; I assumed she would freak out and worry with me like a normal person. But instead, she'd masterfully turned off my worries, or at least put them in perspective.

She continued, "There's something else you can do." I nodded, ready to hear another assignment. "You can get through this without drinking."

I rolled over on the floor and covered my head as the sobs began. I don't know how long I was there, crying and sleeping in bursts between. When I raised my head, it was dark outside. I couldn't see Jenny but heard her rattling in the kitchen. And she was humming... an old Beatles tune, Eleanor Rigby.

My GPS ankle bracelet pulsated, like a short telephone ring in the distance. Jenny had plugged it in and set it up, evidently. After three buzz/rings, it stopped. I was home, where I was supposed to be according to the house arrest schedule.

Reality hit like a shot. *You are a prisoner... you've been robbed... things are destroyed... but you can get through it without drinking. Jenny said so, right? And Eli would say so, too. So... what do you think, Lela? It's all up to you.*

Sober and insane, unstable, dysfunctional... as confused and "unable" as I'd been before going to rehab. Giving up would be easier, I thought.

Then I thought again.

I marveled at how strong I'd been to survive the past thirteen days, how I'd fought through all Stuart threw at me... all that life had thrown at me.

I wanted to fight more, through *all* of it, because I wanted to come out on the other side.

I knew I may never have a perfectly normal life being Bi-Polar, but creative thinking, perhaps, could turn the craziness into an

advantage.

I redefined my priorities, putting calm first. Calm. Quiet. Slow stuff. Because without calm, I couldn't stay sober. I believed that 100 percent.

I pledged to lessen the drama, to learn how to be boring; how to choose low-risk, boring activities and middle-of-the-road boring friends.

I pledged to quit beating myself up for not being perfect and phrase things as my Daddy had taught: "I can" instead of "I can't."

After thirteen days of no Bi-Polar meds, I had red-lined. Frozen between up and down... not depressed and not manic – YET. I insisted it was a good place to start, determined to "manage" the ups and downs I was sure to go through for several months after this clinical catastrophe.

How I pushed through required a pile of notepads and some famous Lela Fox OCD to-do-list behavior. I attacked the problem like a rabid dog, organizing and planning and putting everything in alphabetic order.

I left only one thing dangling and unattended. That one thing would haunt me for the next seventeen years.

BEST BUY & WORST IDEA
CHAPTER 36

I didn't tell anybody about Stuart's thievery but Karen... and I probably shouldn't have told her. She was furious and roared like a lion, literally, cussing a blue streak, using more "f-words" than I use. And it brought up an issue she'd been "fretting over," as she said. "I hate for you to have to spend so much money. Let me send a check to help with replacement expenses."

"Don't, Karen. It's my problem and a problem of my own making. I'm sober and supposedly able to face shit like this, pay my own debts, all that."

"That's another thing!"

"*What's* another thing?"

"Debt!"

"Karen, dammit, settle down." *Haha! I'm trying to calm my big sister, the one who's been trying to calm me for decades.*

"It's not really your debt, of course; it should belong to that sonofabitch!"

"Karen, it is what it is... please don't get upset. I was stupid, I admit it. But I don't like to hear your criticism on top of it all. Believe me – I beat myself up enough already."

"Just don't add to the debt for this, Lela. That's why I want to send you a check."

"Well, I have to get a computer."

"Save and wait to buy it. Trust me! I know how to live on a tiny bit of money! I did it for years when the shop was new! Surely you know how shitty you are at managing money..."

"Ouch, Karen. Kick me when I'm down."

"Oh. No, wait! I don't mean it *that* way."

"Let's just not talk about this now, okay?"

"Just don't get into more debt."

"Goodnight, sister."

"Wait for my check before you buy anything!"

"Sleep well." She was still talking when I hung up.

"I need a laptop with the largest possible screen," I said to the Best Buy "consultant," or so his name tag stated. As young as he was, his tone was professional, and he led me to an aisle with a dozen choices. "And a cheap ink-jet printer? One that takes cheap replacement cartridges?"

After an hour of pros and cons and discussions back and forth, he packed up my purchases, adding Microsoft Office, a printer cartridge and a new external hard drive." Together, we filled out the complicated application for a Best Buy credit card. "And I need an alarm clock, plus two cordless telephones. But only one of them needs to have a message recorder."

"Sure, let me take you to that department."

"I wish I could also replace the camera that was stolen... but I'll have to wait."

"Are you sure? We have a big sale this week."

"No. I'll come back. Maybe after I pay all this off, and by then the technology will be a whole new thing! Know what I mean?"

He didn't laugh. Wanted the sale, I supposed. But he should've been plenty happy with the size of my purchase already. Replacing everything Stuart stole was costly; he even took my hairdryer and an old electric pencil sharpener! He took anything he knew would inconvenience me or simply piss me off.

Before shopping for anything, I went to the neighborhood pawn shop to see if any of my stuff was there. I high-tailed it when I felt the owner's stare burn a target on my back. I felt threatened as hell... like he was going to pounce on me, convince me to buy hot goods. Pawnshops left a bad taste in my mouth.

But now you're in Best Buy, Lela, spending a million dollars.

"Anything else, Ms. Fox?" I didn't want to see the total bill. My right hand purposely covered the bottom line as I signed my name. *More debt... exactly what you need, Lela.*

As if defending myself *to* myself, I argued that I had no choice. I'd said the same thing to the MasterCard rep when I applied for that card, and to my stockbroker when I called to withdraw even more money from my IRA.

It was after 2:30 in the afternoon; I'd left work at Smyth Software at noon to do my shopping. I hated to miss billable hours, but I needed a large chunk of time... more than my anklet would allow outside of work hours.

For the smaller purchases, I'd gone during the time allowed for meetings. I'd missed a full week of AA, shopping instead. The Guilt of skipping those meetings weighed a ton; I had lied to Jenny about it, too, making the Guilt even heavier.

As I unlocked the door to my apartment, I heard the funny pulsating-vibrating semi-silent ring of my ankle bracelet telephone and wondered why they were checking my whereabouts during the day. *Maybe to make sure I was gone... gone to work? That's dumb and I may have to answer for this, but... what's done is done.* It clicked off as my device flashed a blue light.

Inside, I was relieved to see the maintenance men had installed the new deadbolt and replaced the chain-lock on the inside of the door. I'd yet to feel safe in my apartment since coming home from jail, and twice I asked Jenny to stay with me.

I'd begged the apartment office to let me switch apartments, but they refused to do it without a screaming-expensive charge. "You guys should be the ones responsible for a robbery, anyway! Aren't you supposed to provide us with a safe community?" My chest was all puffed out; I looked as indignant as my tone of voice. But their response was nothing but silence. And rightly so.

It took three trips to the van to gather my Best Buy purchases. I knew tonight I'd be knee-deep in power cords and cables, but first... a meeting. The first one of the week, and it was Thursday.

☼ ☼ ☼ ☼ ☼

The POWERLESS club was off A-1-A near the Homing Inn, behind a strip club and beside a 50s-theme diner with kickass burgers. The floor was real wood and real old, with planks running the length of the room, about a hundred-yards-long. Rows of tables and dented metal chairs kept the atmosphere grim and shabby, but the most rousing meetings I'd attended were held there.

The reek of cigarette smoke permeated every inch of the walls; it even choked the smokers. Years before other places dared to ban smoking, there was talk of making the POWERLESS a non-smoking club.

I remember a crotchety old-timer, tufts of gray hair exploding from the sides of a Dolphins cap, declaring, "No club o' mine's gonna tell me I can't smoke!" His index finger hit the table to emphasize each syllable. I was struck by how confident the old man seemed, and how he dared to call the club "his," as if the rules were his to change.

I knew so little about how AA was run at the time.

The meeting started. I loved to hear the opening readings, especially the promises. Despite the bullshit in my life, I still had my eyes on the prize. Everybody but Jenny thought I was bullshitting them, but I was truly that sure of maintaining a sober life. *I have to be sure because I have no choice. Sobriety or death... that's the way I see it.*

When the meeting was over, the after-meeting began. At least twenty of us ended up in the parking lot smoking cigarettes and giving each other shit. For the second time, I noticed a guy, a big guy... tall and muscular... salt and pepper hair with a killer mustache and wide shoulders like my Dad. *The ham hocks that grace those shoulders would feel soooo good wrapped around me.*

My eyes drilled into his profile, noticing his easy smile. *Oh, shit! I'm busted... he sees me watching him! That's NOT what you need, Lela. No dates, no flirting, no way.* I faked interest in the conversation beside me for a few minutes, then sneaked another look. *Oh, hell! He's still looking at me!* I had no choice but to return his smile.

The warmth of that smile carried me all the way home... and all the way, I tried to convince myself that I shouldn't even look a man. *Just ignore them, Lela. Pretend they don't exist.*

The next night, Charlie and Elsa drove up from Serenity Sisters to join me at a POWERLESS meeting. Elsa was pretty chill, seemed to be doing much better, but Charlie was a mess. She bitched about the Serenity Sisters house so much I finally told her to shut the hell up. Yeah, it was mean, and she was hurt, but I think it put things in perspective for her. She kept whispering to me during the meeting, trying to make plans for the rest of her life.

After the meeting in the parking lot, she asked me, "How did you tell your parents you weren't going back home?

"I said this: 'Hey, parents... I'm not going back home.'"

"Just like that?"

"Just like that. I know I'm older than you, Charlie, but nobody over the age of 25 should let their parents decide where they'll live."

"But I'm so new in the program!" It was a nasal whine, but I resisted smacking the crap out of her.

"What does your sponsor say?"

"That I should stay, keep my job, save some money."

"Then why are you asking *me*? Especially because you know I feel the same way!"

"Because I keep thinking somebody will tell me I'm making a bad decision. That's what I'm used to hearing, right?"

I laughed. "Charlie, dear... all that's between you and your Higher Power. Besides, nothing is forever. Get a six-month lease... you've seen my place with second-hand furniture, so you see it can be done on the cheap."

"You just seem to have it all together, Lela. I want what you have."

"Ha! You want this damn ankle bracelet, too?" Charlie laughed. "I'm not kidding, girl! And do you want to pay for the shit I had to buy this week... the stuff Stuart stole?"

"Yeah, all that sucks, Lela."

"You get what you get." I kicked at a cigarette butt on the pavement, wondering if I felt as accepting as that sounded.

I slowly brought my head up and – *oh shit!* – there he was again, smiling at me. "Let's go, girls. Twelve o'clock penis warning."

Nobody moved. Elsa piped in, "Oh, he's nice and big, Lela. Just like you like 'em."

"How would *you* know how I like 'em?"

"Just seems like you would," she said, speaking louder than I'd ever heard her speak.

I thought about Elsa's comment the entire drive home. *Do I have a type? I like big and tall guys? Barrel-chested gorillas? Miller was a little beefy, but Andy and Stuart were both on the small side... maybe that was the problem.*

SPRING TRAINING
CHAPTER 37

"Stop it, Mom, you're embarrassing me."

"You'd be embarrassed if the Chipper Jones himself was picking you up. You've flown down here before, son... you know how they are with unaccompanied minors. They have to assume you're a helpless idiot. But it's just for insurance purposes... nothing personal.

"And now you're acting even *more* protective. I'll be eighteen in just a few months, Mom! Jeez!"

"Don't remind me how old you are... or how much of your childhood I missed. We're just going to have a good four days. I've got the tickets for the game already. And my boss is all cool with giving me the time off."

"My dad said you were about to get fired again."

"What does *he* know, buddy? I've had this job off and on for almost a year."

"Right. You're such a stable and responsible individual now." His eye-roll was so wide he stumbled down the concourse.

I stopped, grabbed his shoulders, and turned him toward me. "Look, Bo. I know it's just been six months, but I *am* sober. And doing everything I can to stay that way. It's like being in school, learning all this stuff. They say I stopped growing when I started drinking so that means I'm still a teenager. I know I have a lot to learn, so can you just give me a break?" Two tears slid from the outside corner of my right eye.

"Aww, Mom, *please* don't start your crying crap! How do you expect me to think you're stable when you just stand there and cry?" I felt his words stab my heart. I didn't expect him to forgive me instantly for everything I'd done, but he seemed to still be pushing me away.

"Bo Winston, your mom will always cry. G-Daddy used to call me Tear Bucket Jim... you've heard us say that, right?" Bo looked at his shoes, nodding. "I am easily touched, easily hurt, or as my Mom says, I have a tender heart. But whatever, don't equate tears with being weak."

"I was talking about you being unstable."

"Okay, don't equate it with being unstable, either. My meds are as straight as they've ever been, buddy. It's just regular, everyday tears you're dealing with and it feels like you're painting me the wrong color, being an insolent child!"

"Insolent child, huh? If I know what it meant, would it be a good thing?"

"Stop with your smart mouth! I refuse to let you hurt me. But you're dissing me, son. It hurts my feelings." A huff escaped Bo's lips, and he raised his arms as if defending himself. I spoke before he could. "And don't roll your eyes again! If you didn't want to come, then you should have stayed home!"

We stood eye to eye in the middle of Concourse A in the Fort Lauderdale airport. Bo's chest seemed to deflate in one whoosh of air. "Sorry, Mom. It's just–"

"It's just *nothing*. Show some respect. I'm sober and I can demand it now. It will take a lifetime for me to make up for what I've done to you, son, but I'm starting here and now. Until you can feel it, fake it. I'm doing the best I can."

The emotion required to put those difficult words together sent a flash of pain to my skull and caused a rash of tears on my cheeks. I didn't wipe them away, staring adamantly at Bo... who stared back at me just as hard.

"Okay, Mom. I get it. I love you and I'm proud of you, okay? Just... please stop crying in public."

"I'll try, Bo. I will." I dove into the black hole of my purse to find a tissue. *Be strong, Lela. Keep your shit together, just for Bo. Swallow your pain for a few days, put on a happy face, fake it 'til you make it.*

Wiped dry, I smiled and pointed forward. We walked in step, aiming for the baggage claim. As we chatted, my mind reeled, thinking about how much work it'd take to prove myself a worthy mother again. *Bo is a tough customer... because I've hurt him badly, more than I know. And it seems he's as scared of the Bi-Polar as the alcoholism. I wonder what's up with that? Does he think he's Bi-Polar, too?*

We were on our way north to Jupiter, Florida to watch the Cardinals in their spring training baseball game against Bo's favorite team, the Atlanta Braves. Spring training games were crazy-popular in South Florida; Stuart and I had been to several, and took Jeremy once, too.

Not the minor leagues like we had in Rockville, but the real McCoy, featuring the full roster of players, with stadiums decent enough call "big league." Bo was fired up, wearing his Braves hat and t-shirt.

"So tell me about your own baseball tourney coming up, kiddo. Think you can stop all of them with your badass third base presence?"

A chuckle. "If I can keep my hamstring healthy. It's been killing me and you know that's a career-killer." It struck me that Bo would consider baseball a "career," but... why not? He still lived and breathed the game, and the level of play in his senior year had been competitive as hell.

"Season is over, right? Only the tournament after Spring Break?"

"Correct. Double-elimination and our field is the host for the South region. Sixty-two high school teams and the odds are good on us."

"That's awesome, Bo. I just wish the recruiter had worked out. I'm sorry about that."

Unbeknownst to me, his dad had hired a promoter for Bo, in search of a college scholarship. In fact, the recruiter worked for three boys from Bo's high school, but only one was offered anything decent. Poor Bo... his offer was more of an insult than an opportunity. A tiny community college offered a full ride, such as it was, and, according to Andy and Ella, Bo had been despondent about "his failure."

The last time I'd talked to Andy, he explained, "I guess you get what you pay for because Bo is twice the player than the kid who got the scholarship.

Bo's dad had acted strangely that night, and I had a hard time getting in touch with him in the first place, which was odd. I tried to pry the truth out of him, but he wasn't talking. I asked if he and Ella were okay, if Bo's little brother was okay, if his job was working out... everything I could think of to identify the problem, but his lips were sealed.

I reasoned I had a right to know if the father or stepmother of my son was in trouble, but Andy disagreed, saying something like, "Just because you're sober doesn't mean you get to run the show all of the sudden."

I suppose he had a point, but I dared to ask Bo for the truth, and the thirty-mile trip to the game was the perfect time. "Why is your dad so weird these days? He acted like something bad is happening up there."

"Uh... I'd rather not say."

"What? Why not? What's going on?"

"Don't make me say it, Mom." Silence and a sigh from Bo. I let the silence ride for a half-mile or so, then he spilled the beans. "They're separated. Dad is with another woman. A woman from work. And he got fired because of it. So now he lives with her."

Surprised as hell, my eyes widened, and steam shot from my ears. *The son of a bitch did it again! He cheated on me with Ella and cheated on Ella with...*

"What's her name?"

"Ginger, if you can believe it. And he wants me to meet her."

"Has he officially filed for divorce?

"Ella did."

"Oh, sweetheart... I'm so sorry. I know this must be a terrible thing for you. Do you want to talk about it?"

"No, I just want Ella to quit talking *to me* about it. I can't help her, and it's like she's expecting me to help."

"No, son. She doesn't want your help. She shouldn't be talking to you at all, but women 'vent' their emotions. You're not supposed to fix it, which I know is hard for a man. She should be talking to her women-friends, not to her stepson. That's unfair. Wrong-wrong-wrong."

"She's begging me to stay home and go to that tiny little college. Said she needs help around the house."

"NO! That's BULLSHIT!"

"Mom! Chill out!"

I was incensed by her immature request; she'd gone too far, trying to hold Bo back from the entrance to adulthood. "Sorry for the screaming, buddy, but you can *bet* I'll call to talk to her about this! It's not cool... not cool at all."

"*Please* don't call her, Mom. I don't want the drama, and she'll know what I said to you! And the−"

"She *needs to know* what you said to me! Let me guess... you haven't told her to stop talking about it, right? You haven't told her how YOU feel. I know you, son. You don't want to make waves." *Then again, he makes waves with* me... *what's up with that?* "I thought you were going to TSU in Rockville, anyway. It's all set up, right?"

"I thought maybe I'd stay home for just one semester. She says she needs somebody to hang the Christmas lights on the gutters."

I exploded in an angry scream. The only intelligible words in my rant: "It's not *your* job to take care of her and I'm going to take care of *this!*"

"Mom, no! Please don't say anything." My heart was racing and my foot shaking on the gas pedal. The daggers of my anger sped to a woman four states away. *What a whiny bitch! She won't be directing Bo in where he goes to college, by God! As soon as this damn divorce goes through, I can get financial aid for him, because I'll be poor. I'm not going to let her hold him back – no way. And now I have the authority and the stability to stop it.*

I paused to consider what I'd do and to think a bit about how Dude might help... thinking I may need to tell him what was happening since it'd been so long since we'd "talked."

But one momentary thought of Dude brought a rash of tears, the overwhelming gratitude I felt when the dramatic-connection thing happened. I tried to hide my tears from Bo but stay in the same grateful place... but the pressure between my ears stopped me; it hurt. My esophagus shrunk, and I thought I'd choke to death. I couldn't help it; the tears flowed naturally.

"Let me explain why I'm crying, son."

"Don't even say. You make me crazy doing that."

I wiped my tears on my shirt sleeve and squeezed my nostrils to catch the drip. "Okay, I'll stop. But it's about God. I asked for his help."

"Right... sure, Mom. You expect me to believe that?"

The rest of the drive was in silence. *Damn, Lela! You messed up again. Just keep it in the road for the sake of your son, you idiot! You may be sober and insane, but he doesn't need to see the insane part; things are already insane in Nashville.*

Help him, Dude. Or help me help him somehow.

FOUR SETS OF TIRES
CHAPTER 38

I left work at noon for the third day in a row. I said goodbye to Dale, but he flipped his wrist at me without bothering to look up from his computer. A relief; on Monday, he'd said, "What good are you if you aren't here to work?"

Considering what was happening, that was an odd comment. I was confused and half-pissed about the crumbling situation at Smyth Software. Dale had dropped a few projects on my desk for critical-update notes, but mostly he left me working on the Microsoft Word document. Still, after all this time... and after he'd told me not to spend much time on it.

I'd told him frequently that I had an open schedule, ready for update notes, but he kept feeding the bulk of the work to his teacher's pets and leaving me flapping in the wind.

The one time I told him how I felt, I overshot the runway – as always. I asked him to give me a purpose for being there. As it came out of my mouth, I heard Jenny scolding me for being too dramatic, and sure enough... Dale rolled his eyes. Starting on that day, he made his dislike of me more obvious every day.

But what could I do? I did what I was asked to do... he just didn't want me to do anything important, it seemed. How could I earn his trust if I wasn't given an opportunity? I was stuck.

You'll have to solve that problem some other day, Lela Fox. Today is a day for Bo and you... and something you dread. I threw a prayer in the air, hoping Dude would catch it.

"I'm back! Up and at 'em, son! I need you and we can make it a fun day, too." He rolled off the sofa, trying to hide his morning boner from me. I looked away, embarrassed. *Next time, Lela. A guest room. A better job, a better apartment.*

For today's errands, I needed Bo's help. The lease was up on my van and I had a big issue with the end-of-contract process at the dealership. A secret issue... and so illegal I cringed to even think about the possible consequences.

I'd waited until the last day to return the vehicle, trying to avoid the problem for as long as I could. I'd driven it for three years, most of them drinking years, and, amazingly, the van was still in one piece. A bit of body damage on two panels, but nothing so bad. *Are you fooling yourself, girl? Or are you just reserving the worry for the bigger deal? It's the bigger deal that could land you in jail.*

To lease a vehicle with a low mileage allowance was one of the stupidest things I'd ever done; another dumb-drunk decision I'd made in my last year in Rockville. I'd fallen for the cheaper payment and disregarded the fact that I traveled most weekends. I was sure to put more miles on the van than even a "heavy driver, as State Farm called them.

Dumbass Lela Fox.

The first time I mentioned this worry to Stuart, he offered an instant solution. "I can roll the odometer back, easily. No problem."

"I thought they'd made it impossible to do that."

"No, they just made it *illegal* to do that."

"Oh, but–"

"But nothing. I'll fix you up." The next day he took my car to work and drove it home after lunch, showing 40,000 fewer miles than it had at breakfast. "Instead of rolling it back, I just installed a new odometer. No way to trace it, you're good to go."

I was paranoid as hell, but he was right; nothing looked amiss on the dash. They'd just think I'd been hard on the interior for so few miles driven.

Then one day when I stayed at the Homing Inn, I opened the glove compartment looking for cash or something; it was the first time I'd opened it in months. Like a jack-in-the-box, a blast of wires, cables, and box-adapters erupted from the tiny compartment.

Oh, no! You could easily see the cords leading to the left toward the odometer. Nothing could be more obvious. I'd be busted, no doubt.

If nothing else, I'd be charged a million dollars for the mileage overage... but maybe also sued by Nissan, or the dealership, for fraud. *Fraud with a capital F.* I didn't know what would happen, exactly, but I knew enough to know I was in big trouble.

Jenny and I had discussed the issue at length. She said, "You must be honest, Lela. If you don't, your old friend Mr. Guilt will eat your lunch... year after year."

"But it wasn't *me* that did wrong! It was *Stuart!*" She flashed "the Jenny look" and I succumbed to common sense. "Yeah, yeah... I know I'm responsible for it."

Your program demands rigorous honesty, right? You can't afford to lie, Lela.

I wasn't sure I believed Jenny's promise that I "would surely drink" if I was dishonest, but I couldn't take any chances. I already felt more Guilt than dread! *Wreckage of the past... be thankful it's in the past and will be gone soon.*

When I told Bo about my dilemma, he flipped out. "I don't want any part of this, Mom! It's fraud! You may be arrested!" Sigh. *There you go again, dumbass Mom, scaring your son with drunken behavior. Why did you feel the need to tell him, anyway?*

I sighed, knowing I'd have to think fast and act totally casual. "Okay, mostly I need your help in buying the new one, anyway. So... you stay here while I handle closing the lease, then we'll go together to look at that '96 Ford Taurus I saw in North Palm Beach... and/or another car at that massive dealership. I need your 'Mr. Cool advice.'"

We agreed on the plan. I dashed out for enough food to feed a small horse then left him to eat. The Nissan dealership was about two blocks away.

Wouldn't you know it... I came when they were slammed. The entire staff was at lunch or wherever; there was only one salesman trying to sell three cars and deal with my return simultaneously. It took forever; he kept going back and forth between customers like a ping-pong ball.

First, he brought a clipboard and checked the tread on my tires, explaining the dilemma of his schedule and bitching about how the manager's day off couldn't have come at a worse time. With a closer inspection of my tires, he said, "Oh, my."

"What?" My nerves were shot; the word sounded like a parrot squawk and I assumed he had already called the police.

"You'll need to replace the tires but there's good news there." I dared not speak, so I let him keep talking. "We keep used tires from our used and demo cars. And I know for a fact I have this tire size. Just brought out a van 'xactly like this one."

"Great, so they're... cheap?"

"Two for about eighty bucks, installed."

"Awesome!"

"Okay, hold on. I'll be back after checking with the guy on the pickup. Hang tight!"

A half-hour later, we sat in the car as he checked this and that. I was in the passenger seat; he sat as the driver with a clipboard balanced on the steering wheel. "I've never seen one with so few miles," he said, "You were a good candidate for a lease, Ms. Fox."

"Uh, that's the problem I was talking about. The 'something' I have to tell you." Showing his impatience, he huffed and slammed the clipboard on his leg. I said nothing but opened the glove box. He immediately understood the problem.

"Oh, hell." That's all he said. Then he flashed a look at my face, furrowing his brow. *Maybe he thinks you don't look like the kind of person who would commit fraud? Is that a scowl? Or maybe he's just confused that I insisted on telling him.*

"Hmm... I don't know exactly what to do about this, Ms. Fox. And like I said, the manager is out today." *Wow. He's just worried about his own paperwork and not about how to punish me? That's a good start.* "Uh, I guess... well," he stumbled, ending with, "I'll see if this situation is covered in our manual, okay? But in the meantime, there's a couple in my office ready to sign on a Sentra. It'll be awhile – can you deal with that?"

"Can I go inside to escape the heat?"

"Absolutely."

I sauntered into the dealership, a typically massive space, two stories high with floor-to-ceiling windows. Also as expected, shiny-new cars and "conversation areas" complete with chocolate candies. I had a free cup of coffee and a free pack of peanut butter crackers. Afterward, I studied each of the models in the showroom, just looking. Killing time.

At last, the salesman came to sit with me in the corner sofa area, his top lip balancing a line of sweat beads. He tipped his head back and rolled his eyes. "Whew! What a day, right? Sorry to keep you waiting."

"No problem." My anxiety had peaked when we were in the car; by that time, I was cool and willing to accept what was to come, good or bad.

"There's nothing in the book about this, Ms. Fox. Nothing at all." *Did you look under 'F' for "Fraud?" or maybe "Fucked-up?* "So I'm going to do what any good employee would do: let the boss handle it!" He laughed loud, then slapped his knee and laughed louder and longer. "Yeah, like a GOOD employee!" More laughter; he'd cracked himself up.

I could only look at the floor, feeling my heart beat against my eardrums as fear returned. *Laugh with him, Lela.* Between fake-chuckles, I said, "That' a good one, Paul! The buck stops on HIS desk, right? Ha, ha, ha." I'd never been so insincere in my years, but I wanted him to think he was doing the right thing. *WRONG!*

Laughs subsiding, he said, "Manager's name is Charles... here's his card. Good news is he can get right on it. He said to keep his desk clean while he was out. I knew what he meant."

"Yeah... sometimes a vacation day is just double-work for the day after."

"But that Charles is a smart cookie," he said, pausing to study my face. Instant paranoia took over. *Oh hell, he's trying to keep me here until the police come. Oh, shit. What should I do?* My heart rate zoomed to a strong ba-BOOM, ba-BOOM. The salesman continued rambling, dropping the study of my face but stumbling over his words. *Maybe this means nothing but get the hell out of here, Lela. Run!*

As I was planning my exit line, I zoned back in to hear him say, "So leave the van, just pay me for the tires, and I'll get this in front of Charles first thing in the morning. If you don't hear from him by noon, don't worry about it. Because *today* is the last day for us to get the report to Nissan. They're strict, and our manager may just send it on through as-is."

I don't know if he saw my lungs collapse with relief; he looked down at the papers and huffed a chuckle. Then he said, "You didn't waste time, did you? Turning it in with just hours to spare!" The laugh again.

He stood up fast, reaching for a handshake. "The cashier's office is through the door on the left, Ms. Fox. Good doing business with you." Dumbstruck, I could only nod. "And if you're in the market for a new Nissan, you know where to find me, right?"

He gave a thumbs up and walked away while I was still frozen in place, unable to speak. But I was able to run, and I did. To the cashier and straight next door to the bakery to call a taxi.

As I waited for the taxi's arrival, I came up with a great campaign for Nissan. The headline would be "Get the hell out of Dodge."

The taxi driver overcharged me, I thought, but I made it home. I didn't see Bo sitting on the sofa and I called out, "I'm back! Sorry it took so long."

Bo's eyebrows pushed together in one line. "I was *worried*, Mom! You should've *called!*" I realized he probably thought I'd been arrested and each minute I'd been gone was a tick up in his worry. My apology didn't satisfy him; he was still so pissed at me.

Hide your heartbreak until he leaves, Lela. He needs time to forgive you... and hell – he's a damn teenager, anyway! Did you expect to be his hero? So keep it light, act like nothing is wrong.

"So are you ready for a trip to the Volkswagen dealership?"

"I think it's cool you want a Volkswagen! And a Jetta! Is it really based on Ella's recommendation?"

"And your dad's too." I saw his face light up further and decided to keep quiet about the other recommendations I'd received, a good one from Damon Toomey, who had called the week before, and some good, ol' fashioned *Consumer Reports* research.

"Do you need something to eat along the way? It's probably twenty miles and we'll be there a long ti–"

"Mom, I *always* need food. No need to ask." We laughed together, and I found myself overtaken with gratitude for him being there with me. I yearned for him to consider me a good mom and I almost cried just thinking about it but turned away and stopped myself. *No crying in front of the kid.*

The Volkswagen dealership had the tall, flopping "people" with random arm movements from a generator and air pump; a new thing at the time. Bo was amazed.

We found the saleswoman I'd talked to on the phone within a few feet of the entrance, while I was still bitching about the cost of the taxi. When she showed me the two used cars in my price range, I had second thoughts about the Volkswagen. "You know that Ford Taurus is nice, too, son. And it'd be a smoother ride. It's one year newer and has fewer miles... might be a better choice."

"It's an old-lady car."

I told the saleswoman I wanted to drive the Taurus first, and the test upped the positives of the car. It was roomy and had a few more bells and whistles. When I asked Bo what he thought, he made grumbling sounds... nothing more. "So I guess you want me to buy the Jetta no matter what, right?" Again, no reply. *Of course he does. He wants you to validate his only "parents" by following their recommendations.*

Despite the saleswoman's insistence that I buy the Taurus on the spot, I said, "I'll test-drive the Jetta, too." It was also a smooth ride, even though it was a manual transmission. She bragged that Volkswagen was "investment-worthy" with a long history, blah, blah, blah. But she'd made a much harder sell for the Ford Taurus. Maybe she'd make more commission on the bigger and newer car.

Still disbelieving, I asked, "And the payments would be exactly the same? Are you sure?"

"Within five dollars of each other. So it's all about which one you like."

"I'm just not sure about the five-speed on the Jetta. I mean, it's sporty, but..." My voice trailed off.

Bo piped in from the back seat. "The Taurus is an old-lady car, Mom. This Volkswagen is the total opposite. It's hot!"

I locked eyes with the saleswoman, about my age, and we smiled at each other... as if saying "Teenage boys are so precocious!" I chuckled and asked Bo, "So maybe I *AM* an old lady. You have a problem with that?"

"Yes! You need to look cool, Mom. Then everybody will like you more."

The saleswoman and I shared laughter openly that time; laughter lasting long enough to make Bo puff up and pout.

Ignoring Bo altogether, the saleswoman said, "Why don't you take the Taurus home tonight, and come back tomorrow for the paperwork. See if you like it after driving it in your own neighborhood and along your typical routes."

"No kidding? You'd let me do that?"

"We do it all the time." As I contemplated this opportunity, she added. "And, of course, you must make sure people still think you're cool."

I smiled, nodded at her. "I'll take the Taurus home."

☼ ☼ ☼ ☼ ☼

On the way south, Bo announced he was again hungry. "You're killing me, kid! You should weigh a thousand pounds, but it all goes to muscle, I guess. You're built so much like your grandfather it's crazy-scary."

We stopped at a fast food place of some kind and both got large Cokes. The problem with the Taurus becoming screamingly evident when we tried to put our drinks in the console holders. Not only were they too small, they were too small for *anything!* I grumbled, "*Nothing* will fit in that hole, Bo! And that's weird 'cause the dash and everything is much more modern. Dammit! I don't know about this car after all. It's not practical."

"And an old-lady car."

"We'll see." About that time, I spilled the entire Coke on the console, and in trying to help me clean it up, Bo got ketchup on the passenger seat.

I closed my eyes and felt my heart sink to the bottom of my stomach.

"Don't lose it, Mom! I'll clean it up!"

"Son, I'm not mad at you at all... why would you even think so?"

"Because you get... mad, sometimes." He looked away, a sad smile on his face. "Sorry." He'd spoken like a child, his eyes batting as if he was afraid of getting swatted.

I took a minute to think. "Are you thinking I will hit you? Or is it that your dad hits you?"

"What? No! Not my dad! Nobody hits me."

"Have *I* ever hit you, son?"

His long pause told me all I needed to know. Eventually, he answered, "Just twice," and the bottom fell out of my heart.

"Oh, Bo! I'm so sorry. I'm sure I was drunk, baby! I'd never do that in my right mind! I'm so, so sorry I did that, sorry I made you feel scared or that you... couldn't trust me. Oh, my sweet Bo! I love you so much!"

"Quit gushing, Mom. Just keep driving."

Yes, you are gushing... and you know how much Bo hates that. Keep it in the road, mind your manners, just put on a happy face. With a deep breath, I put the car in gear and pulled onto the boulevard again. My throat has grown closed, crying without tears, feeling 100 percent ashamed.

I tried to equate it with the "wreckage of the past" that Jenny talked about, anything that would make it less personal and less painful. *But nothing can excuse that, Lela. That's how fucked-up you were. You can NEVER go back to that place again.*

Finally, the tears broke the dam. I cried, "Let me just say one thing, Bo: I don't and won't act like that ever again! I'm sober. And sane."

"Even though insane stuff keeps happening to you?"

I chuckled and cringed at the same time. "It's early." *Here's your chance to use a term he may understand.* "We call it 'wreckage of the past.' Mistreating you is in the past, but I'm sure I have a lot of wreckage to make up for. Some *serious* wreckage."

"Yep."

I wiped my left eye, trying to see the road at least. "But we'll have to talk about this tomorrow. And probably many times over the years, buddy. I can't cry anymore or I'll wreck this new car."

Sullen, Bo said nothing.

I slept late the next day; Bo did, too. Around ten, I woke him so we could work together on getting the Taurus cleaned up. I'd already decided to turn it in and buy the Jetta; I suppose half of that decision was to please Bo. I needed a leg-up in any possible way.

As I was signing the papers at the dealership, someone in a blue uniform, from the back, I supposed, entered the cramped office and passed a note to the saleswoman. As the man left, she cleared her throat. "Ms. Fox, we need to add a charge, a substantial charge."

"What? Why? Are you trying to-"

"Interior detailing on the Ford Taurus. You signed the waiver, initialed the rule of no eating or drinking in an overnight loan car." I didn't know I'd signed anything, but I'd seen the extra charge coming; the ketchup was stubborn, and I didn't have the tools to get to the Coke from deep between the seats.

Red-faced, I muttered a response. "I understand."

From that point forward, her comments were snippy; the "friendly salesman" demeanor was gone. I acted like I didn't notice, but even Bo saw the difference. We winked at each other when I answered her bitchy questions in such a mockingly happy and carefree tone. It was like playing a game.

I decided to take the Expressway home; I hadn't tested the Volkswagen beyond a 65 MPH speed. "Oh, no! Bo! This piece of shit is a rattle-trap!"

"Rattles and clangs and knocks... loud! And sounds are coming from at least six different places – just on this side!"

"Oh, man... I'd take it back if I could."

"But you can't because the lady is a bitch."

"Bo! Language!" After a beat, I realized I was quoting my mother. He didn't reply, just rolled his eyes.

The rattling in that car would be an issue for many years and for many reasons. But fixing the rattles was even more of a problem.

When I sold it, the young couple didn't test drive it at a high speed, just as I hadn't. My husband (at the time) suggested I say nothing, and I didn't... even though I knew better.

My Guilt earned me an extra $250, too, which made the Guilt even heavier. The money was a prize for first place in a short story contest; I wrote about a shyster salesman on Celestial Star Jetta96; the story's ending may have been more truth than fiction, too. The salesman committed suicide, drowning in the guilt caused by a lifetime of sleazy tactics.

I gave the prize money to charity. In the Lifetime that followed, I gave the Shame to Dude, wrapping it around an Alka-Seltzer tablet and dropping it in a tall glass of water.

Works for a headache, too.

THE CONTRACT
CHAPTER 39

On Friday of the week Bo left, I received an email from Kathy Sussex, head of Human Resources.

> Lela,
>
> Your three-month contract is soon to expire, and we need to talk about renewing it. Please come to HR first thing on Monday.
> Kathy

Yay! Maybe the hourly rate has increased like she thought it would! And maybe a new contract will help Dale get me on-task with the critical update notes! Good, good news! I wrote back without delay.

> Kathy,
>
> I'll see you then. I can't believe it's already been three months! Time flies! Or as my son says, "Time sure is fun when you're having flies."
> Lela

I'd be thrilled about the higher pay; my car payment for the Volkswagen Jetta was a bit higher than the van's lease payment, and money wasn't exactly free-flowing in the first place. I was only able to pay the minimum on the Visa Stuart jacked up, and now I had payments to Best Buy and the new MasterCard, too.

I decided the timing was good to ask Dale, again, for work on the manual. He'd been out of the office most of the day already, and by five o'clock, he hadn't returned. I left for the weekend, not saying goodbye to anybody... which had proved to be the best way to avoid Spooky Robert.

On the way home, I realized that re-signing the contract would be the best time to confront Dale, anyway. That way, Kathy would know what I'd been up against and how bad Dale had fucked up.

I went straight to the POWERLESS club, hanging out in the parking lot before the meeting. I'd chosen to hang out with a group of women with much more sober time than I was, though I felt like the crazy one... the know-nothing newcomer. Still, I listened and laughed, wanting a long-time sober friend in addition to Jenny.

That day, the conversation steered to swallowing our pride. An older woman spoke of a disastrous conversation with her boss when she'd admitted she was wrong about one thing... and he went off on her, blaming her for everything wrong in the international company. "Sometimes it's like only alcoholics understand me," she said.

The comment struck me as way-too-true. I'd felt misunderstood by those not trying to delve into their character defects. They huffed at me, asking why I would want to highlight my weaknesses.

All I could add to the group conversation was a sarcastic comment, "Sobriety is hard."

I took the last half of my cigarette inside when it was time for the meeting to start. There weren't many open seats, but one was directly across from the salt-and-pepper hair guy who'd been smiling at me. *What the hell, Lela. Go for it. Sit there. It's not a crime; it's just a seat. And there's a whole table between you.*

I sat without a word, watching the meeting chairman get the laminated pages together. I turned to find the ashtray, keeping my eyes down, and suddenly another hand appeared to "ash off." The beefy hand of Salt and Pepper.

His cancer stick was a mini-cigar... the kind that come five to a pack at 7-Eleven. I looked up. It was the guy, of course, but I acted surprised. "Oh, hi!" I said, and he returned the greeting.

Just then, the chairman called the meeting to order, and I looked away, not flinching and not turning his way for another five minutes. Somebody up front made a joke after the readings and we both chuckled – his a low and gravelly baritone... sincere, sexy, confident.

I dared to look at him, studying his profile without staring. Soon, he turned, looking straight at me. I felt my cheeks redden, something that had never happened when I came upon a man that might be interested in me.

I looked away as soon as it would seem cool, I thought... the buzz between my ears letting me know I was nervous. *No-no, Lela. You can't do this. You can't! Get up and leave... no men, no relationships! Your meat thermometer isn't hot enough for a relationship.*

As if he heard me, the guy stood and took his phone out of his pocket, walking quickly outside. *An emergency call, I guess. Bummer. Maybe he'll come back. I hope he does. I don't even know his name!*

He didn't come back. The circle for saying the prayer broke and I have to admit that my pace to get outside was rushed. He wasn't there.

I didn't even wait for my friends to come outside for after-meeting banter. I just got in the VW and drove home.

Lying in bed, feeling sorry for myself, I heard the semi-silent ring of the GPS receiver box. The blue light of the ankle bracelet flashed in the dark of my bedroom. I shouted, "Fuck you!" to the box, breaking the deafening silence.

I went back to the POWERLESS club both Saturday and Sunday, trying to convince myself I wasn't looking for Salt and Pepper in the room. I searched; he never showed.

Just as well, Lela Fox. Get your ankle bracelet off first, at least! Who wants to explain THAT?

☼ ☼ ☼ ☼ ☼

Monday morning, I turned left entering the Smyth Software building, heading to HR. Kathy's office was the dead-end of the hall and I could see her sitting at the desk. I called out when I approached the door. "Kathy?"

She looked up and waved me in, but her look concerned me. Kathy wasn't exactly the bouncy-happy cheerleader type, but she always carried a genuine smile. But not that day.

My pace slowed, and stepping through the door, I came face to face with Dale. "Oh! I didn't know you were going to be... what? What's wrong?"

"Sit, Lela." Dale's voice was stern.

"I'm not going to renew your contract." The thought had never occurred to me.

"But... *why?*"

"You're not productive in the department, Lela. I've gotten no update notes from you, you just keep working on that Marketing document... like that's all we have going on!"

"Dale! I've been asking you for work the whole time! You never assigned update-notes to me! Maybe three or four! What was I supposed to do... make things up?"

"You never asked."

"BULLSHIT! You *know* I asked!" Dale's smile mocked me; it took a minute to realize I'd been skunked. "I can't believe this! I should have kept a 'they're screwing me over' record. This isn't right, Dale. You *meant* to do this to me. you probably didn't even want me here in the first place! Why did you even hire me? What the hell? I could sue you guys for fraud! Unfair employment practices! You have no idea how unfair this is!" After all those words, I was out of breath and my cheeks were on fire.

"Are you finished?" It was Kathy this time.

"I could go on and on! This is bullshit, Kathy! Are you in on this? Why did you hire me if you knew? Oh, hell... I swear, I'm going to sue! I'm going to–"

Dale interrupted. "You have no grounds as a contract employee. Or maybe I should say EX-contract employee." His smirky grin sickened me and I glared at him.

"You think you're so superior! You don't know what I've been through!"

"Well, I know what *I've* been through and I didn't like it. Don't want any more of it."

"But you–"

Kathy reached her arm toward me, touching the desk. "Lela, I think what Dale is saying is you're fired. And if what you've been through has anything to do with it... we can't make any more allowances for it. Your time at Smyth Software is over. If I were you, I'd quit arguing. Nobody wants to have security escort you out."

My tears started in earnest then; I'd only leaked a few from the outer edges in my tirades.

Kathy's voice oozed like suede. "I understand you also have... stuff... surrounding your workspace?"

Dale spat, "Junk! Kid's toys and clutter! I should have written you up just for that!"

"It's just..." *Damn. Lela, shut up. This is going nowhere. You can't win. You have no power and they can be assholes if they want. You can't stop them. And, face it, has this been a good three-month job? Hell no! So hold your head high, get your stuff, and go. You'll figure it out later.*

"Uh, Kathy... do you have an empty box?"

"I do... why do you–"

"Dale, will you take me to my desk so I can gather my 'junk and clutter?'" The request made me think of being fired from another job... when I'd stashed booze bottles in a Tampax box. What the hell... embarrass him.

"I also have a value-sized box of Tampax and a douche mix in my drawer. You wouldn't want to throw that away yourself. It might mess up your manicure."

He glared at me. "Smartass."

Kathy saw what was coming. Her stern voice warned, "Stop it, guys. Dale? Just take her to her desk, okay. Let's keep it light." She looked at me and stood, reaching for a handshake. "It's been nice working with you, Lela."

I turned, refusing to shake her hand.

☼ ☼ ☼ ☼ ☼

Nobody said a word as I packed my stuff, Dale crowding me and tapping his foot with impatience. He huffed three sighs, each time crossing his arms across his chest. *Fuck you, Dale. Fuck you big-time. I'm not going to accommodate you and your schedule now. You screwed me royally, had it planned all along.*

I had finished packing. Sure enough, I had quite a haul; my box was over-full, and I still had my vowels to carry. Yes, my vowels: the coolest desk decoration *ever* for a writer, in my mind. About two feet tall, my vowels were a 3D combination of "e" and "a" in a script font. They'd been part of the "Sunbeam" sign that workers had removed from the building when I first got the job.

The letters fit perfectly between my desk and the shelf above it in my stupid carrel at Smyth Software, and I was proud of them. *And I'll be proud to find a new home for them in my NEW office, you asshole. Fuck you TWICE, Dale! You can bet I'll find another job in a flash, and it will be a lot better than this piece of shit job.*

Dale huffed the fourth sigh when I put the vowels on my shoulder for carrying. Something hit me... something stupid. But my humor had always been inappropriate when I was nervous. I thrust the letters toward Dale. "Want to buy a vowel?" I asked.

Chuckles came from every corner of the carrel group, even from Red's side farther away. "Just get out," Dale said.

I walked down the hall slowly, forcing Dale to adjust his pace as he followed. He continued to follow through the parking lot and I stomped to my car slowly, purposely... realizing I had once again parked next to the railroad tracks. *My last day... is that too much of a coincidence?* Too numb to cry, I drove to my apartment in a trance, getting caught at every red light, it seemed.

Like a robot, I walked into my living room expressionless and sat on the sofa, staring straight ahead.

Lela-Lela-Lela... aren't you getting tired of asking yourself, "What's next?" I'm over it... sobriety has been a big, fat failure! I'm still doing stupid things - things only a drunk does.

And I can't control the crazy shit that's happening to me. It's too much! I'm losing my mind! Is this the way it's supposed to be? Tears began, irritating me. I shouted out loud, "And I'm so damn tired of crying!"

My first thought was to lay down and kick my feet like a toddler. My second thought was to pray.

I did neither. Instead, I journaled. Using my biggest, blackest Sharpie, my words bled through two layers of paper.

I AM INSANE AND NOTHING CAN CHANGE IT.

Maybe an hour passed before I wrote again, using the same Sharpie.

I AM SOBER AND NOTHING CAN CHANGE IT.

EPILOGUE

What happened next is surprising. Alarming, even. See, there's still much left to say and more left to my story. In fact, this is not even the end of my Lifetime Number Six; more sober insanity is yet to come. After a time, things settle down, but not before I'd lost two more jobs in West Palm Beach and gone through a lot more crap.

The only way to find out what happened is to dive into the next two books in the series, *Honesty,* then *Serenity.* Those books will take you through Lifetimes Seven, Eight, and Nine. But a few things can be wrapped up here... and I think you deserve to know.

As for my Smyth Software coworkers, Spooky Robert was killed in a car crash on the way to meet with another "Grey," another guy supposedly abducted by aliens as a child. Dale's partner broke up with him after seven years, deciding he'd been heterosexual after all. And Joe, the Atkins-diet farter, worked to slim Murphy down to a normal-size dog. The last I heard, Murphy had lost 28 pounds and Joe had lost sixty.

Jenny remained my sponsor for the next six months, a crazy-critical time in my life. Jenny and Damon Toomey, plus a dozen AA friends, took me out for steak on June 30 in the year 2000... then to the POWERLESS club where I received my one-year chip.

My treatment center, Recovery Resources, closed down less than a year after I attended. Simple word-of-mouth from a dissatisfied few can kill a business in the recovery field, especially when surrounded by so many competitors. I was one of the lucky ones, reaping the benefits while R&R was in its prime. Not bad for a random phone-book choice.

Serenity Sisters Halfway House was still going strong in 2004. That's when I went back to tell my story at a speaker meeting and just after Rhonda left as manager. Sometime that July, her redneck roots got the better of her and she beat the shit out of a girl at an NA meeting. She was arrested for assault and sentenced to a year in jail. Serenity Sisters grew in her absence, I hear, and they bought another building next door to accommodate another thirty women and their children.

I'm still in touch with Abby. She moved back to Jersey and took a part-time teller job, somehow avoiding the background checks that would have barred her. But nothing stopped her climb to success; the badass woman was recently promoted to branch manager of the same bank. I can't imagine her in a navy suit, but sobriety can flip a person upside down. Like it did me.

I guess you want to know what became of Stuart after 1999. Unfortunately, I can't tell you the rest of the story because his life remained a part of mine for several more years. Not by *my* choice, be sure of that... but the relationship wasn't closed until it ended in Lifetime Number Eight.

The rest of the story... you'll read within the next two books. I hope you find *Honesty* as powerful and stirring as the final book in the series, *Serenity.*

Here's a warning: the neat, sober ending comes very late in my rollercoaster life. And maybe it wasn't so neat. You'll have to decide for yourself.

SNEAK PEEK AT BOOK 6
HONESTY: WALKING THE WALK

CHAPTER 1: Stitch & Bitch

"I'm walking the walk and doing all the right things! So how could *I* get fired? Why *me?* I mean... I'm six whole months sober! And it wasn't even my fault! I didn't do anything to deserve it!" I stabbed the embroidery needle through the linen fabric with more force than needed and huffed a frustrated sigh.

Murmurs from the thirty-plus women in the AA meeting seemed to challenge the "not my fault" statement. I insisted, "Seriously! Ask Jenny! It really wasn't my fault!" I looked at my sponsor, sitting close beside me in the circle, but her unreadable expression didn't support my point.

"And no matter how much I pray; I still can't find a job."

"How long have you *looked* for a job, Lela?" The question came from Jenny's sponsor, Nancy, from the other side of the circle.

Of course I knew her question was the beginning of a lecture about patience, and that was a problem all around because I hadn't had time to look for a job yet. Maybe she thought I was just a whining newcomer and her judgement pissed me off, so I snapped back, "It just happened two days ago!"

The entire circle of women laughed, and Nancy added, "Maybe you should look a little longer before you bitch about not finding a job." That snarky phrase brought even more laughs.

"But what if there aren't any jobs for a washed-up advertising writer?

That's my fear. And y'all, my rent is due... I'm in a world of hurt."

"Your time is up, Lela."

"But I'm not finished!"

"You actually went over. No matter how serious your issue, newcomers get a max of three minutes of stitching and bitching. So, pass the needlework to the left, please."

"That's another thing! I want to bitch about this stitch and bitch meeting! I thought it was funny at first, but you guys give me so much grief that I don't even feel welcome here! And how can Jenny call this her home group? You guys are flat-out MEAN!"

Chuckles all around, even from Jenny. I clenched my jaw and thrust the embroidery hoop to the next woman, also with more force than needed. She gave me a look of pity and deftly picked up the needle. "Actually, I have only gratitude to share today, so thirty seconds will do." Then she spouted some happy-ass news about something at work; something I cared about NOT ONE BIT.

I leaned to whisper to Jenny. "These women don't believe I have real problems, Jenny, and I *do!* How can you stand this happy-butterflies-out-your-butt meeting?"

"Sounds like this would be a good day for you to just listen, hon. Listen and learn."

I rolled my eyes. *I only need to learn how to find a job... a job worthy of my advertising degree and decades of experience. After all, I deserve a certain level of respect as a professional, an award-winning writer.*

As the embroidery hoop passed from woman to woman, each shared honest wisdom about how to live sober... because this meeting attracted women with long-term sobriety. Only a handful struggled with life the way I did. On good days I admired them but doubted I could ever be sober enough to just need thirty seconds of stitching. Yet I continued to come, every Wednesday before Jenny and I met at the Subway in Pompano Beach, home of the Goodyear blimp.

Getting fired was a smack in the face for me and I still felt buckets of anger toward Smyth Software in general and my boss Dale in particular. Plus, I guess I felt a touch of Shame for not standing up for myself, and for not seeing through his ploy to get me fired. Like ex-husband Stuart, Dale had made me look like a fool and I'd played right into his hands. Now I'd suffer without a reference from my most recent job.

"Actually, I'm double-screwed, Jenny. And I can't let it go. My sense of peace is gone and I'm out of control of things."

"Again?"

"What do you mean 'again?'"

"Sorry... I shouldn't have said that."

"Quit making it worse, Jenny!"

"Your stack of notepads isn't helping you sort through options?"

"Not this time."

"You can't put things in alphabetical order?"

"Hell, I can't even recite the alphabet! Nothing has happened yet but nothing is listed on the job sites or in the classified ads. And the real problem hasn't come yet. See, I drank through the technology revolution in the advertising business. I'm out of the loop and too old to offer a fresh perspective for fast-paced ad agencies."

"Something will come around. Keep looking."

Sarcastic and snippy, I said, "I'm glad you're so sure of that, ma'am. Send some of that assurance my way, please, since you're so in control of it."

"Watch your mouth... Lela. All you need to do is keep walking the walk. You'll get there."

A growl of frustration shot through my lips. "You just don't get it."

"I get that you're upset, I really do. But I can't help you do this... I can't make it go away for you. Why do you seem to expect *me* to fix the problem?"

"You always fix my problems."

Jenny threw her head back and laughed – loud enough to draw the attention of other Subway customers. "You only THINK it's me, Lela! All your progress in sobriety?" I nodded, hoping for a pat on the back. "All that progress has come from *your own hard work*."

"Really?"

"Really. So keep working hard and you'll continue to make progress. I'm sure of that and I don't know what else to tell you."

"Maybe something will show up in the classified ads this Sunday."

"Do you have your résumé ready?"

"The guts of it, and ready to customize for whatever job I'm shooting for."

"A cover letter?"

"Ditto. Ready but for fill-in-the-blanks depending on where it's going."

"Then you're prepared... what are you bitching about?"

"I have nobody to send my perfect cover letter to! Don't you get it?!"

"First... keep your voice down. Second... do some research on how long people look for a job. I bet you'll find that you're not *supposed* to get a job in the first month of looking."

"A month?! I can't wait that long! I have bills!"

"Then get off your high horse and start bagging groceries! Go to the mall and fold clothes... anything, Lela! Why are you so against that?"

I put my head down, knowing I should do exactly as Jenny suggested, but I honestly believed it was beneath me. *Quick comeback, Lela. Think!* I said, "It would be so temporary... is that really fair to the grocery store? Or the clothing store?"

"That's not the point. The point is you're a snob. A job snob."

I looked at my watch, trying to avoid this line of questioning. "Oh, shit! I'm going to be late for house arrest! I gotta go right now!"

"How convenient." Jenny didn't move, but I gathered my papers and jumped up in a frantic rush.

I kissed her left cheek. "See ya next week at the Stitch and Bitch!"

"Call me," she yelled at my back as I flew out the door.

☼ ☼ ☼ ☼ ☼

A job snob! How DARE she say that!? I'm just a down-to-earth alcoholic trying to find my way. I have a lot to offer and a talent sure to be an asset for any ad agency. As long as I realize it may take a while for my salary to reach the six figures it was before, I'll be fine.

The right side of my brain argued with the left side, and I defended myself out loud. "It doesn't *matter* how long ago I earned those awards! They're still in the books. National superlatives don't go away."

A pause for another problem from the doubting side of my brain.

"No! It doesn't *matter* how long it's been since I've been a copywriter! Advertising is advertising. The basic rules don't change."

Another pause, another defense.

"Someone of my caliber can't work for minimum wage. It's unhealthy for me, likely to throw me into a deep Bi-Polar depression cave. Can't do that."

You can prove your talent, Lela... it's there waiting for you. I don't know why I'd avoided putting my portfolio together for so long, but on that frantic ride home, I made a decision to use my anger for a good cause. *Make that portfolio sing, Lela. Show 'em what you're worth.*

Night had fallen as I unlocked the door to my apartment, and I heard the strange, distant buzz-ring of my GPS box, checking the whereabouts of my ankle bracelet. I'd barely made it home in time. *Too close for comfort, Lela. That's all you need now... to go back to jail for breaking probation.* I said aloud, "Yeah... that would help you find a job, for sure. Then bagging groceries would sound pretty damn good."

CHAPTER 2: Three Pictures

I gave myself only an hour for self-pity, then took a deep breath and opened the storage-closet door in my bedroom. Once again, I spotted the box labeled "Lela's Portfolio" on the top shelf... and once again, I cursed the movers under my breath. *Why would they put such a heavy box on the top shelf!? I'll hurt myself getting it down; I can see it coming.*

I'd borrowed a step stool from Jenny for the specific purpose of getting that damn box down. It housed my credibility... a rich-leather binder with transparent sleeves for print samples, plus audio and video tapes of my best multi-media work. Ad reprints, brochures and mailers, annual reports, TV and radio spots – all the projects that represented my talent.

Younger writers would have transferred things over to CDs, I knew, but Lela Fox was old-school by necessity. I didn't know how to upgrade, nor who could do it for me, nor did I have the money for such luxuries. Fingers crossed; I hoped a potential employer would appreciate quality work over presentation format.

Too many pieces crowded the portfolio; I knew that. Weeding it down would take some time. Most things had been done decades ago; the majority of the printed pieces designed by ex-husband and master-creative Miller McKeown, with the TV and videos directed by Augie Highfield. Despite Miller's and Augie's faults, they were still some of the best in the Southeast. Those two names, along with my own, were the cream of the crop in the creative field back in the day.

Yeah, until your drinking brought you down... until your clients couldn't depend on you... until you beat your head against the wall and still couldn't come up with an idea.

Of course, nobody in the West Palm Beach area knew of my reputation, neither the good part or the bad part, but the contents of that box would prove my excellence. My future absolutely depended on it.

Balancing on the stool, I reached to tip the bottom of the box up from the shelf. *Oh, shit. It's too lightweight! What happened? Is there another portfolio box I haven't seen?* The box, literally, fell into my hands. I stepped down from the stool and carried it to the bed.

I shook it; a rustling sound and no more. *I swear... I think it's empty! How can that be?* Then I ripped the not-sticky-anymore tape and opened the flaps. In the bottom, one measly envelope, addressed to... nobody. It said, "Sorry for your loss." *What the hell?*

Inside the envelope, three pictures.

1.) The leather binder licked with flames; a layer of firewood beneath it.

2.) The cassette tape and videotape; melted on top of the burning binder.

3.) Stuart holding a lighter; an evil grin on his red face.

My entire body frozen in shock, the pictures fell through my fingers and onto the bed, face up. I stared at them, drilled my eyes into their detail. *How could he do this? Now I have no future at all. How did he know the worst possible thing to do to me... the cruelest way to hurt me?*

My hand shook as I wiped the sweat from my forehead and upper lip; it had appeared though it was plenty cool inside. Somewhere deep inside, my mind cracked into another sphere, another realm. And as stupid as it sounds, I saw my life flash before my eyes... scenes from my career in advertising. After "seeing" my PR photo with the Best of Show award at the Atlanta Addy award ceremony, I flashed to what I assumed was a premonition: a gray-haired me wearing a blue and yellow Walmart vest, struggling to put a plastic tricycle in a bag.

I couldn't process the thoughts at the speed they came at me... didn't realize I'd flopped onto the bed and cried the proverbial crocodile tears. *Get your shit together, Lela. Don't let yourself get immobilized. That would be the worst.*

Denial seemed to be a way to cope, or so my mind determined. *This simply isn't happening. It's a hallucination, a horrible dream.* Still, minutes passed before I could fathom the reality. *I'm doomed. Fuck you, Stuart. Fuck you very much.*

As if in a daze, I walked to the kitchen and opened the fridge, then drew a blank. *What was I looking for?* I looked in the pantry, hoping to give myself a clue... then figured it out. *I've come for a beer. Oh, hell... I NEED a beer, a hundred beers, a thousand! A fifth of vodka and a truckload of lime. And a gun.*

☼ ☼ ☼ ☼ ☼

I had to dial the number twice; my vision was blurred with tears. And Jenny couldn't understand me at first because my throat diameter was so small, my voice squeaked incoherent words.

She was livid when she heard the news, and more livid when I told her about my robot-walk to the fridge. "Don't you let that sonofabitch make you drink! *He's* the loser, not you! Let *him* drink... and rot in hell, for all I care. But don't you *dare* let him win, Lela Fox! No way. Never. Got it?"

"But Jenny... now I can't get *any* advertising job! Something I've done all my life and now I have nothing to show for it." My voice was flat, ethereal, matching my emotional numbness.

"I'll make you rephrase that, you know."

A whine. "Oh, stop! Don't do this to me tonight, please! Your little teaching tricks won't work this time. Without a portfolio, I have no job. No history despite a lifelong career—"

"You didn't do it all your life."

Shocked, I stopped. "True, but—"

"And why did you *stop* writing?" Jenny drew her words out and up in tone, like a first-grade teacher trying to lead her student to understanding. It was her way of forcing me to answer logically and honestly.

"Yeah-yeah... because I drank my freelance business away."

"And before that?"

"I got mad and quit my job."

"And that's called..." The rise in her voice went off the scale.

"Dammit, Jenny! Wreckage of the past! But please, don't be so—"

"So *what?* Real? Practical?"

"So in-my-face!"

303

She laughed. "That's my *job,* Lela. Here's the truth: your problem is temporary."

"Burning my credibility is pretty damn permanent, Jenny!" Her nonchalance had fired me up again, brought my anger to the top of my pounding head.

"Make more credibility... a new portfolio."

"HA! Right. Create twenty years of award-winning work for make-believe clients... get it printed, produced, hire the models. You're crazy."

"Find an understanding employer."

"That's even *more* ridiculous! Can't you see the magnitude of–"

"Offer to start on a contract basis, to prove yourself. Just tell the truth and you may get the sympathy vote." I stopped. *Could that work? The truth shall set you free? How competitive is the job market right now?* Jenny continued with a string of possible fixes, all unrealistic in my mind. Then she said, "Make a video... tongue in cheek... saying how un-friendly the divorce was, tell the truth but be creative about it. I mean... you two... you can't make that shit up. It's a soap opera!"

My heart was racing, my mind seeing possibilities. I closed my eyes, envisioning intro footage to a video. "It could be the soap opera... 'As the Portfolio Turns.'"

Jenny hooted a laugh. "Perfect! I'll help you! I'll do whatever it takes."

"I could make it even funnier with cheap and cheesy production... on purpose, ya know?"

"Now you're talking!"

"And I could do a magazine ad saying the same thing. Use the pictures he left in the box."

"Be mega-creative... with no client to make changes that ruin it. I know how you hate client changes."

Her voice continued in the background as I zoned her out, reeling with ideas, kernels of hope popping like popcorn. "I think this just might work, Jen!"

"The creative Lela roars back to life!" After a pause, we both cracked up laughing. I laughed chock-full of creativity and confidence, and Jenny laughed, she said later, because I had so easily transformed from gloom to glee.

"Jenny, I can do it. I can!"

"And remember, the Sunday classifieds are coming. I wouldn't be at all surprised if a small agency needs a kickass copywriter. The boss is a woman..."

"A recently divorced woman..."

"Who got screwed in the divorce..." Our laughter tinkled through the line.

"This will work! By being clever about the loss, I show more about what I can do than the portfolio ever could!"

"See, that sonofabitch can't keep you down."

"Hell no! I'm smarter than he is, Jenny. He's evil, but I'm smart."

"Absolutely. Get your ideas on paper, Ms. Writer. Do it now."

I worked until two in the morning, creating a script for a slap-your-knee-hilarious skit. To myself: "Tomorrow, prop-shopping. I need it ASAP."

My prop-shopping list, carefully written on a blue pad, led me on adventures through Delray Beach and further into the depths of West Palm. As I'd done in Rockville when I produced commercials for a living, I created a little pouch for receipts; all props not destroyed during the shoot were returned to the store.

- plastic wedding bands
- ugly wedding or prom dress
- false eyelashes, bigger is better
- ugly bouquet of flowers
- bandit face mask
- fake moustache (handlebar)
- men's black bow tie and weird hat – top hat?
- a joke lighter or fireplace matches, big!
- water hose
- yellow raincoat
- toy fire fighter's helmet
- clothesline rope

Jenny would play the dastardly villain Stuart Weinstein and I'd be the naïve bride, batting her eyelashes and immersed in the sweet smell of the fake flowers. Our wedding... kiss the bride, blah, blah. Then he plays cruel tricks along the way – drops me over the threshold, rolls his eyes a lot, trips me on a walk in the park, makes fun of me behind my back. Stuff like that.

Then, wiggling his eyebrows, he sets fire to a stack of paper and I run into the scene like a frantic maniac, dressed as a firefighter, to douse the fire. In the end, the video goes to super-fast-speed as I chase him around the room, tie his hands to his feet and stand with my foot on his back, raising my water hose in victory.

CHAPTER 3: A Fax for a Deaf Fox

I had an idea and about ten bucks. I also had a lot of fear.

Email attachments weren't a thing yet... documents were printed and faxed, including résumés and cover letters. The good news: fax machines had become affordable by 1999; cheap enough for home businesses.

I wanted one. A cheap, used one like you'd find in a pawn shop. But just the thought of a pawn shop made me shiver with fear and Shame, and it would probably even worse now that I was sober.

On that Friday, I held my breath, pumped out my chest and walked into Boca Pawn like I belonged there. My feelings of confidence lasted about five seconds, melting when the greasy-haired guy behind the counter looked at me and licked his lips. *Creep. Don't you dare come out here! I don't need your help.*

I resisted the urge to run, staying on task. With so much... uh, junk... on the scarred floor, I zigged and zagged through the aisles until I found the business equipment section. Most of the machines were twenty years old and broken, but behind an old electric typewriter, with a curly telephone cord wrapped around it... a fax machine, a tiny one. No bells or whistles, a missing paper tray, and a stretched out spiral phone cord. Perfect. And ten bucks. SOLD!

At the cash register, I avoided looking at the greasy-haired man, but he was determined to talk to me. At his second comment, I looked at him quizzically, pointed to my ears, then used both hands to "sign" a word that was not a word as far as I knew. "Oh, you're deaf!" he said. I nodded and repeated the "sign." The stupid ass kept talking but talked louder. At the end of the transaction, I signed something else and he SCREAMED, "Nice doing business with you!"

Idiot.

On the way home, I counted how much I'd save by faxing at home instead of going to the Fed-Ex store. It was a good purchase; another feather in Lela Fox's hat, according to a Lela Fox full of herself.

When I unlocked my apartment door, my GPS box was buzzing; I'd slid in on the last buzz/ring. *Cutting it too close again, girl. You're going to be busted if you don't be more careful.*

Even worse, Monday was my next probation officer check-in – ugh! – and I'd have to tell the bitch I was job hunting. Changes to my "out with permission" schedule were sure to come. The thought of it turned my stomach.

I despised seeing that woman; she always asked if I'd gone within so many feet of Stuart Weinstein. It gave me the heebie-jeebies to be accused of doing the thing most opposite of my desires. My complaints about Stuart contacting *me* didn't phase her. Once, I took a tape of his five messages for the month; she didn't give a damn. "I don't care what *he* does," she said, "My job is to keep *you* in line."

They just don't get it! I'm so innocent and so stuck.

Those appointments ruined my whole day; feeling misunderstood and powerless caused instant depression... like being a dysfunctional drunk all over again. I shivered with anger just entering the office and sitting with the losers who waited with me. I wanted to scream, "I don't belong here!" even knowing it would do no good.

"Six more weeks, Lela. Only six. You can do that, surely." I had to talk myself into keeping enough hope to survive the humiliation of house arrest. I knew my sobriety could never peak as long as I wore that damn thing on my ankle.

✵ ✵ ✵ ✵ ✵

I set up the fax machine on my dresser and called Jenny at work; we had worked out the timing for her to stand by her office fax for the test. I wrote on a plain paper: FOX IS A FAXIN' FOOL! Then, "send."

To confirm it worked, she faxed me back... a smiley face and, in her perfect script: GO GET 'EM, TIGER!

How lucky I am to have Jenny! She even knows my Dad's famous encouraging words... "Go get 'em, Tiger." Hell-yeah, I'll get 'em. And I may not let go!

CHAPTER 4: Gold Coast Productions

On Sunday, I set my new alarm clock for 7:11 and threw on crappy clothes, dashed to Publix with four quarters I'd found in the sofa cushions, and opened the creaky newspaper box to grab a *Palm Beach Post*. Though I'd lived there for nearly two years, I still marveled at how thick the newspaper was, especially the Sunday edition. It was hey-day for printed newspapers, but the *Post* was especially big because it was "season," when all the snowbirds from Canada and New York caravanned to enjoy always-sunny South Florida. The population almost doubled from September to May, it was a pain to find a table at any decent restaurant.

It's not like you can afford a nice restaurant now, dumbass. You need a job before you can buy a burger at Mickey D's. A few weeks prior, I'd pledged to eat all existing food in my pantry before I bought a single thing at the grocery store; I was down to the gross stuff... like the low-fat, low-sodium canned soup that tasted like sea water. I thought grossing myself out might motivate me to find a job sooner.

That morning I had three boxes of cereal left, but none with enough to make a full bowl, so I combined them. Fruit Loops, Cheerios, and stale Corn Flakes. If I focused on something else, I could pretend it was good, but I also suspected the milk was a bit spoiled. Between gags, I opened the paper to the Classified section, red Sharpie at the ready.

Of the dozen-or-so ad agencies offering jobs, five of them needed a writer. Of those five, four advertised with a large "display ad," not just a listing in tiny type. *Which are you, Lela... a kickass display-ad writer or a writer so small you can't read her?* I didn't bother to circle the small ad. *That leaves four.*

Two made it obvious female-owned, and another listed a woman as the contact person. *Okay, that leaves three. One of these three agencies will be my next employer.*

Google wasn't quite as informative then, but I found background information and client lists for each of the agencies. The tone and attitude of the business showed on their websites, too, giving me a clue about what they might be looking for; that's what I needed to customize the résumés and cover letters. *Bingo! Ready to go!*

I faxed everything around midnight, hoping to be first on the boss's desk. *Go get 'em, tiger!*

I saw the probation officer Monday morning, fighting the typical dive into rage and depression with a clenched jaw and a repetitive chant of "They're just doing their job." Chanting the phrase "Just say moo," something I learned in rehab as a reminder that I'm no better and no worse than others," also helped with the fury.

As if she was new in the job, my probation officer said she had to ask her supervisor about the unemployment scheduling, and in the meantime, I should keep my schedule as it stood. But as always, she reminded me I was lucky to have so much free time. Every damn time I went, she said, "Don't relax with all that time on your own. You must control your urges every moment of every day." *Shut the hell up, woman.*

I was out by noon, as I hoped. Next up: the production studio to film my "substitute portfolio. Jenny met me there; she'd taken the afternoon off to play Stuart, and she was fired up. "I'd never be able to be as mean as he was, but I've got a good evil eye, according to my sponsor."

I'd only been able to afford an hour of the studio's time... so expensive! Timing of each scene was critical to keep shooting time to a minimum, and I used my producer skills to plan it to the second. Turned out, the camera man was having fun with the silliness of the skit and went over on time without charging me.

Jenny said, "You're damn good at this, Lela Fox. I admit... I'm impressed."

"Seems like I have my head on straight these days. I'm getting better, don't you think?"

She thought I wouldn't see her rolling her eyes, I supposed. "You have good days and bad days. Sometimes I think you're 100 percent sober-minded."

"I don't want to hear what you think on the other days, okay? I'm trying like hell, Jenny, but being unemployed... my anxiety is through the roof."

We sat on the sofa at the edge of the studio, waiting for the technician to confirm the tape hadn't screwed up. The sound of a door opening made me look to the back of the studio, where a man in a white shirt and khaki shorts stood, his arms crossed. "Penis alert, two o'clock!" I said.

"Nice! The biceps..."

"And his thigh muscles are long and lean... like a swimmer."

Unaware of our lusty gazing, the man spoke to the tech sitting at the studio monitor. We couldn't hear him, but he pointed back and forth to the monitor and laughed. First, a chuckle that only moved his mouth... a more intense chuckle, and he threw his head back... then an all-out guffaw, leaning over and clutching his stomach.

He spoke to the tech again, who turned and pointed to Jenny and me; the man looked up. Boom. Sizzle. He locked eyes with me.

His direct look made the buzz of anxiety scream behind my ears. *But there's no reason to be afraid, Lela. He's a good-looking, ooh-la-la guy, not an ogre! Look at those eyes – mesmerizing! And the muscles... and oh, shit – he's walking this way!*

Jenny whispered to me as he neared... she spouted a series of warnings, including the bullshit about my meat thermometer not being hot enough.

I could smell his cologne, musky but not overly so. A manly scent that reeked of confidence and sex appeal. "Hi. I'm Dawson Hupp. And you're Lela Fox, right?"

"Yes, I am... and this is my friend Jenny Jenkins." Dawson barely glanced at Jenny, keeping his eyes drilled into mine. *Oh shit, could he be more obvious in flirting?* My blood pressure zoomed, reacting to my dual feelings: half fear and half excitement.

"I'm your video editor," he said, "We're booked for tomorrow?" The question wasn't meant to be answered, I assumed n- and that was a good thing because I melted a bit when he flashed a sincerely proud smile. Not cocky or snooty... just the right amount of pride and fearlessness.

"This video is hilarious! And well done, it seems. Did you really shoot all that in an hour?"

"A little over." My squeaky response shocked me; I didn't think I was that nervous.

Dawson (a name I found funny, like a soap opera star's swoon-worthy name), scratched his head and asked, "But what is the purpose? What kind of client would order that?"

"I'm the client and it will be my portfolio. A substitute portfolio."

His confused look made me laugh; I think it was *meant* to make me laugh. "So... some kind of handle-bar-moustache villain burned something of yours?"

"He burned my portfolio, and this is both the explanation and proof that I can be clever and creative."

His eyes became saucers and he said, "What an asshole! That's a crime... some husband he was, huh?"

"If you only knew."

Finally, his eyes turned to Jenny. "And I must say you make a great villain... love the eyebrows. And not many people can be so convincingly evil."

"I'll take that as a compliment, I guess," Jenny said. Her expression made it clear she was quite taken by the silver-tongued man. Maybe her plan was to take the lead since she was convinced I "wasn't ready." She may have been right about my readiness, but I wasn't going to back down, even with the fear building in my gut.

There'd be no argument; Dawson made it obvious he was into me, not Jenny.

His smile, a sideways grin accented by perfect dimples, sent a shiver down my spine. And what he said caused even more fear/intrigue.

He started with the words, "I'd like to *do* something for you," and I froze solid. That's when Jenny elbowed me again, surely a warning. Evidently Dawson was no dummy... he saw the writing on the wall. "No, no. I mean... knowing you're unemployed, and seeing how funny this video is, I figure you're a fun, creative girl. I can do you a favor."

Another elbow from Jenny. My response tied to her displeasure, and to my own now-piercing scream of anxiety between my ears. "Careful, Dawson. I'm taken."

He shook his head and put his hands up in mock defense. "Wait! It's not that kind of favor!" His innocence was genuine, it seemed, and I laughed.

"Then tell me what kind of favor you mean."

"Sorry, I guess I should've started with the simple offer: I'll do the editing free of charge if we can do it after hours."

After hours. House arrest. Not enough notice. Shit!

Instantly paranoid, I looked at the hem of my pants to make sure the damn ankle bracelet wasn't showing. "Dawson, thanks for the offer, but I have to pass. I turn into a pumpkin at five o'clock."

"That's too bad."

Aha! What am I thinking? I'll just postpone the meeting with Jenny.
"Wait! Unless it's on a Wednesday! Can you do it Wednesday around five?"

"Make it 5:30 and you have a deal."

"5:30"

"Deal!"

Go get 'em, tiger.

CHAPTER 5: Refried Beans

I arrived at Gold Coast Productions early and sat in the editing suite to wait for Dawson. The purposeful dim lighting, combined with his choice of soft jazz music, created a space as romantic as it was mysterious, and much like Augie Highfield's editing suite. *Maybe that's why it seems romantic, Lela. You and Augie sure made it a place for romance. But maybe "half raunchy and half romantic" is more like it.*

Augie, videographer extraordinaire... the one who liked me too much but treated me like shit. I remembered the night years ago when the two of us drank a full fifth of tequila and streaked naked around the building at two AM.

The stupid antics of my drinking days seemed so far away now... as if they happened in another epoch. But thinking of Augie brought the continuing Shame of my promiscuity; it still churned in my gut and tasted like gunpowder. Waiting for Dawson, chewing on a renewed sense of worthlessness, I bashed myself with thoughts to make sure I felt like shit before the smoking-hot, oh-so-flirty man came in. Maybe I thought feeling like worthless scum would help me deal with his sure-to-come attempts to seduce me.

I knew I could remove myself from the sexual confrontation altogether by sitting primly on the client side instead of in the creative pit where the writer/producer and editor typically sat side by side.

Breathe, Lela, breathe. In through your nose, out through your mouth. Slow. Shoooooow. Relaxation came little by little and I felt free to look around at the monitors and knobs and slider buttons. The sultry lighting and mystery of technology created an oasis... if I could only relax.

My eyes focused on Dawson's workstation; like mine, the theme was "funky and eccentric." Decorated like a tiny museum of the weird and twisted... silly kid's meal toys, offbeat artifacts, visual puns... oddball objects accumulated over the years. My favorite was a miniature can of Old El Paso refried beans personified with arms and legs. His head with beady eyes and curly black hair, and his pipe-cleaner arms folded over a colorful Mexican poncho.

I reached to touch it...

"Helloooooo Lela Fox, come on down!" Dawson swept in and threw his briefcase on the client sofa... hopping up the step to the studio space.

"Hey there! Just admiring your workspace. I surround myself with stupid shit, too."

"How dare you call my Museum of the Weird stupid!?"

"Funny."

"Today especially, my friend. I have a present for you."

"You do? I think your editing magic will be gift enough."

He raised his index finger. "Just a sec," then slid through a narrow door. I heard bumps and thumps in a room to the side and an "ooof" from Dawson shortly after. I wondered what the hell he was digging out of what appeared to be a huge closet.

He reappeared with a sly grin and his hands behind his back. "Creative juice!" he said, then showed what he'd hidden: a bottle of cold champagne and two flutes.

My blood pressure shot through the roof. *Oh, no! Alcohol six feet from me... and a celebration. What do I do? Dammit! No Lela, no-no-no. Don't drink it! But what do I say?*

I guess he saw my face fall. "What's wrong? You don't like champagne?"

My jaw was frozen, my mouth in a wide "O." Words wouldn't come. What, Lela? Say something! What do alcoholics say when someone offers them a drink? Oh, my God! Help! Jenny! Dude!

And suddenly... my vision blurred. Dude appeared. As if my mind had snapped to attention in a puff of clouds. There he was - his jeans just as worn, his cigarette still perfectly half-smoked, but his head was moving. *I swear he's shaking his head no! How can that be?* I tried to shake the vision away, catching the twinkle of Dude's eye as he disappeared from my mind. *Did Dude himself just tell me not to drink? Bullshit! My mind is tricking me big-time. Why did he even flash into my head? This is crazy. But what do I say to Dawson? Tell him my Dude told me not to drink the champagne? Help! Somebody! Please help me! What does an alkie do when booze is around? I haven't been trained for this!*

I heard the end of Dawson's question, it seemed; the first few words came from inside a tunnel. All I heard was, "...of course, but I hope this evening turns out to be special so it's a *good* bottle, not my normal two-dollar brand."

"Thank you, Dawson, but I don't drink." My eyes rolled to the back of my head.

"Are you okay, Lela? You're pale and look like your bones have disappeared!"

I sat on my hands so he wouldn't see them shake. "Yeah, I'm fine. But... where is your ladies' room?"

Obviously confused, Dawson raised both arms, the bottle in one hand and the flutes in the other. "You don't look so good. Are you sick? Can I get you something?"

"Seriously, I'm fine. Just need to... powder my nose, as they say."

No response, just a look half-confused and half-pissed. Obviously, I'd not responded the way he'd planned.

I stood, pushing against the desk to steady myself. "Bathrooms off the lobby then?"

He shook his head as if trying to shake off the confusion. "Yes. Those are the closest."

"Do you have the footage cued up?"

"Uh, no... I thought we would discuss it first."

"Well, Dawson, since I'm getting your services at no charge, I thought you'd want to keep it simple and quick." A long, five-second pause; he obviously didn't plan to reply. "I'll be back."

☼ ☼ ☼ ☼ ☼

The vanity was Italian tile, the recessed sinks a bright turquoise ceramic. A great contrast to the loads of vomit it held. Luckily, blasts of hot water cleared the drain but I still to the adjacent sink to drink hungrily from the tap and splash my face with scoops and scoops of cold water.

The mirror showed a fragile child, mascara running in rivers to her chin, her lips swollen and slack. And the fragile child had wet her pants with the force of the purge.

What do I do, Dude? How can I go back in there? But I can't run away. I can't! A visual "pop" of a sweaty Diet Coke bottle brought a thin idea of calm. *Yeah, drink something else. And carbonated. Pretend that's exactly what you wanted all along. Pretend you're a normal person who just doesn't drink... isn't that what you've wanted all along?*

I looked at myself from all three angles. *Wash your face. Dry your pants. Get your shit together.* "Fetch yourself up sharply," as Jenny would say. *You're bigger than this, stronger than this. The book says you can go to a bar if you have a good enough reason, right? You have a good reason to be here.*

You're okay. You're okay. You're okay. I repeated the phrase dozens of times, finally beginning the process of re-grouping my face and clothes. I knew I'd been away too long and Dawson would know something was wrong with me. *But you're the one in charge here, Lela... no matter if it's a favor or not. You came here to do a job. Something that's going to make your future. You have to be okay. You MUST! Find a way to fake it.*

I had a germ of an idea and enough lying experience to pull it off. *Yes, you can. Go get 'em, tiger.*

☀ ☀ ☀ ☀ ☀

I stuck my head in the doorway before going in. "Is there a Diet Coke hiding somewhere?" My smile was meant to dazzle, and I thought I was doing a fine job.

"I'll get it for you. Come on up... and you look better."

"Feel better! Diet Coke to top it off and I'm on fire!"

Dawson's tentative smile said he wasn't so sure, but I didn't care; I'd pretend my ass off. *Focus on the project, Lela. Only the project.*

Dawson stepped past me. "Diet Coke coming up. Is a bottle okay?"

"That's exactly what I was hoping for." I watched him leave and stepped up to the creative area and sat. There was no champagne there, no flute. I said to the can of refried beans, "See? Problem solved."

This was the first of many times I was forced to mingle with drinkers in early sobriety. At the times I felt tempted, I flashed to a

picture of the refried beans to find strength.

In case you don't already know (duh), I'm a very visual person. Even after twenty years sober, I use these conjured scenarios to guide and calm me. My journal, still color-coordinated, includes many such drawings. When married to husband number four, I paid the big bucks to commission a watercolor artist to do one of my sketches; it hangs above my desk. You might guess... the artwork is the Go Get 'Em Tiger in all her leaping glory.

By the way, the video edit proved successful. Dawson behaved himself with no flirting and bushel of friendly banter. We parted with a handshake and, for appearances, I took a handful of his business cards for distribution to "all my advertising friends." (I couldn't bear to tell him I didn't have a single friend in the business.) His prediction that the video would secure a job for me came true... in a round-about way. But that's getting ahead of the story.

-- END OF SAMPLE --

MORE ABOUT ME

First, always first, I'm a proud and grateful recovering alcoholic with 21 years' sobriety. That's who I am.

My life and career have always been about writing, and it started when I was a kid. I gathered a collection of compound words, color-coded and OCD-organized. I still have that tattered paisley notebook on my bookshelf. No shit.

Thirty years a copywriter, then twelve as a certified picture framer, and many jobs in between. Then something happened (it's a huge something), and I began writing for fun in my 50s.

My tidbits landed in AA's *Grapevine* magazine and a few online journals, then a story about my dog was featured in *Chicken Soup for the Soul.*

Hmmmm... maybe this is going somewhere.

As if meant to be, about a week later, an author-friend challenged me to

317

write and publish a full book. "Just one rule," he said, "Write what you know."

I didn't know writer's terminology, so I took his advice literally. I thought it meant writing your life story. Only later did I find that the phrase means *based on* what you know. Huge difference.

The words came easily, and I spent the next three years writing my life story, which became seven top-selling books.

Who'da thunk it?

Mostly, I hope to help others; that was the whole point.

With the series complete, I'm now writing weird books under the pen name Patty Ayers. Updates to come.

I live in East Tennessee with a panoramic view of the Great Smoky Mountains, surrounded with cozy and calm here in my little condo. If I'm not writing, you'll find me tinkering or playing tug-of-war with my distinguished editor, Stormin' Norman the Schnauzer.

Combining creativity with my OCD, I also have a side biz called *Kid's Art in Stitches* – I embroider children's stick-drawings in crazy-bright colors. Stitch by stitch, the result is happy.

By the grace of Dude, I've been sober all day long.

I wish you the same.

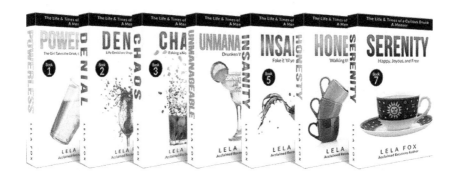

FIND OUT WHAT HAPPENS!

Next up: *HONESTY*
Can sobriety calm the chaos?

Thanks for reading my books!

Find me on lelafox.com

or

Facebook @curlywriter

Made in the USA
Las Vegas, NV
03 March 2023

68458739R00184